Songs of the Night

Singing Sorrow's Songs
Through the Darkness of Grief

Songs of the Night

Singing Sorrow's Songs
Through the Darkness of Grief

Renee Coates Scheidt

Foreword by Ron Dunn

Songs of the Night
Renee Coates Scheidt

Copyright © 1995 by Renee Coates Scheidt

Published in Houston, Texas by Rapha Treatment Centers and Baxter Press.

To my family and friends who have stood with me as I sang Sorrow's Songs in the darkness of night.

Table of Contents

I want to thank Pat Springle for guiding me through this project. His insight, patience, suggestions, and support have contributed greatly to this book.

Foreword

One of the most telling differences between the Christian and the non-Christian is how they respond to tragedy. And it is one of the greatest testimonies that believers can give to those who do not believe.

Paul said to the Thessalonian Christians that we do not "grieve like the rest of men, who have no hope." He didn't say that we do not grieve—we do. But there is a difference between the grief of those who have hope and of those who have no hope.

In recent days, I have been drawn to the story of the death of David's baby in II Samuel 12:15-24:

> After Nathan had gone home, the Lord struck the child that Uriah's wife had borne to David and he became ill. David pleaded with God for the child. He fasted and went into his house and spent the nights lying on the ground. The elders of his household stood beside him to get him up from the ground, but he refused, and he would not eat any food with them.
> On the seventh day the child died. David's servants were afraid to tell him that the child was dead, for they thought, "While the child was still living, we spoke to David but he would not listen to us. How can we tell him the child is dead? *He may do something desperate.*"
> David noticed that his servants were whispering among themselves and he realized the child was dead. "Is the child dead?" he asked.
> "Yes," they replied, "he is dead."
> Then David got up from the ground. After he had washed, put on lotions and changed his clothes, he went into the house of the Lord and worshipped. Then he went to his own house, and

at his request they served him food, and he ate.

His servants asked him, "Why are you acting this way? *Why are you acting this way?"*

Now here's what strikes me about that whole incident: the *surprise* of the servants at David's reaction to the news of the baby's death. Did they expect him to go into an angry rage? Did they think he would be so overwhelmed with grief that he could not function? Whatever the response they feared, it wasn't the one they got.

The simple reason why David was acting that way was because he had *hope*: "He cannot come to me, *but I can go to him."* And on the basis of that sure foundation of hope, he got up, showered, put on some cologne and went to church and worshipped the Lord.

That's the difference. That's the testimony. And as I read Renee's manuscript I thought of David's tragedy and how he responded, and I thought to myself, *That's Renee. How could she act that way? What secret ingredient in her life enabled her to worship the Lord in the midst of such a horrible tragedy?* This book tells the story.

I have known Renee for a number of years, before and after tragedy struck. And I have been amazed at her faith and hope that has enabled her to rise above the ashes of a shattered life and become a mature pilgrim of the Way, leading others by her song and testimony to surprise the world by the way she has responded to the dark enigmas of life.

You will read this book with tears and laughter and be a better person for it. Read it for yourself and pass it on to others. I don't see how anyone can experience what's told in these pages without wanting to kneel at last and worship the Lord.

Ron Dunn
LifeStyle Ministries
Irving, Texas

1

Singing Sorrow's Song

The sun rose on another hot, late summer day in south Louisiana. When I got out of bed, I was looking forward to this special day. I had no idea that my life would be changed—tragically changed—a few hours later.

Early that morning, we prepared for a full day of fun. In a few hours, our family would load up our little Toyota and drive seventy-five miles toward Baton Rouge to celebrate our daughter Nicole's birthday with friends. She would be three the next day, and a big party was waiting for her. I couldn't wait to be with these precious friends!

The last eight weeks had been a nightmare. We needed a break, a time to relax with those we knew loved us. Since my husband Chuck's two month hospitalization in a local psychiatric hospital and his release just one week earlier, our lives had been under almost unbearable pressure. "Lord, please, let us get back to normal!" I silently prayed. "Let this be a good day for us as a family. I pray that it would be a time of refreshment for all of us as we spend time with our friends in Livingston. Thank You for the precious gift of their love and friendship. Please direct us today."

Less than four hours from the time I whispered that early morning prayer, I found myself face to face with death. My entire world turned upside down. Chuck walked out of our home with a shotgun in his hand and ended his life.

This promising young minister, so handsome and intelligent, who seemed to have so much to live for, was dead. Our baby Tara would never know her father. She was just ten-weeks-old when he entered the psychiatric hospital. Our Nicole would recall every year for the rest of her life that her Daddy died the day before she turned three. I was left to wrestle with a myriad of emotions flooding my soul. I wanted the world to stop so I could get off, yet somehow I needed to find strength to carry on for the sake of my girls.

Sorrow invaded every part of me. Grief became my constant companion for months to come. During those long, dark days, I was convinced that I would never be free from pain as long as I lived. Death had become an unwelcome intruder into our lives. Uninvited, it barged in and stole the one we loved with all our hearts. Without permission and with no warning, it robbed us of the one we called "husband" and "father."

Less than four hours from the time I whispered that early morning prayer, I found myself face to face with death.

Certain that sorrow had taken up permanent residence in my heart, I resigned myself to accept its presence. I couldn't do anything to make the sorrow go away. The words written by Moses many years earlier became reality for me, "As for the days of our lives. . . their pride is but labor and sorrow. For soon it is gone and we fly away" (Psalm 90: 10, NASB). Now, life was forced labor; every motion and every decision was drudgery. For the next few years, I learned to sing Sorrow's Song. But I'm not the only one.

My friend Colette has learned to sing this song. She has faced death, sorrow and grief head on, yet continues to affirm her strong faith in the goodness of God and His sovereign rule in her life. Colette and I worked together for over eight years in the church pre-school program I directed. She was the kindergarten teacher for both of my girls. I attribute much of their current success in school to the wonderful foundation Colette laid.

In less than a year's time, Colette said good-bye to both of her parents. Her mom slipped away suddenly. "Mom had been sick and in lots of pain for a long time. I finally came to the point where I quit praying for God to heal her, and began asking Him to take her. She was hurting so much, and I hated to see her suffer. I asked God to be merciful, and He was. One day she laid down for a nap, and didn't wake up. My brother checked on her just forty-five minutes later. He found her dead. She had gone on to be with Jesus. Mom was so afraid she'd die in a hospital, and always said, 'Don't put me in the hospital.' I'm so thankful God was so gracious to us to let her go the way she did."

I asked how her father handled losing his wife of forty years. She replied, "Dad never recovered from Mama's death. He mourned for her the next eleven months until his grief resulted in his own death. He became ill on a Thursday, went to the doctor, and died nine days later. I stayed in the hospital room with my father and watched him die. It was the hardest thing I've ever had to do, but I'm glad I was there. He died very peacefully. Within just a matter of seconds he was gone. Once again, I saw God's mercy in the entire situation."

Since my parents are still living, I don't know what it feels like to lose both of them in such a short period of time. I wondered what Colette felt. Very honestly she told me, "It's now been over five years since my parents died. I'm a grown woman with children of my own, and I even have a grandchild. But since Mama and Daddy died, I've literally felt like an orphan. I felt I had no one, *no one* to listen to me anymore like they did. Every time I go to the mall and see an older mother and daughter shopping, I get angry. Mom was my best friend, and now she's gone. When Dad died, I grieved my Mama's death all over again. In fact, it took me over a year before I really grieved for Mama. Initially, after her death, I just plunged back into my work, refusing to think about the reality of her being gone. When Dad died, I felt guilty that I was still crying for my mother. I fell apart at the slightest thing. I still had a lot of things I needed to work through."

Colette then made a statement that I found both amazing and heartbreaking. She said, "People don't understand—especially Christians. We're supposed to be 'overcomers' and 'victorious in Christ.' I found I couldn't truly express my grief and sorrow with some of my Christian friends. They expected me to be praising God when I was hurting so badly. I found more kindness and understanding among my unsaved friends than from the people in my church. My secular friends let me cry without adding guilt to my grief and without judging me as unspiritual. I finally decided though that it was OK to cry. If Jesus could cry over Lazarus, then I guess it was all right for me, too."

Many people grieve the death of a child they never knew. Whether they lose a baby through miscarriage, still-birth, or abortion, the grief work must be done. Because of legalized abortions in our country, many young women find themselves confronted with grief they didn't anticipate. No amount of rationalization or pat answers can remove the very real sorrow these women feel.

Those who return from the hospital with empty arms after miscarriage or still-birth mourn the death of the child they will not know this side of eternity. Unfortunately, many people don't recognize the pain these women experience. I saw this happen to Mrs. Dunn, Nicole's fourth grade teacher.

Nicole could hardly wait to tell me the news when Mrs. Dunn announced to the class that she was expecting her first child. Mrs. Dunn was raised in a minister's home, and she had a strong Christian faith. She told me, "I was sure this baby was God's blessing for us. I had saved myself for my husband, and I always lived my life for the Lord. My husband and I prayed for God to send us a baby at the right time. After being married four years, we felt it was time. We were so excited when we learned I was pregnant! We had just bought our first home, and the baby's room was the first one we decorated. My Mom came to help us get the room ready. We were so excited! We just knew this was the answer to our prayers."

She continued her story, "But three months into the pregnancy, the spotting began. Stomach cramps soon followed. I called the doctor, and he stated firmly, 'You have to come to my office immediately!' The tone of his voice alarmed us."

In the doctor's office a few hours later, Mrs. Dunn heard the words she feared. Her doctor told her plainly, "You are miscarrying, and there's no way we can save the baby. I'm admitting you to the hospital right now."

In a short time, it was over. Mrs. Dunn left the hospital grieving the death of the baby she carried only a few months. "I was hurt and disappointed," she told me. "I had always been taught God has a reason for everything, but at the time, I was very upset. I told God exactly how I felt." She paused and reflected, "I couldn't help wondering if there was something wrong with my baby. Maybe that was the reason God took it to be with Him."

Some people tried to comfort her, but they only added to her pain. Mrs. Dunn related, "It angered me when people said, 'You can always try again. You'll have other babies.' I wanted to shout, 'But I lost *this one!*' It was my first child, but I'll never know this baby until I reach Heaven."

She described her anguish, "I closed the door of the nursery, and I didn't even enter that room for several weeks. When I did, I spent a lot of time and tears as I went through the things we had expected to be using with our baby. It's been a very painful experience. And many people didn't understand why I cried about losing the baby I never even saw or held. Knowing they didn't understand didn't help at all. In fact, it only intensified the pain." Mrs. Dunn felt alone and misunderstood. She lost the baby she loved without ever having seen it. Mrs. Dunn learned to sing Sorrow's Song.

No family is exempt from experiencing the trauma of death, but it strikes some with unrelenting fury. Time and time again, it knocks on their door and causes floods of sorrow to permeate their lives. Why do some have "more than their fair share" of grief, yet other families know death's intrusion only briefly? I've never known of a family who has had to handle death's sting so many times and in such tragic circumstances as my dear friends, Glen and Annette.

From the first time we met, I knew that Glen and Annette would be the kind of friends everyone wants. Glen was an active deacon in the first church we served, always willing to help in any way. We could always call on Glen. We knew he'd be there.

And sweet Annette! No matter what else she wore, you could be sure that she'd be wearing a smile. She was an encouragement to all of us by her faith and positive attitude. This was especially inspiring to me in view of the fact that at age thirty and a mother of three young children, Annette had a leg amputated. It was her only hope to save her life from the cancer spreading throughout her body. Forced to confront her own immortality at an early age, she experienced great sorrow and grief as she lost one of her limbs, but there was no trace of bitterness or resentment in her. Undoubtedly she struggled with a barrage of questions and doubts and faced the possibility of her own death if the cancer was not arrested. Her faith stood the test of the trial, and she emerged as the victor. Of all people, didn't Glen and Annette now deserve to enjoy some of life's goodness after such a grueling experience?

In less than three years, however, sorrow again enveloped their world. This time it was not just death's shadow they encountered. With sudden fury, death stole their only son. Little Glen was about to turn five. He had decided to walk out to meet his eight-year old sister, Glynette, who was getting off the school bus. Annette was working in the house and talking with her Mom on the phone. When Glynette walked in the door, Annette asked, "Where's Little Glen?"

"I don't know," Glynette answered. "I haven't seen him."

"Didn't he meet you in the driveway?" Annette questioned as her pulse started to rise. Quickly, they walked out of the house calling his name. Almost immediately, Annette spotted Little Glen in the deep end of the pool. Glynette jumped in the water and pulled out his little body. The ambulance soon arrived and attempts were made to revive the boy. For a few agonizing days, Little Glen lay in the Intensive Care Unit lingering between life and death. Because no water was found in his lungs, the doctors surmised that he must have choked on the grapes he was eating. Then he fell unconscious into the pool.

Not many days later, a small casket was placed at the front of our church. At Glen and Annette's request, I sang with a quivering voice and tears streaming down my face, "Jesus loves me, this I know. For the Bible tells me so. Little ones to Him belong. They are weak, but He is strong."

But the song did not numb the pain. My own heart ached. I couldn't even begin to comprehend the depth of this family's sorrow, the guilt they would certainly face, and the questions swirling in their minds! "If only I hadn't been on the phone!" Annette has said a million times.

Glynette, now a young mother herself, still has problems accepting Little Glen's death. "I wish it had been me," she stated. "I feel guilty because he wouldn't have left the house if he hadn't been coming out to meet me. It's still very hard to talk about."

After such a tragedy, Glen and Annette needed a rest from the storms of life. Surely death, grief, and sorrow would leave them alone and give them a break! Yet it was not to be. A mere thirteen months later this family sat in the church with another casket in front of them. Once again, death cruelly invaded their family. This time it was Annette's younger brother, David, just twenty-one years-old, who was violently taken from them. The entire town was in a state of shock, devastated that such a thing could happen in our small community.

On Valentines Day only nineteen days earlier, we had rejoiced with this family as David married the young woman he loved. My husband performed the ceremony at our church, and I sang the songs of love and devotion. David was a special friend who worked closely with us in the music and youth departments of our church. As a two-year member of the Police Department, he loved his work and was excited to have his own wife and home. He expected to have a good life, doing work he found rewarding and having the one he loved by his side.

But on that fateful Thursday morning, the silent alarm from the local bank sounded at the police department. The dispatcher radioed David, the only patrolman on duty. David knew the bank had been having problems with the security system all week long, and he probably believed it was just another false alarm. As he arrived on the scene, he advised the department of his arrival, a normal procedure. Those were the last words he ever spoke. Two robbers were leaving the scene when David drove up. Before David could even pull his gun from it's holster, one of the bandits shot him in the head. David died instantly. The robbers and murderers sped away and to this day have never been caught.

Once again Glen and Annette's family gathered in the church. Two weeks before in this very room, they had laughed and rejoiced with David and his new bride. Now, within just a few short days of this joyous occasion, they gathered with hearts crumbled into a million pieces. Grief enclosed them, enveloping their very souls, making a casket of it's own for these left to carry on.

How much can one family take? Was it not enough that Annette had faced her own death and lost a leg to cancer? Then death took her young son in a freak accident. Now her brother had been shot and killed by a bank robber who was never brought to justice. She recently told me, "I couldn't help but ask 'Why?' I wondered what would be next and how much more I could take. 'How long can I be strong?'" she questioned. Then she added, "My faith is the only thing that's gotten me through."

What would be next? "No, there can be no more!" I cried for them. "Leave them alone, death. You have devastated their lives too many times! Haven't you caused enough pain for them?" But death was not finished seeking to destroy this family.

The year following David's death, Annette's father died. "Daddy gave up," Annette related to me. "He grieved himself to death. The tragedies of our family were all too much to take. He had nothing left, and his will to live was gone." The anguish of his heart was never relieved. Sorrow and grief relentlessly bombarded his soul, bringing about his own death.

The loss of her leg, her son, her brother, her father—and I've since learned she had a miscarriage after her first child's birth and lost a brother to heart failure when he was only thirty five!—forced Annette to learn to grieve. More than any family I know, Glen and Annette have learned to sing the songs of the night.

Each of us must face the reality of death. When I was a child, my father told me: "There are only two things certain in life: death and taxes." Our appointment with death is one that will not be cancelled. "For it is appointed unto men once to die, and after this, the judgment" (Hebrews 9:27, KJV). In reality, death is a part of life. "To everything there is a season, and a time for every purpose under heaven, a time to be born and a time to die" (Ecclesiastes 3:1,2, KJV). Of course I knew this! I was prepared to face my own immortality! I knew that life on earth was only temporary, just the route to our heavenly home. Death is the door into the very presence of God. Chuck and I both had the assurance of our sins forgiven because of our faith in Jesus Christ as Saviour. The issue was not *if* we would die—that was a given. We accepted, even expected to die one day. The issue was not even *where* we would spend eternity. That was settled. We knew according to the word of God that we had eternal life.

Even though death is certain, shouldn't it come after we've lived a rewarding life and are "full of years"? After our bodies grow old, and wear out? This is what we all expect and hope for, and in many cases, this is the case. For those who have lived a long and full life, their exit is anticipated and gentle, yet still sorrowful for those who miss them. For others, death comes unannounced and much too soon. With violent desecration, it unexpectedly rips through their lives, instilling in others a fear that it could happen in their families as well.

Regardless of the means and time of death, it is never easy for those of us left behind to let them go. Their absence leaves a hole in our lives that we initially think can never be filled. The sudden, totally unexpected entrance of death into our home filled my heart with sorrow I had never known. Would I ever recover from knowing that Chuck died by his own choice? Could I ever get over the trauma of his suicide? God's promises brought some comfort to my wounded soul, yet even with this wonderful anchor to which I desperately clung, sorrow was never far away. Any respite from sorrow's presence was brief. I longed for an instant fix. "Can't someone pray a prayer that will take away the pain? Isn't there something I can do that will relieve my agony? God, why don't You instantaneously heal my broken heart?" I sobbed with all my heart.

It has been helpful to realize I am not alone in facing sorrow and mourning. David, the greatest king to rule Israel, cried as he questioned, "How long, O Lord? Wilt Thou forget me forever? How long wilt Thou hide thy face from me? How long shall I take

---

I longed for an instant fix.

---

counsel in my soul, having sorrow in my heart all the day?" (Psalm 13:1,2, NASB). My heart weeps with his as I hear his desperate cry over the untimely death of his son Absalom, "O my son Absalom, my son, my son Absalom! Would I had died instead of you, O Absalom, my son, my son!" (II Samuel 18:33, NASB). Even though Absalom died seeking to overthrow his father as King, David mourned for the son he loved. King David knew how to sing Sorrow's Song.

Since time began, all members of the human race have been forced to deal with death's intrusion into their lives. I was not the first, nor will I be the last, to face this enemy. The first family to dwell on planet earth knew the sting of death, not only from their own disobedience when they died spiritually, but from experiencing first hand the horror of seeing their own flesh and blood murder his very brother. Can you imagine the grief this mother and father felt? Their hearts must have been ripped from their bodies as they actually lost both sons. Abel was dead, killed by a jealous brother: a cold-blooded homicide. It was painful to lose a child who bore your resemblance in so many ways, but to make matters worse, Adam and Eve had to face the reality that their own son, Cain, was the perpetrator responsible for Abel's death! One brother killed another.

For his sin, Cain was driven from his home and family, separated from them for the remainder of his years, and banished for the rest of his days. Though not physically dead, for all practical purposes, as far as his parents were concerned, Cain was gone. These parents sorrowed as they lamented the reality that both sons would no longer gather under their roof, sitting and visiting together as family. With hearts wrenching in torment, Adam and Eve surely must have learned to sing Sorrow's Song.

Let us not forget that the Lord Jesus himself was described as "a man of sorrows and acquainted with grief" (Isaiah 53:5). In the Garden of Gethsemane, just hours before bearing the sins of the world in his own body, he said, "My soul is deeply grieved to the point of death" (Mark 14:34, NASB). If Jesus uttered such cries of despair, then why do I think I should be exempt from experiencing the agony of my own heart?

I wish I could tell you an "abbra-ca-dabbra" formula I've discovered to dispel sorrow immediately. I wish I had a magic wand to wave and make everything all right. It has not worked that way for me. I never found the quick fix I wanted. Nor did any of my friends whose stories I shared earlier. All of us encountered grief in different circumstances. But regardless of the situation which caused our sorrow: the loss of a husband by suicide, parents who grew old and died by natural means, a young child in an accident, a brother who was murdered, an unborn baby we never held, or the facing of our own imminent death because of disease overtaking our bodies, the pain is the same. Sorrow and grief cannot be quantified; no one can claim greater sorrow than another. We all have felt the pain to the depth of our souls. It has saturated every part of our being. Some of you know what I mean.

Through my own experience, I have found God's presence to be sufficient to enable me to deal with the pain. Little by little, one step at a time, as I have struggled to face my great loss, I have rediscovered the joy of living. I have felt God's peace seeping into my heart in the midst of the storm. Gradually, as I have sought the Lord through the dark night of my soul, sorrow and grief have slowly been dispelled. I have been freed from their domination and released from their constant terror. The capacity to regain my equilibrium has been a welcome—and unexpected—discovery. Colette, Mrs. Dunn, Glen, and Annette stand in agreement with me. The Song of Sorrow that we sang in our grief has been replaced by a different song that we now sing.

But let me take you back, and fill in the gaps of my own story. Go back with me to the time I first met the dashing young man who would become my husband. Relive with me my experiences of joy, sorrow, despair, and doubt as I journeyed through the wilderness of pain. Walk with me as the winding road led me back to the promised land to find again the goodness of the Lord in the land of the living. There I discovered that the music of life that died with my husband could begin again.

I share my story with you to encourage you for the times when you too must sing Sorrow's Song. Grief is common to all of us. Each time we encounter a significant loss in our lives, whether through death, divorce, disease, disability or life's trying, everyday circumstances, we need to grieve in order to rebound from the loss. Facing sorrow and pain is necessary to begin to pick up the pieces.

What God has done for me, He can do for you. The same resources that I have found helpful in my time of grief are available to you. I'm no super-spiritual Christian! I'm just a normal person who loves the Lord with an imperfect love, who seeks to follow Him but often falls, and who has a faith that often waivers as I look at tragic situations instead of keeping my eyes on Jesus. If God can resurrect the song that once died in my life, then there is hope for you!

The shattered pieces of our hurting hearts can be put back together again, not just to survive, but to thrive. I offer you the gift of hope from the God on whom we have set our hope. You too can find a new song to sing! The songs of the night are often awkward and unmelodious. They are heard in whispers that are almost imperceptible, but they can lead to the song of resurrection and restoration. It is possible to begin again. But only you can make that choice. The invitation is extended. Will you come and sing with me?

"The Lord will command his lovingkindness in the daytime; and His song will be with me in the night" (Psalm 42:8, NASB).

2

The Love Song Moves to a Minor Key

He had disappeared. No one saw Chuck leave or had any idea where he might be. He didn't leave any message or instructions for the secretary; he walked out of the church office unobserved. As the afternoon hours slipped away, I knew that something was terribly wrong. My heart began to race! Fear began to imprison my mind.

Though the possibility of him being kidnapped or in an accident was not ruled out, I knew that the more likely reality was the depression was back. "Oh no, not again!" I pleaded. It can't be happening again, dear Lord. I thought we had put this behind us. I thought we fought the battle with depression and won. Please don't let it return! Please help my husband, where ever he is, to think clearly and handle these emotions!" No, we were not finished fighting the war against our old foe, depression. Once again it had reared its ugly head and disrupted our lives.

How could this be happening? Where had we gone wrong? It certainly didn't begin like this. No, it began as a Cinderella story, a song of love that was the sweetest I had ever sung.

Marrying Chuck Scheidt had been an answer to my prayers, a dream come true. I was captivated by this handsome, intelligent, and witty young man from the moment I first laid my eyes on him. The crowning touch of all these positive qualities, however, was a heart that loved God and wanted to serve Him. He was everything I ever hoped for, my Prince Charming!

Maybe "love is blind." I failed to see the warning signs following our engagement. After announcing our wedding date and beginning the necessary preparations, a haunting gloom consumed Chuck. Soon, he unexpectedly broke our engagement.

"It's not that I don't love you, Renee, but I'm just not ready for marriage," he said with reservation.

My heart sank. The dream of becoming Mrs. Chuck Scheidt was shattered. He then withdrew from the world, lying in bed in a state of helplessness and hopelessness. It was the first time since meeting him eighteen months earlier that I had ever seen him like this. Chuck's depression continued for a number of weeks before he "pulled out of it." Then without explanation, the sparkle returned to his eyes, and his hardy laugh rang through the halls of our school. Chuck's emotional re-emergence brought another surprise: a second marriage proposal!

I didn't hesitate to accept. Surely the previous waffling was just another case of "cold feet." *He just needed a little time to work through his reservations, I told myself. That's only natural after seeing his parents divorce after many years of marriage.* I never suspected that there might be something deeper involved than just "cold feet." After dating for almost two years, we were married on August 14, 1977. Those first months of marriage were "perfect." There couldn't have been a happier couple on the face of the earth! It didn't matter that our income was small or that we lived in an efficiency apartment during our early days of marriage as we completed college. Our simple home didn't dampen our joy. No one living in any mansion could have matched our happiness! Until the depression came.

Only four months after saying "I do," Chuck's depression crept into our lives and began it's reign of despair. Within a matter of days, I saw Chuck's whole demeanor drastically change—just as it had after our initial engagement. He seemed to be caught in a downward spiral he couldn't escape. For no apparent reason, he began to doubt his abilities and felt totally worthless. Helplessly, I watched the vivacious, confident man I had married change to someone who lacked any motivation even to try. Listlessness and gloom permeated his life.

What could cause such a change in his whole outlook? How could he swing from being so positive and energetic one week to being unable to get out of bed the next? I was at a loss to know how to help him. The words of encouragement and love I offered did no good. They were "like water off a duck's back." In our ignorance, neither of us realized he was suffering a major clinical depression caused by a chemical imbalance in the brain. Manic-depression was still an unknown term to us. It would be ten years later when we discovered this was the cause of the emotional mood swings Chuck fought all of his adult life.

Chuck stayed on that emotional roller coaster of up's and downs for the next eight months before he returned to his old self. During that period, counselors advised him to work on improving his self-esteem. Though it was slow in coming, it finally seemed as if this remedy was beginning to work. Gradually, the truth of his significance to God seeped into his mind. Steadily, as he began to grasp these concepts, the depression began to lift. We assumed that this must obviously be "the answer" to the problem since Chuck was improving.

I was at a loss to know how to help him.

Step by step I saw my husband come out of the deep pit he had been in for months. "I'm fine now, Renee," Chuck tried to assure my fearful heart. "Now that I understand who I am in Christ, I don't have to doubt my abilities anymore or feel insecure about life. I know I'm somebody, 'cause God don't make no junk!" he said with a laugh.

Neither of us had any idea that the enemy we were fighting was much bigger than a simple "change your way of thinking" problem. After months of living with the insecurity and fear of having a husband who could barely perform normal daily duties, I was willing to do just about anything to get back the man I had married. This was the answer the counselor gave us, and it was the one we believed. As long as the dark clouds blew away, that was all that mattered.

Chuck's unstable emotional health had taken it's toll on me as well. The depression not only affected Chuck, but I changed from the upbeat, bubbly person I had always been to someone experiencing great doses of anxiety and mistrust. "Where is the strong young man I married? I don't want to be the strong one, Lord!" I cried in fear and anger.

The constant fear of wondering what each day would bring and the insecurity of not knowing if my husband could function that day weighed heavily upon me. Yet I had to put on a smile and a cheerful face as I went to teach my music classes each day. My energy was sapped by the pain of having to go on with life's routines while I struggled with the fear that Chuck would never get any better. And my struggle was compounded by intense loneliness. I didn't think *anybody* would understand my fear. . . and anger. . and hopelessness.

When you are a "dedicated Christian," the humiliation of being depressed can be overwhelming! Very few people in our world understood us! In the back of our minds, we thought there simply *must* be some biblical truth Chuck could put into action to relieve the turmoil. Wasn't it true that if you did what you knew was right—even when you didn't feel like it—positive feelings would eventually follow? Couldn't we speak the truth and in Jesus' name command the depression to leave? No matter how many Bible verses we quoted on the victory we have in Christ or how hard Chuck worked to apply them, the depression never left for long.

Some people told us, "If you were spiritual enough, you wouldn't have this problem. You must have some unconfessed sin in your life, or you're simply not doing what you know you should."

How very sad that brothers and sisters in Christ judge each other so harshly. It was easier to hide the reality of our situation than try to explain it to people who had pat, cut and dry, black and white answers.

Sometimes Chuck felt better and a semblance of life entered his eyes and his outlook. But soon the dark clouds were back. I felt angry and confused. "Didn't we put this behind us?" I asked with bewilderment. "They said Chuck just needed to improve his self-esteem. I thought we took care of that. I thought we dealt with the problem and could move on now. The reality is we haven't gone anywhere. We're back at square one!" I sobbed.

After a particularly long, gut-wrenching episode with depression, Chuck became adept at masking his true emotions. Unsuspectingly, I thought everything was fine. I had no clue that although he always projected the image of a man "having it all together and under control," inside he was dying. Satan played with my mind as I entertained the condemning thought, *You must not be a very good wife, Renee! He couldn't even tell you, his wife, the one he's supposed to be closer to than anyone in the world, his innermost thoughts!*

Why didn't Chuck confide in me? I wanted to be there for him giving love and support during the times of confusion, but he wouldn't let me in. The depth of his pain was hidden inside, not shared with a single living soul.

He had worn that mask since our recent move from south

Florida (where we met in college), to a little town in central Florida called Frostproof. Only three months earlier, we took our first "real job" as music and youth staff members at a church in this quaint town nested between several lakes and orange groves. The months went by. I thought he was doing so much better now. But it was an illusion.

Then the Monday came that I couldn't find him. My mind was numb as I desperately wondered, *Where could Chuck be?!* I tried to stay calm, giving reasonable explanations for his sudden disappearance. *Maybe he went to the hospital in the neighboring town to visit someone. Or perhaps someone called and wanted to meet with him for lunch,* I nervously tried to assure myself. But as the hours ticked by and Chuck didn't appear, all reasonable explanations vanished. So did my strength. My entire body felt like a bowl of jello.

I phoned local authorities and explained that I couldn't find my husband. Soon, the whole town of Frostproof knew that the new minister of youth was missing. Search groups were dispatched. I was overcome at the display of support shown by the good folks of our town, many whom I had not even met. People dropped what they were doing to help in the search. Groups were formed to begin combing the orange groves. Four-wheel drive vehicles rode through the brush and groves in hopes of finding some sign of Chuck. The Frostproof police department brought in bloodhounds to trace his path. Phone calls were made to friends and family members across the country. I hoped that someone had heard from him.

But no one had heard a word. My husband was gone without leaving any sign or clue. I was in a state of shock as I tried to grapple with the reality of the situation. It seemed as if my mind was only half working. I was unable to make decisions, and I gladly followed the advice of wise, godly people from our church since I was in no condition to think straight. Though I was just getting to know these folks, they cared for me like I was a family member. Praise God for the support a church family gives to one another! I needed them so much!

Soon the night began to fall, and the day's search was halted. A new friend, Jan, brought dinner out to the house and came prepared to stay with me overnight. I had no appetite, but I gladly accepted her offer to spend the night. I needed someone to be with me during this trauma. Her physical presence helped me stay in control of myself.

Every time the phone rang, I jumped, hoping it might be Chuck. The phone rang constantly as more people learned of Chuck's disappearance, but the one call I longed for never came. All night long I lay awake praying that Chuck would come home. I listened for the front door to open. But it never did. The night seemed endless as I waited for the light of dawn when the search could continue. By the next morning it was obvious that the time had come to reach beyond the local boundaries. By noon, twenty-four hours since Chuck was last seen, the state police were contacted and an APB (All Points Bulletin) was issued. Newspapers prepared to run the story.

This can't be real! I thought. *This is all just a bad dream. I'm going to wake up with Chuck lying right beside me. Then he will hold me, and comfort me, and reassure me that everything is fine.* As much as I wanted that to be true, the reality was that my husband had been missing for over twenty-four hours.

I guess it is part of fallen human nature to speculate and make a painful situation into something even worse. When some people learned that Chuck was missing, they started a rumor that Chuck had left me. They said we were having marital problems, and he had walked out on me! My story of Chuck "missing" must have seemed too simple to believe! Sadly, it has been an eye-opening experience for me to realize that the love of gossip is found among all groups, including Christians who appreciate juicy news as much as anyone else.

Tuesday came and went with no evidence to give any lead as to what had happened to Chuck. People from our church graciously stayed with me around the clock and sent food to the house. For the first time in my life, I understood what it was to fast, not for health reasons as I had done in the past, or even for the sake of trying to draw closer to God, but simply because I was so overwhelmed with sorrow and pain that I had no appetite. My digestive system seemed to shut down. The very thought of food repulsed me. I sat or lay on the couch all day as I continued to cry out to God, begging Him to please protect Chuck and send him back to me.

Though I hadn't dismissed the other possibilities completely, I knew the greater probability was that he was very depressed—just like before, only worse this time. A phrase from the parable of the Prodigal Son in Luke 14:17 kept running through my mind: "When he came to himself. . . ." This was my constant prayer for Chuck during this time. "Lord, let him 'come to himself.' Let him think clearly and see that we can work this out and deal with what ever we need to."

Time stood still, dragging by, as we waited all day Tuesday for a call. . . *anything* that would give us a lead to find Chuck. That night, sleep again evaded me. Wednesday morning dawned, and we knew nothing more than we had Monday afternoon. Still not one sign of Chuck. I began to think of what I would do if he were never found. The reality that Chuck might no longer be a part of my life started to seep into my consciousness. I felt even more confused as the situation grew darker.

Everything that could possibility be done in this situation was done. No stone was left unturned in the search for the missing youth minister. Needless to say, this was not only the talk of the town, but outside our area as well, as the search went state-wide and beyond. I knew that only God could help us. Human resources were utilized to the fullest with no results. God and God alone was the only one with any power to change the situation. I continually cried and pleaded with Him to bring my husband back to me!

All day Wednesday, I felt a growing sense of despair. It began to look as if God was not going to answer my cry. "Are my prayers and those of other people across the country even making it past the ceiling, God?" I questioned angrily. No one had seen a trace of Chuck.

"You've *got* to eat something, Renee," my mother and others prodded me. But my appetite was gone. The kitchen was full of delicious food sent by loving people from our church. Normally I would have stuffed myself with such wonderful food, but now the thought of eating only turned my stomach.

The night fell, and as before, the search crews called it a day. Nothing else could be done until the light of morning broke. The phone rang continually as people called, wanting to know if there was any new word. Always, it was the same answer: No.

Wednesday evening at 7:15, the phone rang . Mom answered it to try to protect me from the ordeal of rehashing the same words. But this call was different. It was Connie, our church organist, calling from the church office with the words we had longed to hear. She told my mother, "Chuck's here in the office and wants to see Renee."

Immediately, I was off! I didn't know where he had been, how long he had been in the office, his physical condition, or anything else! I knew nothing—except that Chuck was back! That was all

I needed to hear to fly down to the office. And fly I did! I broke all the speed limits as I raced down the eight mile road to meet my husband. Fear gripped my heart as I drove, uncertain of what I would see or hear.

Nervously I stepped into the office. I was unprepared for what I was about to see. I had never seen Chuck look so bad. As my eyes came upon him, I saw a man whose hair was dirty and matted; he was unshaven, and his nice sport jacket was badly wrinkled. But the most painful sight was the look in Chuck's eyes. Those big, beautiful, brown eyes, usually dancing and filled with light, were dark and full of sadness; his face was long and shallow. *This is only a shell of a man!* I thought as I sobbed. I could hardly stand to see Chuck hurting so deeply.

We quickly moved to the church's guest room to be alone. There were a million questions I wanted to ask, but I waited for Chuck to start to talk. He began to weep as he said, "I've been struggling with depression now for sometime, Renee, but I didn't want you to know it. I knew it would just worry you. For the past few weeks, I'd come to the office and just close myself up in it, reading anything I thought might help me get over this. But nothing worked. Finally, last Monday morning, I just couldn't take it any longer. It was all more than I could handle. So I left the office, went over to the educational building, and hid in the storage room. I lay down under all of those cardboard boxes, curled up in a fetal position, and have been there ever since. I heard you come through Monday afternoon, calling my name, but I couldn't respond. But tonight I heard the people singing during prayer meeting, and I knew I needed to come back. So I walked back to the office and found Connie here. I asked her to call you. I know you've probably been worried to death."

The tears streamed down my face as I said in a soft voice, "I love you, Chuck. I just want you to be happy. I don't know why you're depressed, but you know I'm here for you. I don't care what you do for a living as long as it makes you happy. If this is not what you want to do, we can find something else."

Though Chuck looked horrible, he was coherent and able to comprehend all I said. In fact, he began to smile and gently laugh as our conversation continued. *Has Chuck experienced a 'nervous breakdown'?* I wondered? How could he have been in such a confused mental state several days earlier and now appear to be "in his right mind"? He was weak from going without food for the past three days, but he clearly understood everything that was going on. I was at a loss as to how to evaluate this whole episode. I had never seen such behavior or even heard about anyone else acting in this manner. And to talk with him now only compounded my confusion. He didn't act like a "crazy person." He appeared to have all his mental faculties intact. Had he just "snapped" Monday morning? I had no experience, education, or even common knowledge to understand what had transpired these past three days. I knew we needed to find someone who could evaluate all of these events so we could prevent such a terrible ordeal from ever happening again.

The next few days are a blur in my mind. By this time I was completely worn out—physically, mentally, emotionally and spiritually. Chuck had just gone through a devastating trauma. So had I. Neither of us had much to offer to the other since we were both totally spent. We were in desperate need for someone to bind our wounds and give rest to our tormented minds and bodies so we could recover from this crisis. Though outwardly we both looked whole, inwardly we were suffering something much worse than any physical malady.

I thought, *I don't know what it is, but something is drastically wrong with my husband. He needs help, and I don't know how to give it to him. I have prayed, encouraged, loved, done anything I could to help him and his ministry. But it wasn't enough. I don't know what else to do. We must find someone who knows what to do to help him!*

I had a myriad of questions I wanted to ask Chuck: "Why didn't you let me know you were slipping into depression again? You promised you'd tell me if it started to happen again! Didn't you think about what this was doing to me? Didn't you know I'd be worried sick over you? How could you stay in that small storage room for three days? What were you thinking all of that time? Didn't you realize how this would affect your ministry? The entire foundation that we have tried to establish here for the past three months is gone!" But for now, the questions must wait. The most important thing at this point was that Chuck was back. He needed help, and I would do all I could to be a positive factor in the process of stabilizing his emotions.

I could imagine what the good people of our church and town must have thought! They were probably more befuddled than me in trying to understand Chuck's strange behavior. Would we even have a job at the church after all that had happened? How could parents trust us to train their children in the ways of God when they weren't sure if the youth minister was emotionally stable? Was Chuck responsible enough to handle this job? I know those thoughts were tossed about in their minds and conversations. I fully understood the reservations they had after the events of the last three days. Our lives were in their hands. They had the power—and plenty of reasons—to ask for our resignations.

That's not what they chose to do. Under our pastor's loving, knowledgeable leadership, the majority of the people stood behind us. He knew Chuck needed professional psychological help. He stated, "Chuck, I want you to take the next three weeks off to recover from this traumatic experience. I also want you to make an appointment with a Christian psychologist in Saint Petersburg who is highly recommended. You have an emotional problem that needs to be dealt with properly. I believe he can help you."

In the midst of so much turmoil, I was grateful to have him point us in the right direction! *Perhaps this is what Chuck needs in order to get to the root of all that has plagued him these past few years,* I thought. The call to the psychologist's office was made, and the first appointment was scheduled for the following week.

With great anxiety Chuck and I made the ninety mile trip to Saint Petersburg. Though we tried to keep the conversation in the car upbeat, listening to good Christian music as we drove, we were both nervous and uncertain about what the psychologist would find. I stayed in the waiting room while Chuck was given various psychological tests. I felt so fatigued I could hardly keep my eyes open. Eventually, I fell asleep as I waited for Chuck to finish. Worry and anxiety had drained all of my physical energy. Several hours later, the first visit was over, and we began the long ride home. "What did he say?" I nervously asked.

"Not much," Chuck replied. "He'll look over the tests, and we'll go from there. He recommended I start reading the book, *The Sensation of Being Somebody*, by Maurice Wagner." Was it a coincidence that this was the same book we had read during our first year of marriage while living in south Florida?

The next appointment was scheduled for the following week. I wanted to scream, "That's too far away! Let's get on with this process!" I quickly learned that's not the way it works. Though I wanted so much to find a "quick fix," "take this and you'll be OK" answer to this problem, the reality of the situation was that it wouldn't be that simple. It was going to take some time to deal with whatever was plaguing Chuck. Healing, (barring a sudden, divine intervention from God), whether it's physical or emotional, takes time. As much as I wanted to, I couldn't rush the process. We would have to wait until next week to see Dr. Jones and find out the results of the psychological testing.

During the time Chuck had been missing, I had called anyone who might have heard from him. I didn't care about the phone bill or what anyone thought. I just hoped someone might know something to help us find him. Now I needed to follow through on these conversations and let these people know Chuck had returned and was safe. But I dreaded these calls! What would I say? How could I try to explain his bizarre behavior? One by one, I worked my way through the list of people. I thanked them for their love and concern. Basically I told them that Chuck had suffered an emotional breakdown but was on the road to recovery. I requested their continued prayer support as we sought to recover from this trauma.

For both Chuck and me, this was a very humbling experience. Our wounds were exposed to everyone in the world! There was no pretension of being anything other than what we were—two people who loved and served the Lord but who also faced emotional and psychological problems. Although there were some unkind, critical remarks by a few people, we received great love and support from most.

The counseling sessions in Saint Petersburg continued for the next five weeks. How much I wished I could be in that room to hear all that was said! At the conclusion of the sixth session, the doctor said, "Chuck I don't need to see you every week anymore. Let's meet in two weeks." We were encouraged to see that Dr. Jones felt good about Chuck's progress! In fact, I personally was amazed at how quickly Chuck bounced back from the devastating episode. Within just a few days of his return, he seemed like "the old Chuck" to me. He would have gone back to work the next week if our pastor hadn't insisted that he take some time off. Yet I knew Chuck had successfully hidden his emotional problems from me in the past, and I realized I was not a good judge of his inner feelings. It was encouraging when a professional psychologist confirmed that Chuck was moving forward in a positive way.

After the seventh appointment, Dr. Jones gave us the good news, "Chuck, you've done good work these past eight weeks. I feel you've got a handle on the things you need to know to deal appropriately with your emotions in the future. There really is no need for us to continue with the counseling sessions on a bi-weekly basis. If you start feeling like you are slipping into depression, then call me and make an appointment. We can meet whenever you feel the need. Otherwise, just keep doing the things you're doing."

Sometimes I've wondered, "Why, God?"

What was Dr. Jones' assessment of Chuck's problem? The answers seemed so simple. There were no new revelations or backbreaking tasks required of Chuck. Basic, fundamental truths that we both already knew were emphasized. "Back to the Basics" could have been the summary statement of the entire seven sessions with the psychologist. Dr. Jones stressed to Chuck that he must have the proper self-image and realize his position in Christ and how valuable he was to God. This was the reason he asked Chuck to read Maurice Wagner's book. He also stated that Chuck was too much of a perfectionist. He needed to learn to "lighten up" and not expect so much of himself. Chuck also needed to begin to express his emotions instead of bottling them up. This would prevent his frustrations from building and eventually erupting into a major emotional volcano.

We were elated that this was all Chuck needed to do in order to handle his emotions more effectively! Dr. Jones had found no major problems. He just needed to apply a few foundational truths in his daily actions and attitudes. These were things we could immediately and easily begin to implement. I told a friend, "How wonderful to hear from 'someone who knows' just why Chuck has struggled as he has! Praise God that we can work on these areas, and go on with a normal life!" Needless to say, both Chuck and I were thrilled with the doctor's final conclusions.

Three weeks after his emotional breakdown, Chuck returned to work at the church. He seemed to be doing well. From all outward appearances, he was full of life, laughter, and plans. We wanted to put the nervous breakdown behind us and continue with the ministry. Life returned to what I thought was "normal." I didn't see Chuck in a depressed state again for the next several years. This observation was merely another confirmation to me that those days were behind us.

But later, I began to notice a certain pattern in Chuck's life. I thought back on the years I had known him, and the pattern became clear. I realized there were both depressive and manic episodes—downs and ups which were more pronounced than for most people. He had learned, however, to mask his emotions to me, his church congregation, and friends. There wasn't a single person in the world who knew what was really going on inside. His position as a youth minister gave him the perfect outlet for the manic times. Chuck could be this "wild and crazy" youth director, acting like one of the kids in sports activities. Then he could come into the church and calmly lead them in wonderful Bible studies.

It is almost embarrassing for me to say now, but I truly believed the bouts with depression were over. Had we not sought professional help and gotten to the bottom of the problem? We had the right answers now! We would put them into action, and everything was going to be just fine. How I wish that had been true! How I would have loved for it all to be that simple, that cut and dried! A, B, C. One, Two, Three.

The truth was, however, that although the psychologist gave good, fundamental truths that needed to be activated in Chuck's life, the real root of his strange behavior still had not been uncovered. It was not a lack of application of the truths that caused emotional problems for my husband. The real reason for Chuck's emotional roller coaster ride—past, present, and future—was due to a physiological problem, a chemical imbalance in the brain. Bi-polar disorder, or manic-depression as it is commonly called, still remained undiagnosed.

Sometimes I've wondered, "Why, God? Why didn't You let us discover the real problem back in 1979? We sought professional help, and this is what they told us! We listened to those who should have known about these things, but they missed it! Why didn't they give him a physical then? We were trusting that what they told us was right." There is no easy answer for such questions. It is during the times of hard questions, when our understanding is blackened, we must employ faith in God's sovereignty, goodness and love. When we don't know why, and it doesn't seem right, we have to walk by faith.

The song that began as a song of love in a strong, major key moved into the minor mode. In fact, at times the tones were so discordant I could barely follow the melody. "Lord, I'm not sure

I can sing in this minor key very well. Let's please get back to the major key," I whispered. "This is too hard. I'm not that good of a musician to sing these strange clusters of tone that don't seem to mesh." How I hoped and prayed after the counseling sessions with Dr. Jones that the music was moving back to the original key. From all indications, it appeared we were headed in that direction. But my voice was very shaky from all we had undergone. With a very faltering voice, I softly began to sing the song in it's original version, trying to believe it would crescendo, growing stronger and better as time went by. Little did I know that the worst was yet to come.

3

Same Song, Second Verse

C huck, would you please bring me another box? I'm finished with this one!" I yelled from the kitchen out into the garage where he was packing, too. The winds of change were blowing. Within twenty-four hours we would be gone, lock, stock and barrel, headed for the big city of New Orleans!

I didn't want to leave. The little town of Frostproof had become home for me these past three years. We had wonderful friends, a good ministry, and a lovely home here. And the weather was just the way I liked it! But best of all, Chuck hadn't encountered any more bouts with depression since the nightmare almost three years earlier. I was convinced the dark clouds which shadowed us in the early years of our marriage had blown away for good. Life had become "normal." But now this part of our lives would soon be over. Tomorrow morning we would load the rented truck with all of our "stuff" and head down the long road from central Florida to "The Big Easy" to begin classes at New Orleans Baptist Theological Seminary. We both would begin master level work with Chuck continuing on into the doctoral program in psychology and counseling. The first step of our new journey would start at the crack of dawn.

All week long, I had watched Chuck's level of excitement grow. Never had I seen him as exhilarated as he was that first week of January, 1982. "I'm excited to see my dreams of completing my education become a reality, Renee!" he told me. His thoughts were running a mile a minute.

"He's flying high," I shared with my friend Jan. "You should hear him talk about all the ideas he has. I've never seen him so on fire for the Lord!" In spite of my pleas, he hardly stopped packing to eat or sleep the entire week. "Come to bed, Chuck!" I called from the bedroom late at night where I had already fallen exhausted into bed.

"Not now, Renee! I've got too much I want to finish here!" he yelled back. Then he would burst out in a loud laugh that almost sounded spooky.

"You wouldn't believe how talkative Chuck is now!" I mentioned to Jan. "It's as if someone gave him a talking pill. He's even out-talking me, if you can believe it!" It bothered me that Chuck wasn't eating much, and that he only got a few hours sleep each night. I knew that wasn't normal, but I rationalized that Chuck was just "super excited" to be pursuing his educational goals. In my ignorance, I didn't realize this was the other "pole" of bi-polar disorder. The manic side of manic-depression was in full blossom.

We spent our last night in Frostproof with a group of friends out on the town. Chuck was the life of the party that night, full of jokes and witty comments that kept us all laughing. Even our pastor was somewhat alarmed as he noticed how "high" Chuck was, but he let it go like we all did. Late that evening, the party ended and we left for our last night in our little house.

As he had been doing all week, Chuck refused to come to bed when we arrived home. "You need a good night's sleep. We've got a big day tomorrow," I said as I tried unsuccessfully to get him to get some rest. No amount of coaxing on my part would change his mind. Finally, I gave up and quickly dozed off.

About 2:00 a.m. I was awakened by the sound of water running in the bathroom. "I'm just going to take a bath, Renee!" Chuck yelled.

Good idea! I thought. Maybe the warm water would soothe his hyperactivity and calm him down enough to get some sleep. I dozed off again, thinking that soon Chuck would crawl into bed.

The next thing I knew, I was jolted from my sleep! Chuck came bounding from the bathtub, running through the house like a maniac, ranting and raving like a wild man! "What in the world happened?" I gasped. I was frozen with fright as I saw my husband completely break with reality. *Has he lost his mind? Is this what happens when someone goes insane?* I asked myself.

Chuck ran into the garage and closed the door behind him. I hesitantly followed at a distance. "Don't come out here, Renee!" he yelled through the garage door. "If you know what's good for you, don't come out here!" I knew he meant what he said, and I was terrified! Never in my twenty-seven years had I ever seen anyone act like this. I instinctively took the knife set in front of me which was to be packed in the morning, and I put it out of sight. My eyes caught sight of Chuck's two hunting guns, a shotgun and rifle, that were also laying out to be packed. Quickly, I hid the bullets as a precautionary measure.

"Mike, something has happened to Chuck! I don't know what it is, but he acts like he's gone crazy!"

Somehow, even in my state of shock, I had the insight to know that in this break with reality, Chuck was capable of harming both of us. "Can I call Mike, our pastor, and ask him to come out?" I fearfully asked, talking through the door that separated the kitchen from the garage. To my surprise, Chuck said yes. He later told me that he had agreed for Mike to come over because he knew of Mike's experiences in Vietnam, and he thought Mike might have some understanding of what was happening to him.

I quickly dialed the number I knew so well. "Mike, something has happened to Chuck! I don't know what it is, but he acts like he's gone crazy! We need help. Please come over right now!" I begged.

"I'll be right there," he replied. It wasn't long before Mike arrived with two friends, Larry and Orville. I'm so glad Mike had the wisdom to bring help with him.

By this time, Chuck had calmed down somewhat, but his behavior was still very abnormal. Mike coaxed Chuck back into the house where he then fell into his arms, sobbing.

"We've got to get him to the emergency room, Renee," Mike told me.

As we rode to the hospital, Chuck talked continuously, only half making sense. I sat there by my husband with tears running down my face. *He has lost his mind. He is going to have to go into a mental hospital,* I thought. *This is what happens when someone goes insane.* A numbness began to come over my entire body. My whole world was falling apart. The man I loved had just suffered a major mental breakdown. We planned to leave in just a few hours to start a brand new life in New Orleans. What would we do now? *My husband has gone insane. He is mentally incapable of making this move. Yet, we've sold our house, resigned our jobs, and don't belong here anymore. I don't know what's going to happen to us,* I thought as I sobbed.

Chuck was admitted to the local hospital. *What could have caused Chuck's bizarre behavior?* I wondered. *What caused him to break?*

I earnestly asked one of the men on duty, "What's wrong with my husband?"

"Depression," he curtly answered.

I quickly replied, "I know what depression is. I've seen Chuck so depressed he couldn't get out of bed. I don't know what you call this current experience, but this is *not* depression."

The hospital employee offered no further comments as he watched me sit in the waiting room. I wept while I waited to see my husband. The people on duty at the hospital wouldn't—or couldn't—give me any information, so I didn't understand Chuck had just experienced a week-long manic episode which culminated in a complete mental breakdown.

It was about an hour before I was allowed to see Chuck. When I entered his room, he was lying quietly in the bed. He saw me standing hesitantly at the door and spoke to me in a gentle voice. "Come in, Renee." Amazingly, he was very still, quiet, and subdued. So different from only an hour earlier! I was certain they must have given him something to calm him down.

"What medication did they give you?" I inquired.

"Nothing yet," he answered.

How could there be such a change in only an hour's time? I was sure the difference in his state of mind had to be the result of medication. My mind was boggled as I tried to assimilate all that was happening.

"I love you, Chuck. You'll see the doctor in the morning. He'll help us find the answer to this. For now, you get some sleep." I gave him a hug and left the room.

What else was there to say? I tried to be strong for Chuck, but as soon as I was out of his sight, I burst into tears. I felt so alone and insecure. The man of my dreams had just suffered an emotional and mental collapse. All of our plans were now shattered! What should I do now? *Go home, and try to get some sleep,* my mind whispered.

But how could I sleep when the bottom had just fallen out from under me? Mike, Larry, and Orville took me back home with the promise to come back to see me the next morning. I fell into bed, and cried myself to sleep as the questions and fears bombarded my mind all night. Even in sleep, my mind had no rest.

I awoke early that morning, just a few hours since returning from the hospital, and quickly made my way back there. Chuck was awake and appeared to be sharp and alert as far as I could observe. We were able to talk and carry on a normal conversation. How could he make such dramatic changes and snap back so quickly? I was baffled at the entire situation. Chuck was just as confused about his bazaar behavior the previous night. Neither of us had any explanations. We hoped the doctor would help us understand all these strange events.

Later that morning, the doctor came by. I was seated by the bed and heard the brief conversation. "Tell me what happened last night, Chuck," the doctor began.

Chuck briefly related the events of the previous evening. The doctor was convinced that in view of all the changes taking place so quickly in our lives, Chuck had simply allowed himself to become overworked and overexcited. He prescribed a sedative for Chuck and instructed him, "Don't let yourself get so worked up again. If you see yourself heading in that same direction, get help before you come to a crashing stop like you did this time." With this prescription and admonition, the doctor left.

Soon the release forms were filed and we were on our way home. *That's it?* I questioned. *Is that all there is to it? Was it all this simple? We were free to go on our merry way after my husband had just about lost his mind? Was I overreacting and making more of what I had seen than I should? Had Chuck just allowed himself to become too 'worked up'?* The questions poured through my thoughts.

I was a nervous wreck. All the security systems I had previously depended on were gone. Especially the security that a husband is to provide his wife. How could Chuck provide me with that security when he didn't have it in his own life? Though I still didn't know the reasons why, it was very clear to me that my husband was mentally unstable. To other people, he could project the image of someone having it all together. For a long time, I believed in that image as well. But by the time this twelve-hour episode was over, it was glaringly evident to me that something was terribly wrong with him.

We drove to our home, shaken by the events of the night before. I still couldn't believe we were going to go on just as if nothing had happened! How could we leave this town, the only support system we had, in view of what Chuck had just experienced? When we reached our house, we were greeted by a group of folks from our church who had come to give a hand in the huge task of loading the truck. I was so glad to see them! Yes, the word of Chuck's breakdown had quickly gotten around town, and these people cared enough to come. It helped to have them by my side.

Our pastor took charge of the situation as we began packing the truck. I threw myself into the work before me. As long as I didn't think about what I had just seen a few hours earlier, I could keep going. But when I let up and remembered all that had just transpired, I started to weep.

I didn't want Chuck to know how scared I really was. I felt I must be strong for him, but I didn't want to be the strong one! I wanted to have someone hold me and tell me everything would be all right. I wanted to curl up under someone's strong arm of protection. Since my husband couldn't comfort and protect me, I was forced to turn to the Lord. Was I wrong to want—or need— my husband to provide the security I longed for? Was this a sign of my being "unspiritual," looking to a man instead of the Lord? I don't think so.

By mid-afternoon, the truck was filled, and the house was spotless. Mike then called us to the side and said, "Ed (one of the leading men of our church) and I have decided to drive with you to New Orleans. We'll help you unpack everything and then fly back home. We'll leave early Monday morning for New Orleans. Tonight and tomorrow night, you will stay with Ed and Joyce. They have plenty of room, and everything is already arranged."

You don't know how good those words sounded to me! I was so thankful to have Mike and Ed going with us. I will always be grateful to them for the sacrificial love they showed to us. They gave their time from their own job responsibilities, and their money for their own air fare to help a struggling young couple. God knew how much we needed a strong hand to support us on the journey, and He provided it through Mike and Ed.

We went to Ed's house, where Joyce had a hot meal waiting for us. It felt so good to be in their lovely home. There I found the sense of security I wanted so much. I knew they would take care of me. I told them I was afraid, and I asked them to pray with me. I didn't want to leave this haven of rest that God provided, but I knew it would soon come to an end.

Joyce and Ed realized Chuck needed more than just tranquilizers to deal with Friday night's behavior. They were closely involved with a counselor in Orlando, and they suggested Chuck talk with him. I was 100% in favor of this idea. I knew I didn't know the answers for Chuck's problems, but I knew it had to be more than just getting "too worked up." I hoped this man could give us the answers we had been seeking so long. I sighed with relief when Chuck agreed to see the counselor.

Ted, the counselor, came the next day to meet with Chuck. I liked him from the start. They spent many hours together counseling and praying. After all was said and done, Ted concluded that Chuck's basic problem was the attitude he had towards his father. He told Chuck, "You have bitterness, anger, and resentment in your heart towards your dad because of the divorce, his drinking, and his remarriage. This root of bitterness is the basis of all the emotional problems you've experienced over the years. You need to call your father and ask for his forgiveness for this wrong attitude. You will never have emotional health until you do."

Was this the answer we desperately needed? Had we finally discovered and exposed the root of the problem? After all these years, had we found the answer? I desperately hoped Ted was right! With simplicity of heart, we accepted the counsel he gave and thanked God for leading us to this man. Now the days of fighting depression would be behind us! This root of bitterness that had caused so much pain would be removed, freeing Chuck from the terrible foe he had fought for over nine years! In our naivety and zeal for God's Word, we once again thought we had finished the battle.

We were up at dawn Monday morning to begin the long journey to New Orleans. Mike drove our car, and Ed drove the rental truck. The long trip afforded much opportunity for talks with them. Despairingly, I asked Mike, "Do you really think we should do this? Do you think we'll be OK in this big city? Even after talking with Ted, I'm still scared."

"You're gonna be all right, Renee," Mike calmly said. "Chuck needs to do this. He's cut out for teaching, and he will be much more satisfied working in those positions." Though Mike tried to give me the reassurance I desperately wanted, it didn't work. I could tell he had reservations and wasn't truly convinced of Chuck's emotional stability.

We stopped in Pensacola to spend the night, ready for a break from the road. From our motel room that evening, Chuck phoned his father to ask for his forgiveness for the wrong attitudes Chuck had harbored toward him. It was a very difficult conversation for both of them. His dad was surprised to hear the words that came from his son, but he was receptive. I sat on the bed praying for both Chuck and his dad as they talked. As the conversation ended and Chuck hung up the receiver, he breathed a deep sigh of relief. He had done it! He had followed Ted's advice. Once again, we believed that we had found the key to Chuck's problem. He had put this truth into action. Now the problem with depression would be solved.

I know you must be thinking, *How could they have been so dumb not to see what is so clear!* As I recount our life's story and see it in black and white, it is very apparent to me now. But when I experienced these events, it was not obvious at all. In the midst of traumatic circumstances, we sometimes "can't see the forest for the trees." It was as if I were looking in a mirror that was all fogged up and blurry. *Bi-polar disorder* was still an unknown word to me. No one to whom we turned for help ever suggested there might be a physiological basis for Chuck's emotional problems. As before, the disorder remained undiagnosed, and we continued walking down the wrong road.

Upon arriving in New Orleans, we unpacked the truck, and then drove Mike and Ed to the airport to catch a flight back to Orlando. How could we ever thank them for all they had done for us? I hated to see them leave, and I wanted to hold on to them as long as I could because I was fearful that Chuck might have a relapse. I fought back the tears as they entered the terminal. Now it was just Chuck and me. Here we were—on our own in New Orleans, Louisiana.

I was a fish out of water. I didn't really want to be here in the first place, under the best conditions. And these certainly weren't the best conditions! *Was Ted right in what he had said?* I wondered. I wanted to believe it, and I prayed that the worst was now behind us. But I was still very much afraid and felt very alone. There wasn't a single person here in this big city I could confide in. How could I share with strangers that my husband was mentally unstable? I certainly didn't want to belittle him in their sight. But I couldn't share my insecurities with Chuck either. That would only put more pressure on him, and he couldn't handle it. One of us had to keep some form of self-control. The job clearly fell on my shoulders.

It was very difficult to keep all of this to myself. "I wish I had somebody to talk to, Lord," I softly whimpered. To have no one made my burden seem even heavier. Perhaps you think I am unspiritual. Perhaps you think I should have been able to "give it to the Lord" and find my security and support in Him instead of people. I believe we have a very real need for one another as Christians. God often ministers to us through others. The reality was: I didn't have even one person I could be totally honest with and express my deepest fears.

Thankfully, God soon provided someone in whom I could confide. The director of testing, Dr. Don Minton, had such a caring attitude. He knew how difficult it can be for young people making the move to seminary. I found a genuine warmth in him, and I felt comfortable enough with him during the admissions testing and evaluations to share the traumatic episodes I had experienced with Chuck.

What normally took only one hour to evaluate took four for me! Dr. Minton allowed me to come four different times to talk through the fears I had stuffed inside, feelings I would not reveal to anyone else. After relaying to him what I had experienced with Chuck's up and down emotions, he said, "Your husband might be manic-depressive."

"What's that mean?" I naively asked? I had never heard of it. He briefly explained this condition and it's causes and effects. Little did I realize at the time that Dr. Minton had finally hit the nail on the head! That was the first inkling I had of the true reason for Chuck's emotional problems. A seed of truth had been planted that would later give me understanding about the mood swings I saw in my husband.

We began to make friends with those living around us in the trailer park and in our classes. Emotionally, I could hold myself together while I was in class, and I even enjoyed that time. But as soon as I came home from class, the tears would start to flow. I didn't want to cry in front of Chuck—I knew it would upset him—but I couldn't seem to stop the tears! As soon as Chuck came home, I tried to hide the fact that I had been crying.

Chuck was still not back to his normal personality. The difference in his behavior was clearly visible. He wasn't acting in bizarre ways, but he certainly wasn't himself. Of course, none of the people in our classes and our neighborhood could see the difference in Chuck. I did, but I couldn't say anything. My enforced silence and secrecy only added to my own insecurity.

My mom knew I was having a tough time, though I didn't tell

her the real reason for my struggles. I explained to her, "It's just that our money is tight, and we still haven't found a job or church. It will take time to form deep friendships, and I miss that." I could try to rationalize my tears in a number of ways: lack of friends, or money, missing our home, hard class assignments, time constrictions, and on and on! No doubt these were factors, but the root cause of my emotional turmoil was still the fear that my husband might have another mental breakdown. . . and the insecurity that produces.

Mike and other friends from Frostproof were so good to try to help during this time of transition. They kept in touch with phone calls and letters. It was always uplifting to talk with them. Mike knew our whole story. He knew what I was going through and sincerely tried to undergird me. Our dear friend Charlie, editor of the Frostproof paper, faithfully mailed letters each week, as well as sending us the weekly paper. Though I never told him about Chuck's fight against depression, he had enough insight and wisdom to know we needed these letters. I found a sense of safety in these expressions of love. It was good to know that even though they were far away, these people were watching out for us.

After about four weeks of getting into the new rhythm of school, we began interim work as music and youth staff at a small country church seventy-five miles away toward Baton Rouge. The church was made up of a mixture of different types of people: from those with the college degrees to the ones working on the family farm. To my surprise, I liked this small country church. It felt so good to leave the cement of the city behind, and enjoy the freshness of the country. After going to Pine Grove Baptist Church outside Livingston, Louisiana for three weeks as supply staff, they asked us to serve as their music and youth directors.

This little church proved to be a blessing in our lives in so many ways. They showered us with love. We were amazed at the support they exhibited. The fine people of this church would never have believed the problems Chuck had battled emotionally. He appeared to be so confident, full of energy and plans, with a wonderful, infectious laugh. I certainly wasn't going to tell anyone of what we had gone through. *Perhaps Ted was right,* I began to believe. *Maybe we have truly found and removed the root of the problem,* I told my fearful heart.

Slowly, my own internal fears began to subside. I began to sink my feet into this new life and find true friendships and enjoyment in school and ministry. Little by little, the Chuck that I knew returned. The person I had first met and loved reappeared. I started to relax. I believed the depression of the past was gone for good.

While I was taking a class in psychology and counseling in the summer of 1983, a light bulb turned on inside my head. As we began the study of manic-depressive disorder and listed it's characteristics, my heart began to race. The professor was describing Chuck to a T! It was as if he knew Chuck personally and the emotional struggles he had experienced, and he was sharing all this with the class! I was encouraged to hear that this disorder had been successfully treated in many people by taking lithium carbonate. This was the second time I had heard the words *manic-depressive*. After hearing this in-depth description, I was convinced this was Chuck's problem. I couldn't wait to get home and tell him what I had learned!

As soon as we both got home from class, the words came flying out of my mouth. "Chuck, you won't believe what I learned today! I think I know why you've fought depression for so long, and now I think I have the answer for what happened in Frostproof that last night. I think you're manic-depressive." I went on to describe all we had discussed in class.

Chuck allowed me to finish, and then he said with a laugh, "Sure, Renee, and you're obsessive-compulsive!" Though he refused to be serious about what I had to say, a chord had been struck that rang true. I was convinced I was on the right track.

As we fell into our new routines, life gradually returned to normal. Though there were times I suspected that Chuck was fighting depression, he always denied it when I asked him about it. In retrospect, it is now clear to me that there were a number of occasions when he was depressed, but he used the excuse of physical illness (a cold, flu, or allergies) to stay in bed. This was his escape whenever the darkness began to bear down upon him.

In contrast to the depressive episodes, there were the manic times as well, such as the time he was out at 3:00 a.m. in the morning cutting the hedge at his mother's home. At the time, everyone laughed and said, "Isn't that Chuck crazy!" He had a way of making a joke out of anything. On youth retreats, he stayed up all night every night with the boys in their cabin carrying on with fun and jokes. I now see these times were the full exhibition of the manic phase of his illness.

Chuck was so convincing that I always believed what he told me. After two major episodes and many minor ones, the mask he chose to wear had become permanent. By then he was unwilling (or perhaps unable) to look honestly at himself without it. His mask had become his identity.

We worked with this small country church for over three years. In the middle of our time there (and just a few months before I completed my masters degree in Church Music), we moved our trailer from the seminary campus to the church field. Our first child, Nicole, was born while we lived there. I had initially had reservations about this church, but it carved it's way deep into my heart and will always be dear to me.

As time went on, Chuck finished the master level work and entered the doctoral program in psychology and counseling. (After his death, I realized one of the reasons for his interest in this field: he was looking for an answer to his own problems. With the knowledge gained in this field of study, he hoped to be able to deal with his own emotional ups and downs.) By February, 1985, in his last semester of doctoral work, we accepted a call to work with Grace Memorial Baptist Church in Slidell, Louisiana, where Chuck would be the full time minister of education and counseling. What we had been working for all these years was falling into place. Chuck had not suffered any major mental problems in over three years. *The best is yet to come!* I thought. *Chuck's past emotional problems are history. The pay off for these past years of scrimping and saving is just around the bend.* It would be good to be a "normal family" with school behind us.

Chuck enthusiastically jumped into his new work. Our church was full of young couples with small children, and we were thrilled to have so many families—and new friends—in our own age group. We were well-received by our new church, and we felt good about our decision. We were confident it was the right one.

One of the blessings we experienced in Slidell was the opportunity to build our dream house. We moved in to our new home April 28, 1986. *Yes, the pieces are all coming together now,* I thought. *God is blessing all of our hard work! Chuck will soon be finished with his doctorate, and we have a lovely home, a beautiful daughter, and a great job. The depression is gone, and Chuck is doing great! Thank You, God, for Your goodness to us!* We had only been in our house for three months when I began to feel nauseated. It was the same feeling I had known during my pregnancy with Nicole. Even before visiting a doctor, I knew the cause: our second child was on the way! Again, I felt God was pouring on the blessings. We had wanted this child and prayed for the Lord to give us another baby. He had answered our prayers. The doctor told us that baby number two should arrive around May 8th. "Just make sure I don't miss my husband's graduation ceremonies, Doctor. I've waited and worked too hard to miss seeing Chuck receive his doctorate." Dr. Holmes laughed and assured me he'd do everything he could! We would soon be the "All American Family," two children with Mom and Dad.

So many changes taking place in our lives! The year was absorbed with trying to get things in order at our new home, taking care of our little "Colee" as we affectionately called our daughter, completing the dissertation, ministry work at church, and my gaining forty pounds in pregnancy! Spring of 1987 suddenly arrived, and the due date for both the birth of our second baby and Chuck's graduation ceremonies was close at hand.

How I prayed that Baby Number Two would come early for two reasons! First, I was so big, and had gained so much weight that I was very uncomfortable and didn't sleep well. Second, I wanted to be able to attend the graduation ceremonies scheduled for the weekend of May 15th.

"Please Lord, don't let me miss out on this special time!" I earnestly prayed. As usual, God had everything perfectly timed. Miss Tara Charene arrived early the morning of May 1st. A second baby girl! Healthy and whole! Our cup of joy was running over!

Because Tara was born by Cesarean section, as Nicole had been also, my recovery took longer. "You have to take it easy for six weeks, Renee," Dr. Holmes admonished me. "You need to stay still and allow your body to heal."

"How can I do that and take care of both of these babies?" I asked. "Can I attend Chuck's graduation on May 16th?" Dr. Holmes knew how much it meant to me to be there.

With hesitation, he agreed. "OK, you can go, but only on the condition that you go straight to the graduation and come right back home."

"Yes sir, doctor!" I happily replied. "That suits me fine!" I was just thrilled to know I would see my husband become "Dr. Chuck Scheidt!"

I noticed Chuck's level of excitement steadily increasing as the time began to draw closer for the big, up-coming events. It reminded me of how he had acted five years earlier when we were packing to move to Louisiana. Just as in 1982, Chuck wouldn't eat and had trouble sleeping. He was bursting with energy even though he jogged up to three miles every day trying to wear himself out. The jogs were followed by a dip in our friend's hot tub. We hoped all of this would help him sleep. It didn't. He became very talkative and had a confident answer for any question.

The future looked bright as we peered down the road ahead.

All of the money he received for graduation gifts was quickly spent. Since this was his money, I said nothing. It startled me how easily he let this cash flow through his hands when we had previously always been so careful about handling money matters.

"Chuck, maybe you should go see our doctor and get something to keep you from getting so worked up," I suggested one day.

He quickly convinced me that wasn't necessary. "Look, Renee, I'm just excited about all the good things happening in our lives. How often does a person graduate with a doctoral degree and celebrate the birth of a second beautiful baby girl? My family will be arriving in a few days, and they've never been here before. It's only normal for me to act this way in view of the situation." Once again, Chuck was able to talk me into believing him. And as before, I let it go and accepted my husband's explanations.

On May 16th, 1987, the dream became reality. The long awaited graduation day finally came. Thirteen of Chuck's family members celebrated this event with us. They came from as far away as Alaska. I beamed with pride as I saw Chuck shake hands with the president of the seminary, accept the diploma that read "Dr. Charles H. Scheidt," and have the hood placed over his head. Surrounded by family members from across the country, church members who joined in to congratulate him, and his wife of ten years, Chuck couldn't have been happier. The look of satisfaction on his face from realizing his accomplishment was evident.

It had been a long time coming, a hard row to hoe, but now the payoff had arrived. Chuck finally had the credentials he had desired. Now no one could belittle him as an ignoramus when he proclaimed that God's Word gave the answers for dealing with life's problems. Dr. Chuck (as he jokingly told us to call him now) had a fully-earned doctorate in psychology and counseling.

I realized after his death how hard Chuck tried to apply his knowledge to his own emotional struggles. I am convinced that it was only because of his diligent efforts to put these truths into practice that he was able to survive as long as he did. The chemical imbalance which caused his manic-depression needed proper medication. No amount of "right thinking and right actions" would correct the physiological illness. Working in conjunction with proper medical means, these elements can be very effective to bring about the desired results. One without the other, however, is not always enough to make the needed changes. It's like having only two legs on a three legged stool— very wobbly and unable to support any amount of weight. Chuck's life still was missing a crucial element of support.

All too soon the weekend ended. Family members said good-bye and rushed to get back to their homes and work. Everything had been perfect! At times like this, wouldn't it be great to stop the clock and just hold on to those precious moments a while longer? But time waits for no man. The clock marched on, and we had to move on as well. After everyone had left, Dr. and Mrs. Chuck Scheidt and two little girls, Nicole and Tara, stood ready to begin a new chapter of life. The goals of many years had been accomplished: school was finally behind us. Everything was in place now to begin to blossom forth. We seemed to have it all! Of course, we gave God the glory for where we now found ourselves. We knew fully well that apart from His hand of blessing and His strength and guidance in our lives, we would be nowhere. We had dedicated ourselves fully to Him, and we knew (as the song, "My Tribute," says), "All that I am, or ever hope to be, I owe it all to Thee."[1] The future looked bright as we peered down the road ahead. We were definitely in the best position we had ever been: a good job, our family complete (We had no plans for adding more to our quiver!), a beautiful home, the formal education finished, money in the bank, debt free (with the exception of our mortgage), and perhaps most important of all, a great love for each other. Depression had not reared his ugly head in Chuck's life now for over five years. It was good to know that this monster was now gone. There was nothing we lacked as far as I could see. Hopefully, we would start to enjoy some of the benefits from the labor of the past ten years: more play time together since school work was gone, not having to watch our money so closely now that we no longer were paying a school bill, and enjoy the beautiful daughters God had given us. If any couple seemed to have it "together," we did. There were no clouds on the horizon. "Everything's coming up roses," I hummed around the house.

The sun was shining brightly as summer arrived that year. Unsuspectingly, I smiled as I looked ahead. I didn't have a clue that in less than two months my world would fall apart. Only the grace of God would carry me through the dark days that soon would cause my song to die.

4

The Death of the Song

Have fun girls!" Chuck yelled as he watched the girls and me walk down the ramp to board the plane. The final hugs and kisses were given and the last photos shot.

"We'll call every night," I promised. "See you in a week!" I was excited to introduce "Baby Tara" to the rest of our North Carolina family. At eight weeks of age, she would soon take her first plane trip just as her sister Nicole had done. I couldn't wait to show off our precious girls to my family!

I knew Chuck would be busy that week with projects he was working on. *He can use this extra time to get some things done without us under his feet,* I thought. *This will work well for all of us.* The abundant energy that had characterized Chuck's personality the past few weeks also began to dwindle. *He's balancing out now,* I surmised. The big high Chuck had just experienced was wearing off, and now things would get back to normal.

I kept in close touch with Chuck the entire week while we were away. In our phone conversations, everything seemed to be fine. People from church had Chuck over for supper. He preached on Sunday and felt good about how the message was received. A friend from our former church in Livingston came down over the weekend to help with yard work. Don, a college buddy whom we had not seen in years, arrived for a short visit two days before the girls and I returned home.

Before we knew it, the days sped by and it was time for us to fly back home. "I'm ready to come home," I told Chuck on the phone the night before our flight back. "I want to know everything that's happened since we left. Don't leave out anything!" I said with a laugh.

By 9:00 a.m. our plane landed in New Orleans. Nicole couldn't wait to see Daddy! We rushed down the ramp and found Chuck waiting for us, with Don standing behind him. The minute I looked at him, I knew something was terribly wrong. Chuck looked horrible! His face was long and drawn. His pants were barely hanging on him by his belt. In just a week, he had lost so much weight that his clothes didn't even fit! Though he tried to give us a smile, I could see that it was forced. His lips were tight, and his eyes looked dull. The twinkle was gone.

I desperately wanted to talk with him! But I knew that it was not the right time with Don and the girls there. Chuck sat very quietly as we began the fifty minute drive home. I had to pull every word from him, and this was so different than the talkative person he had been in May. "Tell me all that happened while we've been gone, Chuck," I asked, trying to get him to open up.

"Just the usual stuff," he replied. It was evident that he wasn't going to offer any information he didn't have to.

When we got to the house, I hoped we could have a moment alone to discuss openly how he was feeling. But once the suitcases were brought in and the girls had been given hugs and kisses, Chuck headed to the garage. "I've got to get back to work. I'm behind the eight ball since I've had to make two trips to the airport this week."

I followed him out into the garage. When we were finally alone, I asked him, "Chuck, are you sure you're OK? You're not getting down, are you?"

"No, Renee," he answered. "The work is just piled up at the office. I'm OK."

I then said, "Do you promise you'd tell me if you were becoming depressed?"

"Yes, I would. I'll see you tonight." With those words, Chuck got in the car and went to the church office.

I tried to assure myself that I shouldn't worry. Surely after all we've been through, Chuck would tell me if he started to spiral downward. *Chuck knows better than to bottle up his feelings. He can handle this. You're just worn out from getting up so early to make the flight,* I told myself.

When Tara and Nicole lay down for their morning nap, I decided to lie down with them. I was just beginning to doze off when the phone rang. It was Cheryl, one of the church secretaries. The words she spoke caused my heart to stand still. "Renee,

Chuck just called and asked me to call you. He said he tried to reach you, but the line was busy. He just admitted himself to the psychiatric hospital for depression." My body went limp as the realization hit me that our old enemy had returned to plague us once again.

"Dear God, no!" I silently prayed.

I fought the urge to burst into tears, and asked, "Cheryl, I've got to get there to talk with him. Could someone from the office come give me a ride?"

"Sure, I'll get someone out there right away," she replied.

Since we only had one car, I didn't even have a way to get to the hospital. Jim, our music minister, quickly arrived and took me to the hospital just less than a half mile from the church. Tears rushed down my face as fear began to take hold of my heart. Jim was at a loss for words. He was shocked to hear that his friend and co-worker was overcome by depression. Chuck had never said a word to him or any other staff members about his inner struggles.

"I talked with him earlier this morning, and he seemed fine," Jim said with confusion in his voice. There were no words that would suffice as we made the short ride. I prayed in silence as anxiety filled my heart.

We drove up to a brand new, impressive-looking hospital, but I couldn't have cared less about what the building looked like. My only concern was knowing my husband was inside. I ran into the lobby. My eyes scanned the room as I looked for Chuck. He was seated on one of the couches, waiting for me. As I sat down beside him, his first words to me were, "Are you all right Renee? I just need to know that whatever happens, you and the girls are going to be all right." He could hardly get the words from his mouth. It was almost as if his lips were glued shut.

"We're all right, Chuck, but we want you to be all right," I answered as I held on to his hand.

He then told me that he had been fighting depression all week. "I've done everything I know to do: mentally, spiritually, physically. Nothing will stop the darkness. I wanted to wait until you and the girls got back home to tell you. I didn't want to ruin your time with your family." "We can get help, Chuck, but why did you come to this hospital? This isn't the one you even refer your clients to. Why don't we go where you always send your clients?" I asked with great concern.

Chuck replied, "I've talked with some of the staff, and they've assured me I can get the same things here as I would there, Renee."

I was at a loss to know what to do or say. All I could do was cry. Soon the hospital staff took Chuck back to his room. He asked me to bring his clothes and personal items from the house. My head was throbbing as the questions began: Is Chuck going to be all right? How long will he have to be there? How will this affect his ministry? Will we still have a job? How much will it cost to be in the psychiatric hospital? Will the insurance cover it? How can I handle these little girls by myself? What will I tell Nicole, and people at the church?

But I had no answers for these questions.

About an hour later, I returned to the hospital with Chuck's clothes. I waited to see the doctor who had been assigned to Chuck. I was anxious to talk with him and get some answers to my many questions. He arrived shortly. Tearfully I began to share with him Chuck's history and the many up's and downs he had experienced the past twelve years I had known him. We discussed the strong possibility that Chuck was manic-depressive. The thought began to dawn upon me that perhaps this hospitalization would truly get to the bottom of what was wrong with Chuck. *Maybe a psychiatrist will help us get to the root cause,* I shakingly thought. That was the only glimmer of hope I saw as I tried to put the entire situation in perspective.

We concluded our conversation, and I prepared to leave. Walking out of the psychiatric hospital alone, knowing that my husband was locked behind those doors in a very depressed condition, was one of the darkest days of my life. How do you explain to others that your husband, the handsome minister of counseling with the doctorate degree in psychology, has just admitted himself to the psychiatric hospital for depression? Would he recover from this depressed mental condition? How would the people of our church react? What would I say to our parents? To our neighbors? I drove home sobbing the entire way, too upset even to pray.

The news traveled quickly that Chuck was in the psychiatric hospital. I walked around in a daze. Only by the grace of God did I manage to carry on and take care of my girls. "Daddy got sick and has to be in the hospital. We need to pray that God will help him get well soon," I tearfully said to Nicole. My own heart was breaking, but I didn't want my children's hearts to hurt, too. The mothering instinct in me wanted to shield them from the fear and pain of Daddy being gone. Their little world, which was totally dependant on Chuck and me as their parents, was being shaken.

"How long will Daddy be there, Mommy?" Nicole's sweet little voice asked.

"I don't know, darling. We'll just have to wait and see." I had been told by the hospital staff that they expected Chuck to be hospitalized for six weeks.

How do you explain to others that your husband, the handsome minister of counseling with the doctorate degree in psychology, has just admitted himself to the psychiatric hospital for depression?

"I don't think I can make it by myself, Lord, for six weeks. Please have mercy upon us! Please touch and heal my husband! We need You, God. You are our only hope. Please guide the doctors, and let us once and for all get to the root of this thing." I earnestly and desperately cried out to God and begged Him for mercy and grace.

During these first days of Chuck's hospitalization, I received a phone call that seemed very strange to me. In retrospect, I realize how much I needed this message. A woman in our church named Trish, whom I did not know at the time (but who quickly became one of my dearest friends), called with a very brief but poignant message. "Renee, I just heard about Chuck's admittance to the psychiatric hospital. God has impressed upon my heart to call you and tell you that you will survive all of this. I know it seems overwhelming now, but *you will survive.*"

Not really knowing how to respond I simply said, "Thank you. I appreciate you sharing that with me." I hung up the phone and thought, *Who is this weirdo woman? She sounds like she's half crazy.* Yet this message would resound through my mind in the dark days to come as I continuously wondered, *Am I going to make it?* Her words, "You will survive," proved to be my only sense of support when the night seemed as if it would never end.

The next few weeks were a blur. Somehow I got through them,

but that's really about all I can say of this time. I would love to be able to report to you that I let God's peace rule in my heart during this time of trial, that I stood firm without wavering on the promises of the Bible, and that God gave me a word that everything would be just fine. But that's not the way it was. I was overcome by fear of what would become of my husband. My days and nights were spent crying as I faced the uncertainty of our situation. How could I carry on with joy and peace when the one I had become one with was fighting for his soul?

Friends from church called to offer their support and help. "Please pray for Chuck," I despairingly asked. I hoped that if we bombarded Heaven with enough prayers, perhaps God would give us our request. Though I know we don't have to twist the hand of our Heavenly Father to have Him answer our prayers, I was desperate enough to try anything that might work. *We will give God no rest,* I concluded. *I will wrestle with Him just as Jacob did and not let Him go, except He bless me. I will cry before Him all night as David did when pleading for the life of the child born by Bathsheba, that "perhaps God will be gracious to me." I will keep on asking, seeking and knocking, until God answers my prayer.* How I wanted to hear the words that Eli had spoken to Hannah as she poured her heart out to the Lord in her desire to have a son, "Go in peace, and the God of Israel grant you the petition you have asked of Him (I Samuel. 1:17)."

Every time the hospital allowed visitors, I was there. I did my best to look as good as I could whenever I visited Chuck because I thought it would encourage him. Sometimes I went alone and left the girls with friends from church who came to the house to baby-sit. Other times, all three of us went together to see the man in our lives. I always tried to be positive and supportive. "How did it go today, Chuck?" I asked. I wanted to know all I could. What were they doing? Were there any new insights that were helpful to him? He reviewed the day with me. When the girls were there, he spent time playing with them. Some days he seemed to be improving, but other days he took a turn for the worst and refused to get out of bed as he descended into the pit of darkness.

This scenario went on for about ten days. Toward the end of the first week, Chuck began improving somewhat. He started jogging again and began to care about his appearance. A few days later, the report on the blood work came back. He was anxious to share the results with me. "Renee, they found out I have a chemical imbalance. I'm probably manic-depressive. They said it was largely genetic. They think this is the reason for all the problems I've had. It's a treatable condition. In fact, they are thinking about letting me come home soon!"

Chuck's joy was obvious as he shared the news with me. I asked, "What does this mean? How do they treat a chemical imbalance?"

"With medication such as antidepressants or lithium," he replied.

Knowing there was a valid reason for his emotional problems was a great relief. Chuck's problems were not due to a lack of spirituality or some sin in his life. He actually had a physical problem beyond the realm of his control. We huddled together and offered a prayer of thanksgiving to our Heavenly Father.

I could hardly wait to talk with the doctor. When I saw him walking down the hall, I quickly ran after him, and said,. "May I talk with you?" He suggested we go in a small room so we wouldn't be disturbed.

"I just want to make sure I've got this right," I began. "Chuck told me that he has a chemical imbalance, that he's probably manic-depressive, and that it's a treatable condition. Is this correct?" He affirmed what Chuck had said.

"So how you do treat it?" I inquired. "Does he just take a pill, and then everything will be all right?"

He explained to me that there were no guarantees, but he believed Chuck would do well by taking certain antidepressants. Then he would probably be able to carry on as normal. There were very few side effects from the medication, and he expected good results from all he had observed. I thanked him from my heart and left with a smile on my face.

It was with relief and a happy heart that I began to share the news with others. Our family and church congregation were glad to hear this report. "Daddy's coming home soon, Nicole!" I joyfully exclaimed. Her little heart was overjoyed to know Daddy was going to be OK and back with us at home in just a few days.

Thirteen days after admitting himself to the psychiatric hospital, Chuck walked out smiling with his wife and two young daughters by his side. We believed God had answered the fervent prayers we had offered night and day in Chuck's behalf.

Immediately, Chuck went back to work. Though he had just been released that Wednesday afternoon, he attended church that evening and even held a counseling session! Thursday morning he went to the office and worked all day. I was concerned that this might be too much on him after all he had just been through, but the doctor had given the OK. Who was I to contradict him? We ended that day with a family walk. Daddy pushed "Baby Tara" in the stroller, and Nicole walked next to him holding his hand. All of us were filled with gratefulness to have so quickly resolved the difficulty of the past two weeks. Our pastor, Bob, and the entire church stood strongly by our side. That meant so much to us. When Chuck was admitted to the hospital, I had wondered if his job would be in jeopardy, and if he would be condemned by people in the congregation. It was so good to know they were behind us and wanted to help us through the hard times we had just encountered.

Friday was Chuck's normal day off. He was gone much of the day, visiting a friend in a near-by community. I was glad he could have some time to share with him. By evening, we were all exhausted and went to bed early. The emotional stress we had been under for two weeks quickly sapped all our physical energy. We needed a good night's sleep to rest our bodies and minds.

Saturday morning dawned with the sun beaming through our windows, but it wasn't long before the clouds of anxiety began to darken the sky. Shortly after Chuck awoke, he became very agitated. The look of despair was written all over his face. He looked at me, "Something's wrong, Renee. I don't think the medicine is working. Call the doctor and see what he says."

I hurriedly dialed the number of the doctor's office. I relayed to him Chuck's condition as fear grabbed my heart.

"Please, dear God, please don't let us go through this again. Please help us!" I silently prayed.

After talking with Chuck, the doctor made his decision. "I want to re-admit you to the psychiatric hospital for further treatment, but you can wait until Monday morning to return. Spend the weekend with your family, and I'll see you Monday."

I felt crushed and disillusioned. I wanted to fall down and weep, but I knew I needed to try to keep some semblance of control for Chuck and my little girls. "I can't handle all of this, Lord!" I desperately prayed. "It was bad enough to go to a mental hospital the first time. Now to return is devastating! What a blow! We thought we were through this valley. Now we find we are still smack dab in the center. Is my husband ever going to be all right? What will we say to everyone who had rejoiced with us only a few days earlier? How do we explain that Chuck had to be re-admitted?" The good news we had told everyone was now negated. I had to call family and friends to share this setback. What would I tell little Nicole? We were back to square one. I thought it was difficult the first time Chuck entered the hospital, but the pain was doubled this time.

I knew I didn't have the patience or energy to keep up with my energetic two-year-old daughter that day. I didn't want her to see me upset or her Daddy visibly shaken. I quickly called Bob and Janie. "Chuck's not doing well," I explained. "He's going to have to go back to the hospital, but not until Monday. Would you mind watching Nicole for a few hours this morning while I try to get a grip on things here? I don't think I can keep up with her as upset as I am." Graciously, they told me to bring her over. The love they demonstrated meant more to me than words can express.

Just two nights earlier Chuck had a long conversation with his mom, discussing insights he'd gained during his treatment at the hospital. I dreaded calling her now to say Chuck was going back to the hospital. I knew I had to make the call and putting it off would not make it any easier. I mustered the courage and phoned her. I explained the situation as best I could, then I gave the phone to Chuck so he and his mom could talk. I sat by the foot of the bed, praying silently as they conversed.

Gradually Chuck became more distraught, especially as they mentioned his father. Soon he began sobbing heavily and wept as I'd never seen him before. A gut-wrenching howl came from the depths of his soul. I realized, *I've got to get help right now!* I took the phone and said, "I'll call you back as soon as I can, but I've got to get Chuck to the hospital *now!*"

He needed help beyond what I could offer. Chuck was so upset that he was unable to put his clothes on. It was the only time in my life that I ever helped my husband get dressed. He continued to wail. Nothing I said could calm his emotions. I picked up my baby, and somehow got all three of us in the car. How thankful I was that Nicole was spared from seeing her daddy this way! I realized God directed me to take her to Bob and Janie's earlier that morning. I drove to the hospital trying to comfort my husband. "They will help us, Chuck. It was just too quick the first time. You need more time to work through some of these issues. God is going to help us through this." I was speaking to myself as I said these words to Chuck, trying to convince myself that God wouldn't fail us.

We were the classic picture of depression and despair as we entered the hospital this second time. The hearts of the staff and the other patients—who had wished us well only days before—went out to us as they saw our pain. With tears streaming down my face, I watched my husband go behind the locked doors of the psychiatric hospital. Clutching tightly to my baby, not even three months old, I turned and headed for home, alone once more.

A multitude of emotions overcame me. I cried aloud to the only One who could help us, "Haven't we gone through enough, Lord? Please, I beg You please, have mercy on us. You can do all things; nothing is too hard for You, God. Please, in Your mercy and compassion, touch and heal my husband. I ask for a miracle, Lord. You've done it for others. Please do it for us now. We desperately need You, God!" If desperation could be measured, there could not have been a more desperate prayer. I begged God with all of my being to intervene in our situation. . . but the intervention I prayed for never came.

For the next six weeks, Chuck was a patient at the psychiatric hospital. It was one of the most grueling experiences of my life. The uncertainly of Chuck's mental health weighed heavily upon me. Trying to carry on with my daily responsibilities took every ounce of strength I could gather. Chuck's mom flew from Texas to be with me almost immediately after Chuck went back into the hospital. She was a wonderful help to all of us for five weeks. I couldn't have made it without her. The girls loved having "Granny Scheidt" in our home, and it helped them feel more secure since Daddy was in the hospital. We sat up talking and praying many nights as we both pleaded for God to heal the one who meant so much to both of us.

During this hospitalization, Chuck experienced incredible mood swings. Sometimes he seemed almost like his old self. It was during these times that we had great conversations as he shared with me from his heart. But other times he was so deep in depression that he would not participate in the group sessions at the hospital. He simply lay in bed around the clock. I well remember one time I was allowed to visit him when he was terribly depressed. It was like looking at a dead man. Yes, he was still breathing, but there was no life left in him. My Chuck was gone. I was looking at an empty shell.

There were several occasions when he was so depressed that no visitors were allowed. During one of these times, he telephoned to talk with me. His voice was very weak, and the words were forced. "Renee, I'm sorry I've ruined your life. I now see that I'm not cut out to be a husband, father, or minister. I want you to sell the house, take the girls and go back to North Carolina with your family. I'm sorry for what I've done to you."

As in other times of crisis, God gave me the strength and words to respond. "Chuck, I don't care what you say, or what you do, but I'm not quitting! I love you and am committed to you. We're going to keep fighting this thing until we beat it. I'm not quitting."

As soon as he hung up, two of the nurses who had overheard his conversation called back. "Don't let this upset you, Renee," they said. "That's the depression talking, not Chuck."

"I know," I responded. "I know my Chuck loves me, and he knows I love him. I realize that's not how he really feels."

Chuck's mother heard all of this conversation and reiterated what the nurses had said. Though my words to Chuck had sounded strong and firm, I fell apart as soon as we finished talking. I knew in my head that Chuck truly loved me, but it hurt deeply to hear those words come from his lips.

The days dragged on, and we seemed to be getting nowhere. I learned to live with a constant throbbing headache and always needed a cup of coffee just to keep going. I forced myself to eat for my baby's sake, even though food had no appeal to me. I continued to nurse her and I knew if I didn't eat, I would be hurting Tara. I spent many hours in our yard planting monkey grass around the house. Gardening gave me a way to be alone out of the girls sight where I was free to cry. Digging in the dirt seemed to release some of the stress I faced. Because I didn't want little Nicole to be totally shaken, I tried to put on a happy face whenever she was around. She was already upset by the lack of her father's presence. She needed to know Mama was still there. I learned to play the part of "the stable and happy parent," just as Chuck had done for years, to present a smiling face on the outside when actually my heart was breaking. Only when my girls were safe in bed could I release the pain I had bottled up all day.

During the fourth week of this hospitalization, Chuck took a turn for the worst. I didn't know until after his death that he had been put on "constant observation," a term used by the hospital to keep a close eye on patients they felt might be contemplating suicide. I was never informed of this situation by the doctor or hospital staff.

Though I called numerous times, rarely was I able to talk with the doctor. I left messages requesting that he return my call, but these went unheeded. Finally, after leaving messages for three weeks, he called to tell me that Chuck's was a very difficult case and needed long-term therapy.

"How long do you mean?" I demanded. "Are you talking about three months, six months, a year? What does 'long' mean?"

He said he expected Chuck to be in therapy for several years! He had decided to call in another doctor for a second opinion. The antidepressant he had prescribed for Chuck was still not up to a therapeutic level, and he planned to increase the dosage. "Unless he starts to respond to treatment, we will either have to put him on MAO Inhibitors or do shock treatments," he stated. He then explained what these procedures were.

After listening to his explanations, I said, "Neither one sounds good to me." I hung up the receiver and spent the night crying and praying. The thought that my husband might never recover from this manic-depression seeped into my mind. I knew I might very well have to go to work full-time to support our family if the situation didn't change. I started figuring how much our income would be if Chuck were put on disability. I wrote down expenses and projected income. I realized that we may not be able to afford to stay in our home. *I guess we could sell the house if we had to and put a trailer on the farm back in North Carolina,* I tried to reason.

I had a lot of questions about this entire situation, but the hardest of all were about the Lord: Where was God? Why won't He answer us? The seriousness of Chuck's condition was very evident, and I was willing to do anything that might help him recover from this black hole that had enveloped him. Though I had always attended prayer meeting at our church on Wednesday nights, I went with a determination to do more this time than just say, "Please pray for Chuck." That Wednesday night in August, I stood before the people gathered in our church auditorium and said, "We need your help. I want to ask you to fervently pray for my husband. His condition is very serious. The medication still is not up to a therapeutic level. The doctor told me it could be years before he is back to normal. Could we bow down on our knees right now and have special prayer for him?" Everyone who was physically able got off the padded pew, and we all knelt before the throne of God begging for Chuck's recovery. The following Sunday, our pastor allowed me to speak in both of our morning worship services. My message was: "I am hear to ask you to stand with me in upholding Chuck during this time of great trial. The situation is not good. We need a miracle from the Lord. I am asking as many of you who are able to fast and pray in Chuck's behalf. Just as Moses needed his arms uplifted in the fight against the enemy, let us uphold Chuck's now by fasting and praying for him. Please help us." It is the only time I know of that our church set aside a day for prayer and fasting. Members of our church came to me to share that they would join in this effort. The call had gone forth. *Maybe this will persuade the Lord to be gracious to us,* I desperately hoped.

During each of the hospitalizations, Chuck asked to be anointed with oil by the leadership of our church. Anointing people is not the usual practice of our church, but we were simply trying to be obedient to anything that might help and follow the words of James 5:14, "Is any sick among you? Let him call for the elders of the church; and let them pray over him, anointing him with oil in the name of the Lord."

We not only prayed around the clock, fasted, and anointed Chuck with oil as the elders prayed for him, we also bound Satan and all spirits of darkness from having any way or influence in his life. By the blood of Jesus, and in the name of the King of Kings and Lord of Lords, we commanded them to leave Chuck alone. I called churches of different denominations all across town to request prayer for Chuck. In fact, the district leader of one denomination drove from New Orleans to come and pray over Chuck at my request. He altered his schedule and made the drive, but the hospital refused to let him talk with Chuck. They wouldn't even allow Chuck to come to the lobby where he was waiting. I was completely devastated by this action. Yet, what could I do? I had to comply with the hospital's orders.

The Lord brought me a group of ladies who upheld me during these dark days. I really did not know any of them very well until Chuck went into the hospital. These ladies were Chuck's "prayer warriors." He called on them to pray for him anytime he was going to speak or had some event for which he wanted extra prayer support. They took it upon themselves to undergird me as we all joined together in this fight for Chuck's well-being. Many different times, Linda, Trish, Karen, and Charlene came to my house to pray with me. They fasted for days, pleading for my husband's mental health. I was humbled to see this show of support from people I really had not known before we found ourselves in the midst of this warfare.

September rolled around, bringing with it the time for me to return to my part-time work at the church's Early Learning Center. I dreaded it because I realized it would force me into contact with many people. I felt very awkward in meeting people in our community. I knew they knew my husband, Dr. Scheidt, was in the psychiatric hospital, but they probably didn't understanding why. It hurt me to see some of them use our tragedy as an opportunity to laugh at our Christian faith and practices. I determined to meet the public in a gracious manner, holding my head up as I walked down the twisting road before me.

Our pastor, Brother Bob, came over early that morning as I began my work. "What are they doing for Chuck, Renee?" he questioned.

As we talked, my own frustrations mounted until they were ready to explode! Neither of us saw any improvement in Chuck's condition. In fact, he had actually gotten worse the past six weeks. "I've got to go and talk with the hospital, Bob," I answered. "I want to know what's really going on. I'll be back as soon as I can." With those words, I dashed off for the hospital. I didn't know who I would talk with or exactly what I would say, but I knew we weren't making progress, and I was totally upset with the entire scenario.

I entered the lobby and asked to speak to the head of the nursing staff. This nurse, Cindy, arrived within minutes, soon followed by two other staff members who had also worked closely with Chuck. I got straight to the point. "Your program is not working. We've been here six weeks, spent thousands of dollars, and we're not any better off than the day we started. I want to leave this hospital and go to a Christian hospital program in Dallas. Chuck has a sister in that area I can stay with while he's in the hospital. What you're doing *is not working!*"

All of them agreed it would be a mistake for me to move Chuck now. "He's beginning to respond, Renee," Cindy told me. "Don't interrupt what is starting to take place. He's getting the same treatment here that he'd get anywhere else. They can't do anything for him that we're not. He needs to stay and continue in this program. It would be a set-back to move him now."

With great hesitation, I gave up my resistance. Who was I to contradict the professionals? These people were the ones who were trained and skilled in this field. In comparison to them, I knew nothing. Yet many times I have looked back, and wished

I had followed my first instinct. If I could turn back the clock and relive that moment, I most certainly would have taken Chuck to another hospital.

Over the next few days, however, I began to see a difference in Chuck's condition. Gradually, he started emerging from the pit he had been in for so long. *I guess the staff was right in what they told me,* I concluded. The hardy laugh and twinkle in his eyes returned. Very quickly, the Chuck I knew and loved seemed to slip back into place. In fact, he was doing so well that his mom began making plans to return to Texas on Labor Day. Chuck received a pass for the weekend and we were delighted to be able to spend the holiday weekend together. We got out the grill and enjoyed being together as a family. Granny Scheidt, the girls, and I were glad to see the one we loved laughing and energetic once more. Monday morning, we all drove to the airport, and saw Granny off.

We stopped at City Park on the way back home. I had packed everything we would need for a picnic, including the movie camera. The strawberry pie we picked up at Shoney's was quickly gone! How good it felt to be able to enjoy such simple pleasures again! Nicole was elated to have this much time with Daddy, something she had missed for the past seven weeks.

The day slipped by and soon it was time for Chuck to return to the hospital. I was so thankful to see his improvement. Our weekend together couldn't have been any better. Yet I knew from past experiences that we were still on shaky ground. Too often I had seen him up one day and down the next. I was cautiously optimistic as he entered the doors of the psychiatric hospital that evening.

Chuck's possible release from the hospital became the topic of conversation in the next few days. Yes, he seemed to be doing well. He looked great and talked a good talk, but something deep within me knew he wasn't ready. I discussed my reservations at length with his doctor's associate. I knew they were still having problems getting the antidepressant up to a therapeutic level. They had released him too soon the first time. Only a week earlier, Chuck had been in a deep depression. How could they possibly discharge him just one week later? How could they have dealt with that situation so quickly? They should be able see how quickly his complete demeanor could change! My concerns were registered and then cast aside.

When I arrived at the hospital for a visit on Thursday,

September 10th, I was given the news by the doctor's associate: "Chuck is being discharged tomorrow, Renee."

Instead of being happy that my husband was finally getting out of the psychiatric hospital, I began to cry. "He's not ready. You know he's not ready!" He may appear to some to be back to his normal self, but you and I both know he's not ready," I said with tears rushing down my face. Though I protested, my efforts were to no avail. "I want to talk to the doctor. Please ask him to call me. Let him know I'm not in favor of this decision." I left the hospital with a heavy heart because I realized no one was listening to me.

I waited all evening for the doctor to call. It wasn't until early the next morning that he finally phoned from his car while he was on his way to work.

I told him firmly, "Doctor, you know I'm opposed to Chuck's release today. He's not ready. I can tell that he is not back to normal." The doctor replied that the maximum benefit from hospitalization had been reached, and Chuck's needs could now be met on an outpatient basis. Nothing I said made any difference. I knew I was getting nowhere. It was clear the plan was already determined. Once again, I deferred to the professionals, following their advice and instructions even though I didn't agree. What other choice did I have?

Little Nicole was thrilled when I told her Daddy was coming home. "Forever Mama? Is Daddy coming home forever this time?" her sweet little voice asked. This beautiful child had been hurt to see her daddy come home only to have to return to the hospital the first time.

"Yes, darling, this time is for good! Daddy won't have to go back anymore to the hospital," I said, hoping that the words I spoke in faith would prove to be true.

Nicole, Tara, and I arrived at the hospital a few hours later. The car was packed with suitcases filled with beach towels, bathing suits, and sand buckets. The beach vacation we had originally planned in July had been cancelled when Chuck went into the hospital. Now we were set for a great family weekend together at Gulf Shores, Alabama. The four of us walked out of the psychiatric hospital hand in hand. Chuck was beaming, filled with thankfulness to be leaving this place and returning to his own world. It had been eight long, excruciating weeks. All of us had run the gamut of emotions, fighting together to deal a death blow to manic-depression. We had bombarded Heaven day and night, begging God to heal my husband. How I hoped that the doctor was right in spite of my own fears. I wanted to put this behind us and move forward. I hoped and prayed that the medicine was right and would work for Chuck. We all wanted to get back to the good life when plans, and love, and work all fell in the right place. With anticipation and joy, our family headed for a much needed and deserved weekend at the beach.

There is no more soothing place in the world for me than the beach. The beauty of the ocean, the breeze blowing across my face, the warmth of the sun, even the crunching of the sand beneath my feet all combine to say, "Relax. Take a deep breath, and let it out slowly." For the next three days, our little family of four took in all the pleasures afforded by the seashore. Sometimes Chuck would stay in the apartment with Tara during the heat of the day while Nicole and I went romping on the beach. Late in the afternoon when the sun was beginning to set, the four of us went walking on the beach. Chuck took Nicole for a swim in the ocean, then we built the biggest sand castle we could build and decorated it with seashells found along the shore. It was a cherished time for us, and I'm thankful to have such wonderful memories of that weekend together.

"He's not ready. You know he's not ready!"

We arrived home Monday afternoon. Chuck planned to spend the week at home and return to working at the church Sunday. He had many projects he wanted to accomplish before going back to work full time, such as getting the yard ready for sod and looking for a new car. I was relieved to see Chuck feeling good again, motivated to do things instead of lying in bed. All day Tuesday he worked in the yard while I worked at the church. Wednesday, Janie kept the girls while we went to buy a new car.For the ten years we had been married, we had always managed with only one automobile. Since that vehicle had 140,000 miles on it and our family had increased to four, we wanted something a little bigger and more dependable for the long trips we took to see our families. Initially we had planned to buy a car earlier in the summer, but those plans were scrapped when Chuck went into the psychiatric hospital. We had already decided on the model we wanted; we just had to agree on a price. Several hours later we picked up the girls and drove home in a new vehicle. Chuck was so excited, he didn't come in till late that night after every spot on that car was polished to a dazzling shine! We declined the offer of credit life insurance on the car.

I went to work Thursday at the church as usual, leaving Chuck home to continue working on his projects. Brother Bob planned to take Chuck to lunch later that day. Chuck wanted to discuss with him what he should say to the congregation Sunday morning regarding his illness the past eight weeks. As I began my work, for some reason a nervousness overtook me. I found it hard to concentrate, and fear took hold of my heart. I knew I needed prayer support behind me, so I quickly called Linda. "I'm scared, Linda. Something's not right. Please pray for Chuck and me. Do you think maybe you and Trish could go by the house and check on him? I need to know that he's all right."

"Sure, we'll go right away," she answered.

Was I just letting my emotions run away with me? Or was my spirit sensing that danger lay ahead? It wasn't long before Linda, Trish, and Charlene stopped by my office at the church to report on their visit with Chuck. It was the first time in weeks they had seen him because very few visitors were allowed at the psychiatric hospital. "You can tell by looking at him that he's been through a very hard time, but I think he's on the upward trail," Linda stated.

"I think he's concerned about what to say to the church Sunday," Trish said. "I told him just to thank them for their support and not feel like he had to give an in-depth report."

The worry on my face was evident to my dear friends, and they tried to console me. "Let's pray," Linda said, grabbing my hand. Once again, as we had done time, and time again the past eight weeks, we brought Chuck before the throne of the Lord God Almighty, asking Jehovah Rapha, the God who heals, to heal my husband. We resisted Satan and all spirits of darkness, commanding them in the name of the Lord Jesus Christ, the King of Kings and Lord of Lords, to be gone, taking authority over them. We knew we had done all we could do. Now we would have to trust that God was working and would answer our fervent call to Him.

As I drove up the driveway coming home from work, my heart sank. The garage door was down. Immediately I knew this was not a good sign. If Chuck were feeling good, the garage door would be up, and he would be out in the yard. I entered the house, and found it to be quiet. When I walked into the bedroom, I saw Chuck in the bed. Trying to act calm and not let him see my alarm, I sat down beside him. "Hey Chuck, get out of bed, you sleepy head," I said forcing a laugh.

"I was so tired today, Renee," he began. "I just needed some extra rest."

"That's fine," I replied. "After all you've been through, it's only natural you need some extra sleep."

I tried to convince my own heart that what I had just said to Chuck made perfectly good sense. *Quit letting fear control you, Renee,* I told myself. *You've got to trust God in this situation, and stop worrying!* I scolded my heart.

"How did lunch go with Brother Bob?" I inquired.

"Oh, fine," Chuck answered. "I decided to fix something here instead of going out somewhere though."

I was shocked to hear Chuck say he'd rather eat at home than go out. I knew there was very little in the cabinet and refrigerator to offer anyone. Chuck was known for his hearty appetite, but he had passed up an opportunity to eat anywhere he wanted. Hearing this did not help in my fight to control my own fears.

Soon I entered the kitchen and started fixing supper. It didn't take long though for Chuck to tell me he really wasn't very hungry. "Just fix something light, like tuna sandwiches tonight."

His loss of appetite was another sign that things weren't right, but I still tried to keep from being overly alarmed. *I've got to talk with someone. I need a friend to help me keep everything in perspective,* I said to myself. I didn't want to bother Linda and Trish again. *Karen... call Karen, Renee,* the thought popped into my mind. Karen was part of the inner circle who had surrounded me with prayer and support the past two months. She had been unable to come out earlier that morning. Hurriedly, I slipped off to speak to her in private over the phone.

"Karen, could you come over?" I pleaded. "I don't think Chuck's doing well, but maybe I'm just overreacting. Would you please come by and see what you think?" She agreed to be there as soon as she could.

Karen arrived as we were finishing our tuna sandwiches. How sweet and comforting her words were! The love she had for us was flowing forth with every word. It made me feel better just having her there. As my other friends had done, Karen suggested we pray together. She took our hands, and the three of us bowed our heads in reverence to our Heavenly Father, thanking Him for what He had done in Chuck's life and what He was continuing to do.

After Karen departed, Chuck played with the girls a short while. We soon put them to bed and went back into the family room. I couldn't wait to show Chuck the decorations I had bought for Nicole's birthday party and the party bags we needed to prepare to give to her little friends. The party was planned for Saturday morning at our house.

Nicole had decided back in the summer that she wanted a dog for her birthday. Chuck had checked with friends from our church in Livingston who had told us they could get a cocker spaniel for a good price. It was still more than we wanted to spend, so our dear friends informed us they were going to all pitch in to buy the dog for Nicole's third birthday. We planned to drive to Livingston the next morning and have a birthday party with our friends there. Then we'd bring the dog back home to Slidell. It was going to be a full weekend with birthday parties both Friday and Saturday.

I will never forget what Chuck said to me when we went to bed that evening. Both of us were very tired. We prayed together as we usually did. Then Chuck hugged me very tightly and said, "I love you, Renee, and I want to thank you for how you've stood by me all these years. I appreciate you." He gave me a kiss, and then turned over to go to sleep. I'm so thankful that Chuck knew how much I loved him, and he let me know he loved me. This was a precious gift from God that I will always hold onto.

Though both of us were worn out physically and emotionally, our sleep was restless that night. I sensed throughout the night that Chuck was not really asleep. The morning finally dawned, and I was up by 6:00 o'clock. Baby Tara was ready for breakfast, and I was the only one who could supply it! I nursed my baby and then went outside to water the plants.

About 7:15, the phone rang. That was unusual for that time of the day at our house. It was Brenda, one of our dearest friends. Brenda could always bring a laugh and was so much fun to be around. "I've just finished feeding breakfast to the high school dance team and have loads of food left over. Why don't you come down and eat?"

I told Chuck about Brenda's offer, but he just laughed, "You know I don't eat breakfast."

I told Brenda that Chuck wasn't hungry, and she said, "Come on down anyway." But no amount of coaxing on her part could change his mind.

Slowly Chuck got out of bed. His movements seemed to be in slow motion. At eight o'clock when "Sesame Street" came on, he sat and held little Nicole on his lap as they watched the show together. It was plainly obvious that something was very wrong with Chuck, but I hesitated to say anything.

I went into the laundry room and called Karen again. "Chuck seems so anxious this morning, almost shaking. Something is still not right!" I fearfully said to her.

Karen replied graciously, "I'll come over after Bible study this morning and bring him some banana pudding. I know he loves that. He's been through such a terrible ordeal. He's probably just worn out and needs some time to recoup. It might be good for him to try to rest before coming back to the church Sunday."

At 9 o'clock, when the television program was finished and Nicole had gone to get in the bathtub, Chuck said in a halting voice, "Renee, I'm not feeling right. I'm very anxious, and I think I better talk with the doctor." He could hardly get the words out because he was shaking so much. My heart froze as I saw the pain on my husband's face. I realized the battle wasn't over. "But I don't want to go back to the hospital," he explained. "I want them to see me on an outpatient basis."

"OK Chuck, I'll call right now." I dialed the doctor's office, but he wasn't in yet. I left a message with the answering service. I then called the hospital and asked for Cindy, the head of nursing. "Cindy, Chuck's not doing well. He's shaking, and he's very anxious."

"We'll get someone out there to talk with him, Renee. I'll call you back," she said.

"Maybe Karen was right. Maybe I'm just overly tired," Chuck stated. "I'm going to go lay down in the bed until the doctor calls."

I knew I needed to finish dressing in order to meet those who would be coming to the house. I put Baby Tara down in her crib to take a nap, while Nicole played in the bathtub. Since I had been up early, I was basically dressed, but I needed to put in my contacts and finish fixing my hair. I went into the master bathroom and closed the door behind me so I wouldn't disturb Chuck. I made a quick call to Linda for prayer support. "Linda, Chuck is very anxious and is becoming depressed again. Please pray for him," I earnestly said.

"I've got twenty ladies coming over in just a few minutes for Bible study, Renee. Can I share with them and ask them to pray?"

"Yes, please do! We need all the prayer power we can get!" I replied.

I silently lifted my own cry to God. "Please God, please hear and answer us! Please don't make us go through this again! How long, O Lord? Have mercy upon us. We need Chuck. I beg You in Jesus Name to heal him!"

She gently took my arm and said, "He's in the empty field right across the road. But you can't go over there and see him. Stay here. There's nothing you can do."

I couldn't have been in the bathroom for more than ten minutes. When I opened the bathroom door and entered the bedroom, I immediately noticed Chuck was not in the bed. My first thoughts were, *Oh no! He's left again just like he did in Frostproof. He is so depressed that he has curled up in some place that no one will find him!*

I ran through the house calling his name. "Chuck, it's all right! We're not going to quit fighting this thing. It's OK, Chuck!"

With the cordless phone in my hand, I walked out the front door, continuing to call his name. There was no reply. I started out across the front yard. Suddenly I felt a sharp pain run through my foot. A nail! I had just stepped on a roofing nail right in the center of my foot. I couldn't believe it! All of us including Nicole had run around barefoot for over a year in that yard, and no one had ever found any nails!

I went back into the house, and called the church office. I spoke with Cheryl, one of the secretaries. "Chuck's missing, Cheryl. He started getting depressed again, and he's gone. We need to get some men out here to look for him."

She immediately relayed the message to the other church staff members. It wasn't long before a group of men arrived at the house and started looking all over our subdivision. I had already been around hoping to spot Chuck sitting under some tree. I asked my neighbors if they had seen Chuck, hoping against hope that he was just jogging, but no one had. One of them kindly offered to keep Nicole, and I gladly accepted.

All during this time, I tried to appear calm. I didn't want to frighten little Nicole. Inwardly, however, my heart was beating furiously as fear overtook me. When I returned to the house, I found Trish and Karen had arrived as the word began to spread that Chuck was missing.

I was anxious to keep looking for Chuck. Trish and Karen offered to watch Baby Tara to allow me to ride with the chairman of the deacons as we continued the search. While I was riding with Bill, about an hour and a half since I discovered Chuck was gone, his car phone rang. He answered, talked briefly to the person on the other end of the line, and then said to me, "They've found Chuck."

That was all he said. He gave no more information. We raced back to the house, up the driveway, and I ran in. "Where's Chuck?" I asked, looking all around the house but not seeing him anywhere. With a somber look on her face, Trish gently said, "Renee, Chuck shot himself. He's not dead yet, but they don't expect him to live. An ambulance is on the way."

I stood in disbelief as the reality of what she said penetrated my mind. It couldn't be true! Chuck would never do something like that!

"I've got to go to him! Where is he?" I screamed.

She gently took my arm and said, "He's in the empty field right across the road. But you can't go over there and see him. Stay here. There's nothing you can do."

"Let me go!" I yelled. "He needs me. I've got to go. If you don't let me go, I will fight you to go! Chuck needs me!" I screamed.

"No, Renee!" they all said as they began to grip my arm even tighter. "You don't need to see him like this."

My friends stood firm in their determination not to allow me to see Chuck's mangled body. Though I wanted to go to him, I knew deep in my heart they were right. It would only hurt me more to see the man I loved mutilated. That mental image would haunt me for the rest of my life. Unwillingly, I gave up my resistance and sank to the floor.

My whole body went numb. I was unable to feel anything as my dear friends picked me up and helped me to the couch. Though my heart was shattered, I just sat there with a blank stare on my face, unable to comprehend all that was happening. Inside my heart, a voice seemed to say, *This can't be real. This isn't really happening.* But it *was* true.

The ambulance soon arrived to take Chuck to the emergency room. One of the paramedics came over and started asking me questions, but I was in too much shock to answer them.

Then the phone rang. It was Cindy, the nurse from the hospital, calling to tell me they were sending someone out to talk with Chuck.

"It's too late, Cindy," I flatly stated. "Chuck's dead. He shot himself in the head with his shotgun."

Mechanically, I got in the car with Trish and Karen to follow the ambulance to the hospital. My friends were praying aloud as we rode. "Please God, have mercy! We beg You for a miracle!"

Suddenly, the flood gates sprang open as the tears rushed down my face. *This is real!* I realized. *I'm not dreaming! My husband has just shot himself and is probably going to die!* I began to wail as the reality of the situation slapped me in the face.

Walking into the emergency room, I looked down and saw blood on the cement. *That's Chuck's blood,* I realized. My sobbing became even more intense.

We were taken to a small waiting room where I was soon surrounded by dear friends. In this room, I would sit and wait for my husband to die. How would I tell our families this horrible news? What was I to say?

I went to the pay phone and dialed the number to my mother's office. With a trembling voice, I said, "Mom, Chuck shot himself this morning with one of his hunting guns. He's still alive. Some of his bodily functions are still working, but they say there's no way he can live." My voice gave way to pain in my heart.

I hung up the phone and dialed Chuck's mom's number in Texas. There was no easy way to speak such a hard message, and there was no easy way to receive it. Our hearts and minds were flooded with despair and devastation.

It wasn't long before a man with a white coat walked into the waiting room. I assumed him to be a doctor. As our eyes met, I knew what he had come to say.

"He's dead isn't he?" I cried

Softly he replied, "Yes."

I broke into sobs, as did all my friends.

How could this happen? Where did we go wrong? What did we fail to do? Where was God when we needed Him? Suddenly, from out of nowhere, a Bible verse I had learned in my college days popped into my mind. I knew it was God's word to me as I hit rock bottom. How much we needed a word from God! Only by the strength of the Lord could I have done what I did. Instinctively I knew we had to pray. To everyone's amazement I started to pray aloud. "Thank You, God, that You have said 'Precious in Your sight is the death of Your saint.' Thank You that I know Chuck is safe in Your arms, free from the body of pain he struggled with for so long. Thank You that he doesn't hurt anymore. He fought long and hard. Thank You, God, for receiving him into Heaven."

As soon as I finished praying, the floodgates opened again, and the questions overwhelmed my mind. All of us were completely shaken at this turn of events. Hadn't we prayed enough? Had God refused to answer our heart's cries because of some seed of unbelief on our part? Was there some sin in our lives that made Him turn his ear from answering our prayers? Had Satan won the battle we fought so hard for? Were there some secret words if we had spoken with perfect faith that would have twisted the arm of God to answer our pleas?

No one had the answers for these questions. This hadn't been just Renee and Chuck's fight. Trish, Linda, Karen, Charlene, Brenda, Bob, Janie, and on and on—they had all stood in the gap with us. All of us had fought in this battle as hard as we knew how. Now, it certainly felt and looked like we had lost. Big Time.

This wasn't some pretend war, fighting for pennies. The stakes were much higher. No, my husband was dead. Gone. The one I loved with all my heart, the father of our two precious little girls, the one I had expected to grow old with and see our children's children was dead. Twelve years of our lives being intermingled as one were finished, the dreams and work of all those years destroyed. The reality of John 10:10a came to my mind. Up until this point, I had always concentrated on the second part of that verse where Jesus said he came that we might have life more abundantly. But suddenly, the first part of John 10:10 hit me like a brick, "The thief has come to steal, kill and destroy." *He won!* I lamented. *Satan won. He did it!* I wailed.

Slowly, I walked out of the emergency waiting room. At that moment, I was too overwhelmed by grief even to start to comprehend the complexity of my situation. All I could think was that Chuck was gone. A million decisions needed to be made, but for right now, all I could see was the face of death. The decisions would be made in time. Right now, I needed to cry and begin to grieve the loss of my husband.

The girls! How would I tell the girls? My greatest concern was for these precious babies. Little Nicole's heart would be crushed! And Baby Tara would never even know her father. At least Nicole had almost three years with him, but Tara would have no memory of Daddy! How would I explain to my sensitive toddler that Daddy won't be coming home anymore? How do you tell a child not even three-years-old what death is? Heaven would sound like just another city. She never even got to say good-bye!

"God give me wisdom!" I pleaded. "Please don't let my babies hurt! Let me take their pain. Do what You want to me, God, but please don't let my little girls suffer!" I begged. The mothering instinct in me wanted to protect my children, but I knew I couldn't shield them from this pain. My heart broke even more to realize how this would affect them the rest of their lives.

With great apprehension, I called my neighbor and asked her to bring Nicole home. Seeing this beautiful blond-haired, brown-eyed bundle of energy made me want to cry all the more. I asked my dear friend Linda to go with me into Nicole's room and help me explain this horrible tragedy to her.

The girls! How would I tell the girls?

Nicole was sitting on her bed coloring when we entered. "Colee, I need to talk to you," I began. "Daddy got real sick today, and the doctor couldn't help him get better. His body died, and Daddy won't be coming home anymore. But he went to Heaven where he'll get a new body that won't ever get sick again. Daddy's waiting for us in Heaven, and we'll be with him again when we all get there. But that will probably be a long time because God's got work for us to do here on earth. When we finish our work, then we'll go to Heaven and be with Daddy and Jesus. Until then, God has said He will be your father. He has promised to take extra good care of us now since there's no Daddy in our house. We are His special girls."

The tears rolled down my checks. Whether I said the right things or not, I don't know. It was the best I knew to do. I felt I was going out on a limb for God, and I hoped He wouldn't let these precious girls down. Nicole didn't fully understood what I tried to say, but she knew something very bad had happened. She continued coloring and said very little.

The word of Chuck's suicide spread like wildfire. Soon the house was filled with people. Because of the wound in my foot from stepping on the nail, I was unable to move very easily. I laid on the couch all day with my leg propped up. Dr. Taylor, a friend from church, examined the puncture and decided to give me a tetanus shot. Everyone tried as best as they knew how to express their sympathy, but words failed us all that day.

Our friends from Livingston with whom we had planned to celebrate Nicole's birthday soon arrived. They brought the puppy they had bought for her birthday present. As soon as I saw these precious people enter the room, I burst into tears. Hugging me tightly, we cried together. No one knew what to say. They were as stunned as I was. There were no words that were adequate in such a time of intense grief and shock. We sat together and cried as the cruel reality of Chuck's death overwhelmed us.

Bob and Janie had been en route to Atlanta when Chuck died. Someone called and left a message for them there, telling them the shocking news. As soon as they got the word, they turned around and drove all night long to get back to me and the girls. They grieved with us. Bob could hardly believe that his co-worker and friend—with whom he had lunch just the day before—was dead by suicide.

Mom and Dad also drove immediately from North Carolina, and arrived late that evening. Though they too were overcome with sorrow, they tried to be strong for me and the girls. I knew my parents would do anything they possibly could to help in any way we needed them, from emotional support to making the house payment.

The evening hours grew late, and I prepared to go to bed. Dr. Taylor had left some sleeping pills for me, but I didn't want to take them. I remember going and lying down in my bed. . . alone. *Just last night, Chuck was beside me, holding me and telling me how much he loved me,* I thought. *Now he's gone forever.* I couldn't stop crying.

I forced myself to quote Scripture out loud: "God is our refuge, a very present help in trouble," (Psalm 46:10), I tried to tell myself. I spoke the words to some of the great hymns of our faith, such as "A Mighty Fortress is Our God" and "Great is Thy Faithfulness." But I couldn't keep my mind from wandering and envisioning my husband walking out of the house with the shotgun in his hand. It only made me more upset to imagine Chuck putting the gun to his head. As hard as I fought to keep my mind focused on God's comfort and care for me, I couldn't control my thoughts. I finally gave up the battle, walked out into the family room, and asked for the sleeping pills.

With the aid of the sleeping pills, I managed to get some sleep. When I awoke the next morning, pain was waiting right by my bed to knock me down. For a few hours while I slept, I had found some relief, but upon awaking, the grief immediately grabbed hold of me again. "I wish I could die, too!" I wailed. "Life is too hard. If I didn't have Nicole and Tara, I'd give up. It's too hard to try to carry on. I can't do this!" I sobbed.

But this day, Saturday, September 19th, was Nicole' birthday! How could I quit? My precious girls needed me. I was all they had now. We had built this day up so much to Nicole in anticipation of celebrating her birth. In my heart I knew the party must go on. I couldn't rob her of this special day. How I would make it through, I didn't know. I only knew my daughter would have her party as we had planned. Wasn't it enough that she suddenly had her daddy taken out of her life? How could I take away the party she had so looked forward to?

The word moved quickly that the party was still on. My wonderful friends and family all pitched in. At least a dozen three-year-olds came to join the celebration. We played musical chairs, pin the tail on the donkey, and took turns swinging on the swing set. All the decorations were done with a "Sesame Street" theme. The cake had a big yellow "Big Bird" face on it. Colee received loads of gifts and enjoyed the party, but no amount of gifts or games could make up for the tragic loss both of my girls would now suffer. I would have traded anything to have Chuck back, healthy and whole, in place of what we now had.

As I have looked back at pictures and home movies from that day, I can't believe I made it through the party. Only God's grace and strength could enable me to carry on. I know beyond a shadow of a doubt that I could never have done it apart from Him.

Funeral arrangements had to be made. No one expects to be planning their spouse's own burial service at age thirty-two. We had never given it any serious thought. Now in the midst of my shock and despair, decisions concerning funeral arrangements were thrown on me. My parents accompanied me to the funeral home that our pastor recommended. Though much of that time is very vague in my memory, I recall selecting the least expensive casket available. What did it matter what the box looked like? Who cared how plush the interior was? I had nothing to prove by choosing an elaborate coffin. "This will serve our purpose," I stated flatly. We then went to the florist Bob had suggested. I didn't know the people working at the shop, but I found them to be especially kind. Again, as I had done in the selection of the coffin, I chose the least expensive floral arrangement available. The cold reality was that I had no idea of how much money I had or what kind of income I would now be making, I knew I must exercise caution in monetary matters—starting here and now.

At the memorial service held the following day, I noticed the flowers were different than the ones I had chosen. Beautiful red roses covered the casket. I didn't learn until three years later that after I left the store, the owner instructed the florist to "give her the best." This was their way of showing love to me, even though I was a stranger to them.

I wanted to have an opportunity to speak to our many friends. I felt it would be best to receive these friends at our church, and I decided to see them on Sunday afternoon. For several hours, friends from across the area lined up outside the church waiting their turn to speak to me. Though some people were concerned that this might be too hard on me, and they tried to persuade me not to put myself through this, I am so glad I followed my initial instinct. I needed this time to look our loved ones in the eyes, feel their arms around me, and know they cared. I needed to be able to cry with these friends in the Lord's house.

The memorial service was held at our church in Slidell Monday morning. Almost mechanically, I began to dress to attend Chuck's funeral service. My sweet neighbor, Janice, in collaboration with my mother, had taken it upon herself to find something suitable for me to wear. She arrived with a beautiful two-piece outfit. For the first time in my life, I understood why black is the appropriate color to wear for a funeral. Anything else would have been out of place. How could I wear cheerful, bright colors that represented life when I buried my husband? No, black expressed my heart's attitude, and black I would wear.

With great effort, I put on my make-up and fixed my hair. Actually, I couldn't have cared less how I looked. And besides, the make-up would soon be gone, washed away by the endless stream of tears that raced down my face. Soon it was time for my family and me to make the short ride from our house to the church.

I found it ironic that I was the one who had always told Chuck what I wanted done at my funeral. "If I die, sing this song, and use this Bible verse Chuck," I chirped. He'd laugh and say, "OK, Renee, whatever you want!" Now, the same songs and same verses of Scripture I had asked to be used at my funeral were being used to bury my husband.

Brother Bob later told me this was one of the hardest funerals he ever had to preach. All of us were crushed, with millions of questions bombarding our minds. We were badly beaten from standing on the front lines of the battlefield the past eight weeks. Yet the word of God stands secure and firm, even when we are shaken down to our very foundation. Though everything around us falls apart, "the word of the Lord endures forever" (I Pet. 1:25). Bob spoke forth the words of truth. It was a time to express our great sorrow, admit our questions, acknowledge our lack of understanding, and yet reaffirm our faith in God, and the truth of His Word.

One would have thought that the receiving of friends at the church, followed by the memorial service the next day would be more than enough official mourning. Yet, for me, there was more to come. Chuck's body was to be buried in Texas at their family plot. Tuesday morning, Brother Bob, Linda, Karen, and I boarded a plane to fly to San Antonio for the grave side service. In the past, whenever I flew, I always prayed for a safe flight. This time however, it didn't matter. *I don't care God if this plane crashes,* I thought to myself. *I'm ready to die, too. Life is too hard.* Death would be a welcome relief from the tormenting pain that enveloped my mind and body.

Our dear friend, Shelby Smith, with whom we had worked at our country church while in seminary, drove from west Texas to have a part in the service. Seeing Chuck's family for the first time since his death was difficult. They had as many questions as I had, but the answers were no where to be found. *Do they blame me?* I wondered?

Late that evening, the four of us flew back from San Antonio to New Orleans. Mom and Dad had stayed at my house with the girls while I was gone. In just a few more days my parents would return to North Carolina. What then? What was I to do without them?

My life was shattered. The worst possible thing that I could ever have imagined had just happened to me. I was sapped of all energy and motivation to live. We had done everything we knew to do, and it certainly felt and looked like God had ignored our fervent cries. I felt abandoned by both Chuck and God. My life with Chuck was over. Twelve years of dreams, love, and work were gone. Chuck's body was buried, and I was left to carry on. A widow at age thirty-two, with a four-month-old baby, and a young three-year-old, and a life insurance policy that refused to pay. I didn't know where I belonged anymore. How will we make it? What am I to do now? Thoughts of the future only boggled my mind more. It was all I could do to cope with the present, much less try to think ahead. I didn't even know how I would make it through today! I prayed, "Just get me through today, God. Somehow, someway, I've got to survive today."

The song had died. What had begun as a prelude to a beautiful symphony now suddenly ended on a crashing, dissonant chord. How I wished I could resolve it! "Can't we change these chords, God? Can't we rewrite these notes to a beautiful melody in a major key? I don't like this dissonance! Throw the keyboard out the window. I don't care if I never hear another strain from this song! My heart will never sing again! The music is finished."

Abruptly, the music ended. The song was over. I was left alone, wondering why. Only the Master Musician could ever resurrect the music. As far as I was concerned, it was gone forever.

5

Major? Minor? Sharp? Flat?— Now What?

Critical Decisions

What do you mean it's not valid? Are you saying it's not going to pay?" I said incredulously to the insurance agent. I sat in disbelief as the cold hard facts were explained to me once more. The situation was even more grim than I had previously thought. Our life insurance policy was not going to pay. The shocking news trampled on the shattered pieces of my heart.

For the first few days following Chuck's death, I had found some relief in believing that the girls and I would be taken care of financially because of our life insurance policy. "Thank God, we covered that base. At least we won't be bankrupt," I had uttered. Now I was being told the policy was no good. Wasn't it bad enough that Chuck was dead without throwing more bad news at me? Just how much more did God think I could bear?

This was only one of a million critical concerns that now confronted me. Everything had changed. Crucial, life-changing decisions in numerous areas now needed to be made. And the buck stopped with me. It fell in my lap. Oh, I could receive advice and counsel from others, but the bottom line was that I had to make the final decision. How could I make wise decisions when my mind could hardly think straight? When I needed to be at my best mentally and emotionally to deal with such major issues, I was an emotional wreck.

We thought we had followed the wise, responsible way when we originally took out a life insurance policy shortly after Nicole was born in 1984. Until that time, we never felt a great need for insurance since we were young and healthy, and both of us knew we could take care of ourselves if something happened to the other one. But when a baby came along, that changed things. We wanted to insure that if anything happened to either of us, our child would be provided for.

That initial policy had been in effect for two-and-a-half years when Chuck came home one day and said, "Honey, John (a leader in our church) just got laid off from his job. He's decided to sell life insurance to make ends meet. I think we need to support him. Let's cancel our other policy and take out a life insurance plan with him. It's a way we can help him and his family."

Without giving it a second's thought, I replied, "Whatever you think. That's fine with me." Little did I know that only six months later my husband would be dead by his own hand, and the new policy would not have been in effect long enough to cover death by suicide.

In my ignorance, I didn't realize what our insurance policy stated regarding death by suicide, and I wrongly assumed that the girls and I were covered. Unfortunately, many others also find out too late that for various reasons, their policy isn't what they thought it was. That hard, cold fact leaves them in a predicament that only adds to the emotional pain they face.

I wrongly assumed that the girls and I were covered.

Many have no idea of the insurance coverage they have (life, health, disability, home, auto, etc.), or where to locate the policies. This is an area that should be thoroughly discussed with your spouse so that if a crisis occurs, the policies can be easily retrieved and the claim process initiated. It is the way of wisdom not only to prepare for the unknown storms of life by having adequate insurance coverage to meet the needs of your family and also to know what the policy says. Read the fine print so there are no unwelcome surprises thrown at you when you are already in a confused, emotionally distraught state of mind.

The area of finances was just one of many, immediate, crucial concerns. It was now totally in my hands. Responsible money management was essential because I quickly saw our family income significantly decrease with Chuck's death. I couldn't fall back on money from a life insurance policy that wouldn't pay. And to make matters worse (if that were possible), I faced not only a reduction of income, but a high increase in monthly bills since we purchased a new car less than forty-eight hours before Chuck died. How were we going to survive financially? If I didn't handle this appropriately, we could be financially devastated.

My pastor asked two businessmen in our church to sit down with me and offer their suggestions for getting my finances in order. While I appreciated their concern, even before they arrived I knew exactly what I was facing. I knew they couldn't pull any tricks out of the bag to change things. There was no money tree in the back yard.

When they arrived, I showed them my own calculations. "This is my monthly income, and these are my monthly expenditures. Barring any major repairs and breakdowns, we should be able to barely skim by until I get this car paid for. In two years, when it's paid off, things should be easier. In the meantime, it's a good thing that I know how to stretch a dollar. God's going to have to fill in the gaps for us. He said he'd take care of the widow and fatherless children. We have no other choice but to trust Him. If He doesn't do it, then it's not going to be done." The men could see I had the budget in order, and they had nothing to add to what I had shown them. They prayed with me and then left.

If you have never prepared a budget and followed it, now is the time to start. Learning to be a smart shopper, as well as wisely using what you have, can also save you many dollars. I owe much of my ability to get the most for my dollar from my Grandpa Thomason. As a little girl, I followed him around like a puppy while he worked outside on the farm. Papaw came through The Great Depression, and if ever a man was financially conservative and wise, he was. Papaw parked the car three blocks away when we went to town so he wouldn't have to put money in the parking meter. He cut the car off a quarter mile before we got home and coasted in to save gas.

Papaw was a "scrapper." He saved all kinds of scrap metal—copper, tin, aluminum—and then would take it to the salvage store for money. He was recycling long before it became socially popular! In fact, when people asked me, "What are you going to do when you grow up?" I always said, "I'm going to be a scrapper like Papaw." Though some may call me "tight," I prefer to think of myself as a scrapper. No, I didn't go through the Great Depression, but I learned from one who did, and still today, I benefit from the lessons he taught me to trim the fat and cut the corners. It's not always how much money you make, but how you manage the money you have that determines your lifestyle. Due to my grandfather's influence, my skills for managing my income have enabled the girls and me to continue in our previous lifestyle. Thankfully, Chuck and I had been very conservative in handling our money, and I was not over my head in debt when he died. Otherwise my situation could have been very different.

Some people have no option but to sell the house and move into a smaller dwelling, add another job to try to make ends meet, go back to school at night while working all day, or put the kids in day-care while they work full-time. I am thankful that, although money was very tight especially the first two years, we didn't have to make major alterations in our lifestyle. Good money management is more essential than ever when you've lost the chief bread winner.

Preparing a budget is a must if you are now going to be living on a lower income (which is most often the case). Learning to live on a new revised budget will put your financial house in good shape. An accountant, banker, or a good businessman can guide you through this process. Many good books are also available to guide you in preparing a budget that will work for you. Depending on your resources, it may be wise to work with a licensed financial planner. Most certainly if you come into a surplus of funds, a financial planner should be consulted. This will help prevent losing the money through unwise or uninformed investments or the possibility of squandering it by undisciplined spending.

I soon found myself bombarded with another shock following Chuck's death. This time it was in relation to our wills. Once again, just as in the area of life insurance, I thought we had followed the responsible path. In the early years of our marriage in central Florida, we made reciprocal wills, and each of us named the other as beneficiary. It was a very simple matter. We congratulated ourselves on being ahead of the game by drawing up wills while we were only in our mid-twenties. How many young couples ever think about this area? This was the smart thing to do, right?

When Chuck suddenly died, I was thankful that we had properly taken care of this area and could avoid the unnecessary hassle that comes from not having a will. Little did I know that wills made in the state of Florida were not considered valid in the state of Louisiana. Since Louisiana has what is called "forced heirship," Chuck's will leaving everything to me was overruled, and the girls received part of his estate. Though I had no problem with a portion of Chuck's estate automatically going to Nicole and Tara, I just never realized that a will made in one state might not stand up in another state.

It is always smart to check the legal specifications of each state if you move. Much unnecessary red tape, worry, and unexpected surprises can be spared by taking the time to make a will. An attorney can very easily and quickly take care of this matter. As with the insurance policies, be sure you know where the will is stored. Those left to pick up the pieces after the death of one they love will be immensely grateful this area was not left unattended.

Even before dealing with these important matters of insurance, financial concerns, and wills, immediate decisions have to be made regarding the funeral service and disposing of the body. When and where should the service be held? Who will conduct the service? What will be the total cost of the funeral expenses? Will the body be buried, entombed, or cremated? Do you want to donate any body organs to medical science or organizations to benefit others? Some people pre-plan for their funeral service and burial. This planning can be of great benefit to those making the arrangements. Though I had often given Chuck instructions to follow pertaining to my own death, when I was suddenly faced with his death, I couldn't remember one time he ever mentioned his own funeral. I never fully understood the value and purpose of the funeral ceremony until it was my loved one lying in the casket at the front of the church. Prior to that, I grimaced at the thought of going through such a ritual. Wasn't the purpose of such an event simply "closing the book" on the person's life on earth? Now I realize that funerals are much more than that; they are for the living, not just the dead. It has been said that these rituals are "the glue that hold us together at the beginning of grieving." They have the power to propel us through these painful, initial days of grief. During a time when we are emotionally devastated, the funeral rituals give much needed structure to a time that could otherwise be totally chaotic. As hard as it is, the funeral service makes us face the reality that our loved one is dead. Though we may either consciously, or unconsciously, fight against acceptance of this truth, the funeral forces us to begin to respond to the reality of the situation and breaks down the defense mechanisms our emotions automatically set up. We can no longer deny that our loved one is gone. With this acknowledgement, the beginning stages of grief work are free to begin.

Because we had made no prior preparations for the service and burial, I was suddenly confronted with a multitude of decisions which I felt inadequate to make. Fortunately, my family and church guided me and led me from one decision to the next. The initial decision of which funeral home to use was made simply by accepting my pastor's recommendation. Shortly thereafter, my parents went with me to choose a casket. No matter how modern and nice a funeral home may be, who cannot be even more depressed after walking through a room filled with coffins?

It was amazing to me to see the lengths some would go to dress up a box that would be buried in the ground. Even in my shock and sorrow, my conservative nature cringed at the price of some of the coffins. There is no one right answer for the question: "What coffin should I choose?" It is a matter of personal taste, temperament, and finances. Out of guilt, some people choose to buy the most elaborate casket available in an effort to "make up" for their failure to the deceased. It is a way to "prove" their love. Some aren't constrained by a lack of finances. They choose "the best" because that's their style, and they can afford it. In my case, I wanted one that was simple and adequate for the purpose; "decent," but not elaborate. Money was a factor I had to consider.

The funeral director asked me, "What do you want Chuck to be buried in, Renee?"

This was another decision to make that only made the tears flow more quickly. "Use the new navy suit my parents gave him last Christmas," I answered. What did it matter? No one would see it anyway since the casket would remain closed (due to his body being mangled from the gunshot wound).

But actually, it mattered a great deal to me. This was still my Chuck, even though some considered it just a dead body. Because of my love for him, it was important to me that his body be dressed in a manner both he and I would have deemed appropriate. This was yet another hard question that must be asked and answered immediately, and this series of decisions continued to impress deep into my subconscious the most painful reality I had ever had to face: Chuck was dead.

Part of the burial ritual is the viewing of the body, or "wake" as it is called in some parts of the country. Some may choose to omit this service, but I consider it one of the most significant aspects of the burial process. I have known family members who refuse to attend the viewing (even when the casket remains closed) because they think, *I don't want to go and see everybody crying. I can't take it. My loved one's not there anyway.* How much they miss! It is an opportunity for friends and family to gather and show their support and comfort to the bereaved. Sharing this grief with those who mean so much to us offers the opportunity for the healing to begin. It allows the bereaved to publicly acknowledge their loss. In this informal setting, friends can give their words of love as their embrace wraps around your arms and heart. I count this as a cherished time, when our friends came to say, "We loved Chuck, and we love you. We sorrow with you."

Yes, I cried, and even sobbed. But the expression of my grief was necessary. This active participation in beginning to grieve Chuck's death prevented me from submerging my pain, and thereby extending and expanding the sorrow. By facing my grief, and even embracing it, I began the difficult and painful process of working through it.

Friends can give their words of love as their embrace wraps around your arms and heart. I count this as a cherished time.

It seemed only natural to me that the wake be held at our church, though it is more commonly held at the funeral home. I made this decision because it was what I felt was most appropriate for us even though it broke the pattern normally followed. The church had been the center of our life as a married couple, the place around which our lives revolved. It was fitting that this should be the place where I begin to work through the closure of my life with Chuck. I have never regretted this decision. I only become more affirmed in it as time has passed. Sometimes it is best to follow your gut instincts and have the type of service you desire instead of bowing to convention. Listen to your heart in these matters even if your choice may be somewhat unconventional. If not, you may later regret that you did what everyone told you to do instead of what you really preferred.

The funeral service for Chuck was held the following day. Though ours was a simple service, it's meaning is beyond calculation. The funeral service plays a valuable, positive role in the grief experience. Unfortunately, this is often diminished today in a society that seeks to deny death and looks with disdain upon "rituals" as a meaningless tradition. We often rush through the funeral and want to "get it over as soon as possible," as if putting it behind us will instantly reduce our pain. Yet holding the funeral too quickly excludes people who must travel a great distance. Their presence and support during this agonizing time is worth waiting to schedule the service one day later.

Many purposes are accomplished by the funeral ceremony. This was the time to say our last good-byes and give ourselves permission to grieve Chuck's untimely death. It was a time to validate what Chuck's life meant to so many as we recalled how much he had given to others. It was a time for me to receive comfort and strength from those who came. For some, it was a time to consider their own immortality, to ask if they were spiritually prepared should death call for them. Perhaps above all, it was a time to reaffirm our faith in God, even in the midst of our devastation and turmoil.

A pastor's presence and guidance during this time is of immense value. He will gently direct you through the myriad details that must be considered. Even though wrestling with his own sorrow, my pastor stood "steady on" while I was being tossed about to and fro emotionally. To some degree, I participated in the planning of the funeral service. Even in the midst of my sorrow, there were certain matters of importance to me which I did not want overlooked. Be involved in the planning of this ceremony to the degree that is comfortable for you. The experience will be a source of comfort to you in the days to come, as well as being a positive step towards restoration and healing of your hurting heart.

I requested specific songs of hope and faith to be played by the musicians. "A Mighty Fortress is Our God, A bulwark never failing; Our helper He amid the flood of mortal ills prevailing" rang throughout the walls of the building. *How appropriate for such a time of crises,* I thought. I had sung those words from the time I was a small child growing up in the Lutheran church. But this day the message had an impact on me as never before. The last words of the final verse stood out in particular, perfectly suited for our time of grief: "The body they may kill; God's truth abideth still, His kingdom is forever." Yes, it was a time to fully express our sorrow. Yet for the believer in Christ Jesus, even our sorrow is laced with hope. These hymns proclaiming our trust—even through the darkness—brought a sense of security to a world that was shattered.

There were particular verses of Scripture I requested our pastor to use. I wanted the plan of salvation to be "as clear as a bell. Make it clear, Brother Bob," I asked of our pastor. "There will be people here today who have never seriously considered what happens when this mortal body dies. If ever someone will consider the question of their eternal welfare, it will be today." Other verses, which proclaimed God's grace and strength during our storm-tossed days, served as an anchor for us.

If no prearrangements have been made for a burial plot, another immediate decision will have to be made. Since Chuck's family had bought burial plots in their Texas hometown, I was spared from having to make a decision on where he would be buried. I was thankful for that. His body was flown to Texas following the funeral. A grave side service was held there the next day. Emotional and financial anguish can be avoided by pre-planning in this area. Since death is certain, why not take the necessary steps to prepare for it and thereby alleviate some of the pain for your loved ones? One less decision they have to make during such a tumultuous time will be a welcome relief.

A major decision I confronted immediately after losing Chuck was, Where do I belong? I had to ask myself, *Where is home now? Should I stay here in Louisiana or go back home to North Carolina?* My only reason for being in Louisiana prior to Chuck's death was because that's where my husband's work was. Though we called it "home," it didn't feel like home in my heart. Now that he was gone, wasn't it only logical that I should return to what was "home" for me, North Carolina, to be close to my family? Wouldn't this be best for my two babies, to have Mamma and Papaw close by?

Though I had no prior knowledge or study of "the rules" to follow in a situation like mine, I sensed deep in my spirit that I should make as few major changes as possible until I began to get back on my feet. I needed the support so wonderfully given by my church family. If I made a sudden move, I would cut myself off from that source of comfort. In particular, I felt that my Nicole, though she just turned three, needed the security and safety of seeing that her entire world was not completely shaken. I tried to explain to my family and friends, "She needs to hold on to her little friends and the familiarity of her preschool class and church. Even staying in this house and in her room is important at this time. She's experienced more than enough change. I've got to keep as much consistency in her life as I can for right now."

It was a necessity that I work, and the position I held at my church was ideal for me, especially now that I would be single parenting. If I moved, I'd be hard-pressed to find something with the hours and salary I needed. Plus I already had plenty of music students, and my schedule was in place. A move would mean starting from scratch and rebuilding my reputation as a music teacher.

I still have the list I made so long ago of the "pros" and "cons" of staying in Louisiana or moving to North Carolina. I haven't ruled out the possibility of one day going back home, but I have been even more convinced as time has passed that my initial decision to remain in Louisiana was the right one for that time. However, I wouldn't make this a hard, concrete rule that everyone must follow. Each situation is unique, and all the angles must be considered.

A move or a change of residence (perhaps even in the same area) may be the best option for some people. But a good, general rule to follow after encountering a great loss is "make as few major changes as possible during the first year." Postpone major decisions that can be delayed, and keep decision making to a minimum. Understand that your judgement is unclear because of the trauma you have just encountered. There's been enough change. You need to step back, take a deep breath, and recoup before plunging into something else. Choosing to wait to make major choices will allow time for you to recover sufficiently to the point that you can think rationally and be more objective regarding the overall picture.

One by one, other decisions threw themselves before me in the days that followed. I discovered it wasn't only the major, life-changing decisions that were tough to make. Even the simple ones proved difficult, too. What do I say when the phone rings, and the caller says, "May I please speak to Chuck?" Do I say, "Sorry, he's dead," or go into an explanation of the whole scenario?

What about the friend from college who just called to say "Hello" and had not heard of Chuck's death? Unsuspectingly, he called to "catch up." Now, I was forced to be the one to give him the overwhelming news. I hated throwing this bombshell in his lap, but it must be said.

Sometimes I wished I could just lie, and say, "We're doing fine. Chuck's gone for now, but I'll tell him you called when he gets back." Wouldn't that be easier than blowing them away with the truth? But lying would only prolong the agony. If I were ever going to rebound from this crisis, I knew I must face it head on.

Mail addressed to "Mr. and Mrs. Chuck Scheidt" seemed like a cruel joke. Even my checkbook reminded me of my loss. "Two names don't need to be on this account anymore," I cried. The telephone company, electric company, water company, and on and on—all those who sent monthly bills had to be notified of Chuck's death, and the name on the bill had to be changed. Would all the decisions and changes ever end? Every day, at every turn, something else jumped out at me demanding my attention, awaiting my response, reminding me again (as if I could forget) that Chuck was dead.

Not long after the funeral, I suddenly noticed myself turning my wedding band around my finger, unconsciously playing with it. All at once I was stricken with the thought, *What about our rings? What do I do with our wedding rings?* This was the outward symbol to the world of the vows we made to one another "to love and cherish till death do us part." Now it had happened. The unthinkable had become reality. We had been parted by death. Did that mean I was just to remove the ring and try to forget that part of my life? Taking off the ring seemed so final, as if to say, "It's over. The end." I was unable to face this harsh reality immediately. Hadn't I lost enough without suffering this loss, too? No, I couldn't let the ring go at that point. It would remain on my finger. At least the ring announced: "I'm not available!" to any strange men I may meet. More than this, however, I still felt married. Wearing the ring was my way of saying, "Chuck, I still belong to you. Legally and technically, I know we are no longer married. But in my heart, I still consider myself as your wife." This may sound totally ridiculous, but I felt comfortable with it.

I chose to wear my wedding ring for the first year after Chuck's death. When that day came, it was with mixed emotions that I removed the ring and put it in a safe place. The time had come for me to go on. Even one year after his death, it was a difficult thing to do. But I knew it was time. To cling to the past would only destroy the future. One day, I plan to give the rings to our girls.

Shortly after removing my wedding band I purchased a "family ring." It is much like a mother's ring, but with larger birthstones for Chuck and me and smaller ones for Nicole and Tara. It is my way of wearing an outward symbol of my life with Chuck and the fruit of that union. It is a precious reminder of the love we shared.

Some wear their wedding ring for the rest of their life or move it to the other hand. Others may choose to remove the ring immediately. If that's their choice, it is perfectly all right. I've known people to take the ring and have a necklace or earrings made out of it. There is not just one right answer. You should do what makes you feel comfortable. Removing the ring does not mean you didn't love your mate and that you are being disloyal. How insensitive of others to try to tell you what to do regarding this matter or dare to criticize your decision! It is none of their business! Until they have walked in your shoes, they have no right to fault you for your choice. It is a very personal matter that each person must decide in his or her own heart.

The music of life came to a screeching halt the day Chuck died. In many ways, much of me died as well. I still continued to breathe, but I was half dead, only able to partially function. Even in this weakened, numbed condition, numerous decisions lined up and waited for me to give direction. They didn't seem to understand that I wasn't ready to handle making these choices. I wanted to scream, "Let me push the 'pause' button please, until I'm ready to make up my mind!" Yes, some decisions could wait, but others couldn't. They demanded immediate resolution. Friends and family did all they could to simplify my choices, and that certainly helped, but even they couldn't answer some of the questions. I had to make these decisions, and hope and pray I would choose the right path.

It's smart to discuss as many of these issues as possible before the need arises. Plan and prepare ahead of time. Then, when the music of life suddenly ceases, you won't be forced to make decisions when you can barely think straight. Proper preparations will ease some of the pain and prevent more unexpected crises.

Still, even in the midst of my trauma and shock, with a multitude of issues presenting themselves, I firmly believe that the Spirit of God guided me in each matter that lay before me. At the time, I wondered if I made the right choice. When facing a dilemma, we often aren't sure we are truly being led by the hand of God. Hindsight, however, enables us to see His leading. Faith calls us to trust Him in the midst of the storm. Though some of the crisis may be caused by our own neglect, failure, short-sightedness, or inadequate preparation, God still shows himself to be faithful as He lovingly guides us through the chaos. I remember an old hymn I used to sing. The tune and lyrics swirl through my mind:

> He giveth more grace when the burdens grow greater,
> He sendeth more strength when the labors increase;
> To added affliction, He addeth His mercy,
> To multiplied trials, His multiplied peace.
> His love has no limit, His grace has no measure,
> His power no boundary known unto men;
> For out of His infinite riches in Jesus,
> He giveth and giveth and giveth again.

Lyrics to the hymn "He Giveth More Grace" by Annie Johnson Flint

6

What Happened to the Music?
Picking Up the Pieces

Face to face with death. In spite of all our prayers and efforts, we lost. Death won. And in the worst possible way—by suicide. The very sound of the word repulsed me. I had the hardest time with this type of death. I was caught entirely off-guard; it was totally unexpected; I was devastated by the fact that "it didn't have to be."

In cases of suicide, the stigma, shame and questions that may possibly never be answered can haunt the survivors the rest of their lives. For Christians, the issue can be even more painful because they have to face such statements as: "A true believer wouldn't commit suicide," or "Anyone who commits suicide goes straight to hell!"

The fragility of our human lives was brought sharply into focus when I suddenly found my world turned upside down. I had no control over the events that had changed my entire realm of living. My life would never be the same. It was shocking to me to realize how drastically my position in life changed within the span of a few minutes. No longer was I the wife of the dashing young minister. Now at thirty-two years of age, I was a widow, a full-fledged member of the "single again" crowd, thrust into a dreaded position. "Single again" sounded like a curse word to me. I didn't want to be a part of "those people." More than just being widowed, I was also a "single parent," forced to raise our two little girls by myself, doing alone what God had intended two people to do.

"Lord, it's not supposed to be this way!" I cried. "I'm not supposed to be a widow when I'm thirty-two! That's for the older ladies God. Look at these babies. They have no daddy. How are we going to make it now? What are we going to do? I don't even know where home is anymore! It's not supposed to be this way God!"

Thousands of questions bombarded my mind: "Where are You, God? How could You let this happen? We loved You; we served You. We dedicated everything to You. You know Lord, we were willing to do anything You asked. This doesn't seem fair! After all we've tried to do for You, You wouldn't even help us when we needed You the most! The greatest cry of my life, and You wouldn't answer. For eight weeks, we have not stopped knocking on Heaven's door begging You to touch and heal Chuck. You're the one who said, 'Ask and it shall be given unto you!' (Matthew 7:7). All of those sleepless nights crying out to You were for nothing! We were wasting our time, weren't we God! What about the fasting? Didn't that count for anything? God, we did *everything* we knew to do from praying, praising, fasting, anointing with oil, standing on the promises, binding Satan. . . *everything*! And nothing worked. After all we've tried to do in Your service, this is the payoff. Why didn't You intervene and help us when we begged You to? I'm as disappointed with You as I am with Chuck!"

A full spectrum of emotions flooded my soul. How I wanted to believe that there was a God who showed himself strong in behalf of those who loved him, who still answered the pleas of his children! But He didn't do it for us! As I saw it, the bottom line was that God didn't answer our prayers the way I thought He should. In fact, from all I could see and feel, from all that my emotions were telling me, it looked like God had deserted us when we needed Him the most. I understood the cry of Mary and Martha following the death of their brother, Lazarus, "Lord, if You had been here, he wouldn't have died" (John 11:21,32). I felt the same way. "Lord, if You had been here, Chuck wouldn't have died!"

Satan took full advantage of my situation to hurl his darts at me. He mocked me, "In the time of your greatest crisis, God abandoned you. This is what you get, Renee, for trying to follow the Lord! You thought the years of scrimping and working your tail off were going to start to pay off now, didn't you, Renee! You thought you were going to have the great job, husband, and kids," Satan sarcastically taunted me. "Welcome to reality," he snidely remarked.

Were Satan's remarks true? I wondered. *Were my emotions*

telling me the truth? I knew in my head what the Bible said, yet all I could see and feel contradicted the Biblical teaching. I didn't *feel* like God loved me and had a wonderful plan for my life! I could not imagine how such a horrible tragedy could ever be used for God's glory. My life was destroyed.

In the midst of my devastation, I somehow knew I had to make a decision about God and His Word. The Scriptures that I had zealously proclaimed to be true since my salvation at age seventeen now seemingly stood in glaring contradiction to the reality of my circumstances. For me, the matter boiled down to one simple point: Is the Word of God true or not? The same Bible that promised salvation for anyone that believed in the Lord Jesus Christ (John 3:16, Acts 16:31) also said in Romans 8:28 that "All things work together for good to them that love God and are called for His purpose." I knew these verses came in the same book. I certainly didn't have the authority to pick and choose which verses I liked and and throw the others out. If I can't know that one verse is true, then how can I know any of it is? Either the Bible is true... or it's not. If it's not, I don't need it and I would be through with the whole mess! I'm straightforward enough to say, "Thank you, but I'm not going to play your little church game anymore. I don't need 'churchianity.' I have better things to do with my time. So don't come calling me to say, 'We missed you in Sunday School, Renee.' You can take my name off the roll! I won't be back. I won't darken the door of the church, and there will be no Bibles in this house. Do you understand? I've put out the 'do not disturb' sign. Can you read?"

Though a great part of me wanted to renounce God, the Bible, and anything to do with church, I couldn't escape the fact that I knew in my heart of hearts that God's Word is truth. Period. Because of that deep conviction and knowledge, I felt I had no choice but to stand upon it. There were no other options. Though it was a struggle to overcome all that my emotions, circumstances, and the devil were shouting to me, I knew I couldn't forsake my faith. Where else could I go when the Lord is the only one who had the words of life? Truth is the only foundation that will last. Everything else is sinking sand. If the foundation is not right, sooner or later the entire structure will fall. I didn't know much, but I knew enough to know I must stand on truth regardless of what I felt or saw.

With this conviction planted deep in my heart, I made a conscious, deliberate decision. It most definitely was an act of my will and not my emotions. "Lord," I cried, "I can't believe what has happened in our lives. I never ever dreamed I would wind up in a situation like this. I'm confused, hurt, and angry that You allowed all of this to happen. I don't like it a bit! I don't want this, and I'd change it right now if I could. But I really don't have a choice in the matter. This is reality. These are the cards that have been dealt to me. Now I must choose how I'm going to play this hand. And I choose to believe that somehow, in Your sovereignty, Your great love, mercy, and compassion, that You will work even the tragic death of my husband together for good to me, Nicole, and Tara, because we do love You, and are called for Your purpose."

Life will never be meaningful for me again. That's gone forever.

I knew that Chuck was now experiencing the presence of God. For Chuck, to live was Christ, and now to die was gain (Philippians 1:21). For Chuck, to be absent from the body meant that he was at home with the Lord (II Corinthians 5:8). I want to emphasize that suicide is never the will of God for anyone. It is a sin. It is wrong. Those left behind suffer the immeasurable consequences. But for those who have placed their faith in Christ as Savior, the blood of Jesus washes away *all* sin. That includes the sin of suicide, just as it does the sin of pride, the sin of divorce, and the sin of gossip. All sin is "paid in full" by the blood of Jesus. The Bible doesn't teach that suicide is the unpardonable sin. Hebrews 10:10 says that those who believe are " sanctified through the offering of the body of Jesus Christ once for all." Verse fourteen goes on to add, "for by one offering he hath perfected forever them that are sanctified."

Justification means that we are declared righteous the moment we believe. The righteousness of Christ is credited to our account, removing the penalty of our sin—past, present and future! These promises are for all who come in faith to Jesus. The sinful action of suicide does not negate these truths! If you have lost a friend or family member by suicide, you don't have to live with the lie so often heard that they are automatically condemned to hell. That is not the Biblical teaching.

I now see in retrospect that the decision to stand on God's Word was one of the most important decisions I have ever made. It set the stage for everything that followed. Please don't misunderstand. My pain and hurt didn't suddenly vanish because I made a conscious choice to hold onto God's truth. I didn't "just skip on down the road because God's working it all together for good. La-di-da-di-da!" No! Standing on truth doesn't mean that my girls and I haven't suffered. We have! After Chuck's death, I wished I could die, too! My only reason for living was because my babies needed me. I was forced to function when in reality, I wanted to curl up and die. My naivety had been stripped from me. I now saw the cold, harsh realities of life. Whoever said, "If you do right, things will be right"? Who ever said, "Life was fair"? I realized that I had fallen for the "American Dream" mentality, believing our hard work and faithful service would pay off in this life! I was jolted back to reality as I saw from my own personal experiences that is doesn't always work that way.

God has obviously called me to a life of sorrow and suffering, I thought. *The abundant life Jesus talked about is over.*

Why was I surprised? Had I forgotten the teaching of the Scripture, "For unto you it is given in the behalf of Christ, not only to believe on Him but also to suffer for His sake"? (Philippines 1:29 KJV). Had I forgotten the price that followers of Christ through the ages have paid? Why should I be any different? Who was I to think I could get out of this life without paying my dues to hardship? I knew fully well that being a Christian didn't grant me immunity from the hurts and pains of living in a fallen, sin-cursed world. Yet in spite of my Biblical knowledge, I was hurt and disappointed that God let this happen to us. I discovered it's one thing to know the Biblical teaching; it's another when it happens to you.

The words to an old hymn I had always loved came to my mind. Let me share them with you:

> Must Jesus bear the cross alone
> and all the world go free?
> No there's a cross for every one
> And there's a cross for me

This is your cross, Renee, I thought. *Life will never be meaningful for me again. I will simply function in a mechanical way and do what I am required to do until I can leave this hard life behind. I will do my best to raise Nicole and Tara to fear God and serve*

*Him in truth all the days of their lives, but I don't think I'll ever
be truly happy again. That's gone forever.*

I wondered if there would ever be a day in my life again when
I could make it through a twenty-four hour period without
crying. For a very long time, crying was part of my nightly
routine. After putting my girls to bed at 8:30, I lay on my couch
and sobbed. "Lord, You said You put all of our tears in a bottle
(Psalm 56:8). Well, You better bring out the buckets for me. A
bottle won't hold them all!" I wailed.

Church was one of the hardest places I had to go. You can
imagine how I felt walking into the church auditorium for
worship service nine days after Chuck died. Our life had revolved around this very place. My eyes looked up to the seat on
the platform where he used to sit each Sunday. Now it was
empty. *Chuck should be welcoming these guests, He should lead
this prayer or preach this message,* I fumed. The tears rolled
down my cheeks as I remembered how it used to be—in contrast
to the harsh reality I now faced.

After a number of months, I still sat in the pew each Sunday
with tears streaming down my face. Some well-meaning friends
tried to help by saying things like, "Come on, Renee. You can't sit
here and cry forever. You've got to get a grip and move on with
your life."

Quite frankly, I didn't think I could get a grip, and I really had
no desire to "move on with my life." It all seemed like a futile
game, and I didn't want to play anymore. What was the purpose
of it all? I agreed with the writer of Ecclesiastes, and understood
what he meant when he said, "Vanity of vanities; all is vanity"
(Ecclesiastes 1:2 KJV).

I share these very personal feelings with you simply to say I
know what it is to hit rock bottom. Many of you do as well. Yes,
I made a conscious deliberate decision to hold on to God and His
Word, but that didn't immediately take away my pain, anger, or
confusion. I know what it is to function in spite of constant
mental pain and physical exhaustion. I know what it is to wish
you could leave it all behind and be swept up to Heaven's
doorstep, but have to carry on because someone here is dependant
on you. I am reminded of what Pilgrim said in John Bunyon's
Pilgrim's Progress, "I've been to the bottom and I found it was
rock solid!" I wondered if I would ever be able to say the same.

During my Bible college days I had been required to take
theology classes where we studied the character and attributes

of our God. At the time, it was merely a mental exercise of lists to learn and recite for the tests. I now see how valuable this training was for me. Many years later when my world was torn to pieces, I found hope to carry on by focusing on just what our Heavenly Father is like. After the initial decision to hold onto the truth of God's Word in spite of my fears, doubts, and pain, reminding myself of the character of God was the second most critical factor in facing my crisis.

Daniel wrote, "The people who know their God will display strength and take action" (Daniel 11:32 NASB). As we realize who God is and what He has done to provide our salvation, our trust in Him is strengthened. This awesome, almighty One who simply spoke the word and the world came into being is our loving Father who only desires our best and His glory! His heart is that of a Father lovingly taking care of His children.

I knew I didn't know it all. In fact, I didn't even have all the information to make intelligent decisions about many of the challenges I faced. Any decision I made based on partial information would probably be an inaccurate one. I didn't have all the pieces of the puzzle, and some of the pieces were all black. I groused, "I don't like this color, Lord! Can't we change these dark tones for bright, cheerful colors? What does the cover of the puzzle box look like God? How can I put this together when I don't even know what the cover looks like?" Here I was with my few pieces trying to cram this piece into a spot it didn't fit, shoving another one here, trying to make it work but accomplishing very little. I was ready to scream! "I'm so frustrated, Lord, and I don't understand!"

I knew that although I was finite, my God isn't. I realized I must remember that God is all-knowing. Omniscience is the theological word! Nothing takes Him by surprise. He knows the end from the beginning. He knew from eternity past that Chuck would end his life on September 18, 1987. He didn't have to say, "Angels, we've got a problem. They messed up Plan A. Let's see if we can come up with Plan B." No, He knew from before time began that this would be in my path. The good news for me is that He prepared everything I would need for that moment in time before the moment ever arrived!

From His vantage point outside of time, God can see the entire picture complete with every piece of the puzzle in place. I certainly can't! If I could see the puzzle completed right now the way God already does, I hope I would say the same thing

Abraham did several thousand years ago, "The Judge of all the earth has done right" (Genesis 18:25). Doesn't it make sense for one like me who doesn't know it all to put my trust and faith in One who does? He is all knowing.

I also reminded my hurting heart that God is all powerful. . . omnipotent. He is the One who said, "Behold I am the God of all flesh. Is there anything too hard for me?" (Jeremiah 32:27). At first, this only made my pain greater. I expressed my anger at Him: "God, I don't even want to hear those words! Those are the very words I've said hundreds of times the last eight weeks. You could have changed this whole picture, but You didn't. You could have intervened, but You didn't. You could have touched and healed. You could have stopped the flow of events that led to Chuck shooting himself in the head that day, but You didn't. You could have, but You didn't!"

No, God didn't answer my prayer like I thought He should. But as I continued to mull this over, I understood that there are reasons—unknown to me—that God doesn't always do what we think is best. It wasn't that God lacked the power or ability to answer my very specific request. When He says "no" to our pleas, I believe it is because He, in His sovereignty, grace, and love, has a higher purpose and plan than we do. In our earthly finite state, we can't comprehend or understand all His plans. That's what Isaiah meant when he wrote, "His ways are higher than our ways, His thoughts beyond our thoughts" (Isaiah 55:9).

Sometimes I attempt to explain certain things to my Tara, but no matter how simply I try to put them, she doesn't understand. "Mommy, look. Why do the lights light up when I do this?" she asks with both amazement and astonishment in her voice as she continues to flip the light switch up and down. No matter how simply I explained the flow of electrical current to Tara, she's not going to get it! It is beyond her capacity to comprehend at such a young age.

Likewise, if God himself left Heaven, revealed Himself to me here and now and said, "OK, Renee, all the explanations you've been seeking, here they are. . . ," I'd probably have to say, "Whoa God! Could you slow down? Run that by me one more time. What do you mean by that phrase? Oh God, I'm sorry to be so slow and dumb, but I just don't get it!" With our human limitations, we simply can't conceive all that the Father is doing. It is beyond the realm of our comprehension.

Paul was in awe of this truth and wrote, "Oh the depth of the riches both of the wisdom and knowledge of God! How unsearchable are his judgments, and his way past finding out!" (Romans 11:33, KJV).

Daniel said, "He does according to His will in the army of Heaven, and among the inhabitants of the earth, and none can stay his hand, or say unto him, 'What are you doing?'" (Daniel 4:35, KJV). God is all powerful and does as He knows is best. We can rest assured that "all his ways are just, [He is] a faithful God, who does no wrong" (Deuteronomy 32:4 NIV).

In the midst of my pain, I must confess that the thought occurred to me that God must not love me. Oh, I knew the Bible said otherwise, but if He did, how could He allow such a terrible event to happen? I forced myself to meditate on the biblical teaching that God is all-loving.

It's one thing to talk about love, but it's another thing to show it. God did more than just talk. He proved His love by giving Himself "even unto death" (Philippians. 2:8). The ultimate sacrifice was shown when the One who was perfect and never sinned became sin for us (II Corinthians 5:21). No greater love could be displayed than this! He took the initiative and reached out to us when we could have cared less! In fact, it goes much farther than just being indifferent toward God. The Bible says we were His enemies! (Romans 5:10). We weren't seeking God— He sought us! Now He says that "if He spared not His own Son, won't He also freely give us all things?" (Romans 8:32).

I realized that there was nothing God might do for us that would cost Him more than He had already given! Was God trying to see how miserable He could make my life before I finally buckled under? Was He in Heaven just waiting to "zap" me with terrible trials to make my life unbearable? The answer is an unequivocal "No!" He loved me enough to die for me. I knew in my heart that He only wanted what was best for me and His glory. He said that He came that we might have life and have it more abundantly (John 10:10). In spite of my questions and lack of understanding, I knew that God truly loved me. No, it didn't look like it, and it didn't feel like it at the time. Yet, deep in my heart I knew the truth.

I also spent time considering the Biblical teaching that God is all-wise. According to the Bible, He doesn't make mistakes. "As for the Lord, His way is perfect" (Psalm 18:30). Quite honestly, I've wondered about that. "Are You sure You didn't mess up a little bit on me this time Lord?" I questioned. "My times are in

His hands" the psalmist wrote (Psalm 31:15). The thought occurred to me that maybe God turned His head, and I slipped through the cracks! How could my times be in God's hands, and my husband die by suicide?

Once again, I faced a dilemma. Are these verses true? Do the promises of the Bible still hold water in such a time of pain? In a very shaking voice, I slowly and softly answered "yes." It was easy to see I didn't have all the answers. Admittedly, there were legitimate questions that seemed to contradict the things I read in the Bible. Yet when it came down to the rock bottom, I chose to put my faith in the truth of God's Word instead of my swirling emotions and upside-down world.

I struggled to put all of this together in my mind. When I began to understand that the One I belonged to, the One who bought me with His own blood, was perfect in knowledge, power, love, and wisdom, then I realized that I should trust Him! Would God do me wrong? Was He out to play a dirty trick on me, pulling the rug out from under me and laughing when I fall? No way! Charles Spurgeon, the great English preacher of the 1800's said it like this, "When you can't trace His hand, you can always trust His heart." Though I can't trace God's hand in all the pain and difficult times that have come my way, I can trust that He will work even the tragic death of my husband together for my benefit because of His loving nature and character. This was a much better choice as far as I was concerned than discarding my faith.

Some years later as I read and studied various books on the subject of suffering, I found Margaret Clarkson, author of *Grace Grows Best in Winter*, concurring with my thoughts. She writes,

"God gives only good; His will and His ways are perfect. If we believe these things implicitly, we must learn to make use of the strength they can impart. . . . Such an experience may take place within a short time; more likely it will take months—even years. Always it is initiated by an act of will on our part; we set ourselves to believe in the overruling goodness, providence, and sovereignty of God and refuse to turn aside no matter what may come, no matter how we feel."[1]

I found a glimmer of hope when I recalled Joseph's experiences recorded in the book of Genesis. What a wonderful example of how God took terrible events and turned them around to work for Joseph's advantage. You are probably very familiar with the story. Permit me to summarize.

Joseph was hated by his brothers because of the special love shown to him by his father, Jacob. They wanted to kill him but decided to make a little money off of him. So they sold him into slavery in Egypt. There in Egypt, God raised him up to rule Potiphar's house. Sometime later, Potiphar's wife noticed this young good-looking Hebrew man working for her husband. She made sexual advances toward him, but Joseph resisted and fled from her. He chose to do right. What do you think it profited him? Do you think Potiphar came along and offered him a promotion because Joseph refused to be immoral with his wife? No sir! Joseph landed in the jail! He suffered for doing right! Have you?

There in the jailhouse, Joseph interpreted the dream for two of Pharaoh's servants. "Would you remember me to Pharaoh?" Joseph requested. "Sure, buddy, no problem. Just relax, you'll be out of here in no time," they answered.

But two years later, do you know where we find Joseph? Still sitting in the jail! How do you think he felt? I may be wrong, but I think Joseph struggled with emotions like you and I do. Things like, "This isn't fair, God! I didn't cause this to happen. It's not my fault! I'm innocent! Do You care that I'm hurting? Do You even know what's going on down here? If You do, why don't You do something! You said if I'd call, You'd answer. Well, I've called a long time, and I haven't seen any answers yet! God, I wouldn't do my own children the way You are doing me!"

But when Pharaoh had a dream that none of his wise men could interpret, the one servant whose life had been spared remembered Joseph still sitting in the jail. Pharaoh called for him, and he interpreted Pharaoh's dream. Pharaoh was so impressed that he immediately set him up as prime minister of Egypt. Ron Dunn, well-known speaker and writer said, "For Joseph, the path to the palace was through the prison." As prime minister of Egypt, Joseph saved thousands of people from famine. All of those years of feeling abandoned and forsaken by God turned out to be God's hand guiding Joseph to make him the man he needed to be in that place and time.

Joseph's brothers came, and unknown to them, knelt before their baby brother. When he was young, Joseph had told them they would bow to him some day, but this prophecy only in-creased their hatred for him. I can imagine them saying, "You're crazy baby brother! If you think we'll ever bow our knee to you, boy, you better think again!"

Do you know what Joseph said as his brothers were bowed

down before him? If it had been me, I may well have had their heads cut off and thanked God that justice had finally arrived! Yet Joseph was gracious. Three different times he told them, "It wasn't you, but God" (Genesis 45: 5,7,8). "You meant it for evil (Genesis 50:20), yes, your intentions were wrong! You did want to hurt me. But God meant it for good!"

How could he say such a thing? Could evil ever be turned around to be for our good? I wondered if I could say the same as I viewed the broken pieces of my own life. Joseph could only make such a statement because he knew that God sovereignly rules. He turns the hearts of men like rivers of water, wherever He will (Proverbs 21:1). Joseph also knew that God takes the fragmented bits of shattered lives and can rebuild them into a vessel that is more beautiful, bringing more glory to God than before it was ever broken. So it's not evil, it's actually for our good (More on this in another chapter!)

God takes the fragmented bits of shattered lives and can rebuild them.

It's almost as if the question were asked, "Who's in charge here anyway? Is anyone in control?" When viewed as isolated incidents, the pain and disappointments we all have to face seem to shout "No!" How often Joseph must have wondered what in the world was going on! Where was God when he needed Him? I can relate! But when taken as a whole, years later Joseph could see the overriding hand of God on all that had taken place in his life. He realized that he was part of a bigger plan, something that went beyond his own comfort and security. That's why I must not be too quick to accuse God of wrongdoing when my life doesn't make sense. Robert Wise, author of *When There Is No Miracle*, clearly makes this point when he wrote, "Right now, suspend judgment on what is happening to you and why it is happening. Wait and see. You may be surprised at the end of the story."[2]

Author R.C. Sproul agrees as he poignantly says, "Over all injustice, all pain, all suffering stands a sovereign God who works His plan of salvation over, against, and even through evil."[3]

Well, I'm still staring at a lot of broken pieces, listening to dissonance chords. In fact, I've wondered what happened to the music. Did someone pull the plug on the jukebox? Death's devastating blow to our family seemed greater than I would ever be able to overcome. Reminding myself of the example of Joseph helps me to hope that in time to come, I can say the same things he did. When I remember who my God is and what He has done, I am encouraged to hold on to Him and His truth in the darkness of the night. That gives me hope that one day the light will shine again, hope that one day the music will return, and even in the dark night of my soul, I might still at least hear a note or two of the melodies I used to sing.

> I must tell Jesus all of my trials;
> I cannot bear these burdens alone;
> In my distress He kindly will help me;
> He ever loves and cares for His own.
> I must tell Jesus, I must tell Jesus,
> I cannot bear these burdens alone.
> I must tell Jesus, I must tell Jesus,
> Jesus can help me, Jesus alone.

Lyrics to the hymn "I Must Tell Jesus" by Elisha Hoffman

7

Song Sung Blue
Ups and Downs

As a young girl, one of my favorite weeks of the entire year was the week my family vacationed at Myrtle Beach, South Carolina. After spending all day on the beach, at night we would go out to eat, and then head for what we called "the rides!"—a large amusement park. I loved them all! The more I was jostled up, down, and around, the better! The gigantic Ferris Wheel made my stomach drop; the wild roller coaster turned me upside down; the bumper cars hit me at all angles; and the Tilt-a-Whirl spun me around in circles. Each one produced a thrill—and a plea to ride "just one more time, please?!" The ups and downs of these rides remind me of the little tune I sang as a child, "Round and around and around she goes. Where she stops nobody knows." *Why would anyone would want to ride some baby ride with no adventure to it?* I wondered!

Now I'm an adult, and I still find myself "riding the rides." I'm not talking about the ones at Myrtle Beach, though. I'm speaking of the emotional rides I have encountered since death tore through my life. Just as the amusement park had a variety of rides to offer, I'm sure I've ridden every emotional ride there is. Some have lasted longer than others. And this time it wasn't an activity I did for fun. This time, against my will I was pushed onto a ride I didn't want to take. It wasn't by my own choice that I found myself being tossed every which way but loose! Grief threw me on and belted me in. The music in the background seemed to mock and taunt me, adding to my pain. There was no way I could get off. I would have to hold tight, and endure the agony till the ride came to a stop.

For a brief time following Chuck's death, I rode the emotional ride of shock and disbelief. *This can't be happening!* my mind declared, making every effort to deny the reality of the situation. My body also responded in this way. Shock is the body's way to deal with emotional overload. When we encounter a situation that is literally more than we can physically bear, the body goes into a state of shock. It is the body's way of protecting us from the full impact of the blow, a sort of "shock absorber" to reduce the initial, violent strike we have encountered. Shock serves as a physiological buffer that acts to protect us, allowing us to begin to deal with the trauma emotionally, physically, and psychologically.

No, I didn't faint and loose consciousness. I just felt numb all over. The pace of my thoughts and actions was greatly reduced as if I were moving in slow motion. I knew it was true; I knew Chuck was dead and this wasn't just a bad dream—still it all seemed unreal. There was a fuzziness, a blurring of all that was going on, like I was walking through a fog. Feelings of helplessness overwhelmed me because all that had happened was beyond my realm of control. Nothing I could do would bring back my Chuck. My appetite vanished as my own body system went into a defensive reaction. Friends who were with me from the very start of that terrible day have told me things that happened, but I don't remember them. I found it hard to concentrate, and I lost my thoughts in the middle of a sentence. Confusion ruled in my mind.

There's one emotional ride I've gotten on and off of a number of times. It really surprised me at first because I had never reacted in this manner, to this degree, until Chuck died. Time and time again I have resisted riding the bumper cars of anger. I didn't even know I had such anger in my heart until it came oozing out. *Where in the world is this coming from?* I wondered. *I've never had a temper like this!* Seemingly unimportant, trivial remarks and events could trigger a volcanic eruption within me. "I can't believe I'm responding with such wrath to such an insignificant thing!" I said as I shook my head in amazement and confusion.

At first I wasn't sure I could put my finger on who or what caused my anger. Was I mad at Chuck? Did I subconsciously blame him and feel he had deserted me and the girls? In reality, yes. Even though I could understand reasons for his death and give explanations for the ways the medication adversely affected him, I finally had to face the fact: Yes, I felt angry toward Chuck.

"How could you leave us like this?" I wanted to ask him. "Why did you just bail out and throw everything in my lap? Now it's up to me alone! Why do I have to be the one to carry this load when you're the one who left us? I've followed you around from state to state, going from one job to another, from this school to that sacrificing for you, just making enough to barely get by. All so you could get to where you wanted to be. Now after all of that, you abandon us. How could you do this to us?"

The rational side of my mind responds by saying, *Come on Renee! How can you be angry at someone who was sick? You know Chuck didn't fully understand what he was doing! You know the medicine only hindered his mental abilities and confused his thinking even more! It wasn't really his fault. He didn't know what he was doing. It's ridiculous for you to be angry at someone who was sick and died.*

How dare I be angry with God?

Maybe so. Though all of that is true, and my mind comprehends these statements, my emotions responded differently. I couldn't deny what I was feeling. What I felt was what I felt, and I was forced to deal with it. I've learned that I must admit these emotions if I am to move on from anger's clutches. To acknowledge the anger is the first step toward releasing it.

But anger towards Chuck was not the only avenue of the fury in my life. I wanted to scream from the highest mountain to the medical professionals, "I told you he wasn't ready! I did everything I possibly could to stop you from releasing him. You always treated me like I was the dumb wife. You never valued the input I tried to give. You told me, 'We're the professionals! Let us do our work without you constantly bothering us.' If you had listened to me, Chuck would probably be alive today! Do you realize what you have done to us? . . . to me? Do you want to try to explain to my girls what happened to their daddy? Do you care that we are in a mess financially? It's nothing to you. You'll just go on to the next room with the next patient. But our lives are forever altered because of your negligence and malpractice!"

To admit anger in my heart toward Chuck and the medical staff was not nearly as difficult as the third area I had to face. The hardest area of all for me to honestly acknowledge was anger toward God. How dare I be angry with God? Who am I to contend with the Almighty? Though I had always heard the phrase, "It's all right—God can handle your anger," it still seemed wrong. *I have no right or place to question what He has allowed to happen,* I reminded my heart. I kept recalling the time when God responded to Job's questions and accusations (See Job, chapters 38 through 41). I knew very well that if I were to debate God, He would be the winner. I'd wind up saying the same thing Job did, "I have declared that which I did not understand, things too wonderful for me, which I did not know. . . I have heard of Thee by the hearing of the ear; but now my eyes see Thee; therefore I retract and I repent in dust and ashes" (Job 42:3b, 5-6 NASB).

As much as I have tried to deny my anger toward God, I must admit it. "Lord, I confess to being mad at You. Deep in my heart, I cringe to even say the words. I am embarrassed to confess it, but I ultimately blame You. You heard our desperate cries, yet You did nothing! I don't understand. It's not like we were the heathen, God. We're Your children! You could have healed Chuck. You could have interrupted the events that day he walked out of the house to kill himself. Why didn't the phone ring or someone drive by as he crossed the yard? This didn't have to end this way, God! You could have helped us!"

I am ashamed to admit that I struggled with these emotions. I wish I were so spiritual that I never doubted the Lord, that I always believed He really is in control when my world is out of control. But I would be a liar to both myself and you if I tried to paint the picture that way.

Thankfully, however, as I have acknowledged these feelings, confessed them to God, and released them, I have been freed from them. It didn't happen overnight, and it wasn't just a one-time choice. Over and over I've had to "let it go." But as time has passed, I've found that each time anger returned, the ride became shorter. Now, it can no longer take control as it previously did. No longer is anger in charge calling the shots. He may show up from time to time, but now I can handle him. Now I know how to make him leave.

Of all the emotional rides I've been on, the one that lasted the longest was the Ferris Wheel of depression. As the reality of Chuck's death sunk in, depression moved in as well. I soon learned that sorrow and grief were its best friends. The three seemed to be inseparable. No matter how much I wanted them to leave me alone, to "just go away," they wouldn't. They ignored my wishes and set up house in my heart.

As soon as the initial impact of Chuck's suicide struck me with all of it's wrath, the depression began. What was the purpose of living? What's the point? Why even try? We played by the rules, and now look what happened! What did it matter? Life was meaningless for me for a very long time. Chuck's sudden death made a gapping hole in my life, a vacuum I was certain would never be filled again. High motivation, which had previously been so characteristic of me, disappeared. I had no motivation to do anything. Apathy, hopelessness, emptiness, indifference, loss of direction, passivity, listless, loneliness: these are the words that characterized my disposition and energy level. Even getting out of bed, and getting dressed seemed too great a task. Left to myself, I would have stayed in bed all day. "Leave me alone. I don't want to live anymore either," I sobbed. "The sorrow and pain are more than I can take."

My precious friends refused to abandon me to the grips of depression. With tender mercy and understanding, they stayed by my side and allowed me to grieve and fully experience the pain. They knew I needed to cry, and they patiently watched as the healing stream that flowed from my eyes released pent-up tension. They were wise enough to realize that the many tears I shed kept me from exploding inside. I was just like a tea kettle letting off steam. They listened as I mourned, and they permitted me to put my feelings on the table. There were no words of judgement and condemnation at some of the startling things I said. They shared the depth of my despair with me and allowed me to get all the hurt, anger, and doubts out in the open. The pat, trite answers that so easily fall from the lips of many people in times of crisis were not to be found coming from their mouths.

As much as I wished I could die, too, I couldn't. Even with the overwhelming sorrow that flooded my soul, my love for my children compelled me to action. How could I forsake these precious little ones? As their large brown eyes peered into mine, eyes that looked just like their daddy's, they reminded me so much of him. I knew I must carry on for them. I prayed,"OK, Lord, I'll do what I'm required to do. I will do my best to raise Nicole and Tara to love you and serve you in truth all the days of their lives, but I know life will never be meaningful for me again. Real living is over. I'll be a robot, performing the necessary functions, but I'll never experience real joy and happiness again. I'll simply hang on, till you finally let me be relieved of the weariness of this life and come home to Heaven."

It seemed that the words penned by Paul in Philippians 1:23-25 were written to describe me, "I desire to depart and be with Christ, for that is very much better; yet to remain on in the flesh is more necessary for your sake, and convinced of this, I know that I shall remain and continue with you for your progress and joy in the faith." In the margin of my Bible I wrote, "This is my work for Nicole and Tara." Apart from them, I had no purpose to survive. My sole reason for forcing myself to function was for the well-being of my babies.

The long, burdensome days turned into months, and the months into years. Time became my opponent and always emerged the winner. There was no way I could win. Part of me wanted to make time stop. I lamented, *I can't let go of my life with Chuck. I've got to cling to what we had. But as time goes on, it only takes me further away from him. I can't face that!* The other part of me was crying, *Why can't I make the hands go round the clock faster so that I can get away from this terrible nightmare I face daily!*

Yet nothing I did made time change its tempo. With grueling slowness, the hands on the clock went round. Each "tick, tock" sounded as a jeering, mocking remark that sought to traumatize me even more. I was frozen in time, stuck in a devastating place from which I would never be freed. Day after day it was the "same old same old." *Will this largo tempo never end? It will be this way for the rest of my days?* I questioned.

Facing all the "firsts" alone without Chuck was like pouring salt into my open wound, adding fuel to the fire of depression that already consumed me. I was the vocal soloist in the first wedding I attended after Chuck's death. It was almost more than I could handle. Listening to this young couple recite their wedding vows and promise to love and cherish one another "till death do us part" took me back to the time Chuck and I stood before our minister and made those very same vows to one another.

The first New Year's Eve following Chuck's death, I breathed a deep sigh of relief as the clock struck midnight. *Thank God, this year is over. It's been the worst year of my life.* Then I was smitten by a contradictory thought, *But this is the year God gave you Tara. How can you hate this year when you received such a precious gift?* The irony of death and life—all rolled into one year—boggled my mind. I didn't know how to compute the seemingly opposite events, except to say, "This is life. Welcome to the real world."

And on, and on, and on, the ride goes: the first Valentines Day but this time with no one to buy that special "I Love You" card for or anyone to send one to me; the first Father's Day, hoping and praying that my girls could handle not having a daddy to make a card for in school; sitting in church listening to the sermon about the importance of the father to the home (I almost got up and walked out); the first trip to the cemetery with the girls as I tried to explain one more time how Daddy died.

Every "first" that concerns Nicole and Tara is bittersweet. The joy of seeing each new landmark in their lives is also mixed with the regret that Chuck is not a part of their lives. "I wish he were here to share this moment with us," I confided to a friend, when Nicole's kindergarten class had their "graduation." I've thought that same thought at least a thousand times on different occasions.

The first year following Chuck's death, I shut myself up in my house whenever I wasn't required to be at work. I had no energy for additional activities. It was all I could do to extend the needed physical and emotional strength to complete required functions, much less have any strength remaining for extra activities. I was constantly fatigued, always wishing I could say "What the heck?" and go take a nap. No matter how much sleep I got, it was never enough. At that point, I didn't understand that withdrawal and the conservation of energy is needed for the hard work of grief. Physically, mentally, and emotionally, our bodies need time to rest and restore themselves and replenish the reserves that have been exhausted. The adrenalin that raced through my body during the initial impact of Chuck's death was gone. It left me depleted. My entire body now pleaded for additional sleep and rest. This time of hibernation allowed my body to recover and my mind to begin to assimilate my life with Chuck. This time of convalescence is greatly needed for healing to occur. Frenzied activity, used as a distraction and means to keep from facing the pain, is comparable to trying to walk on a broken leg. It only delays the healing process. Though I didn't realize it then, this time of withdrawal was working to get me back on my feet again.

It is only by the grace of God that depression never became so severe that I had a total mental breakdown. By the strength of the Lord (probably because so many people were holding me up in prayer), I managed to function and meet the daily responsibilities required of me. Depression's presence, however, overshadowed every moment of my life for several years. As time passed, only my closest friends were aware of the depth of my gloom. To most people, I appeared to be doing well. I continued working at my church position, taught music students in my home, took care of the house and yard, and attended church regularly with my girls by my side. From all outward signs, I appeared to be "doing fine."

In spite of appearances, there was no song in my heart. As far as I was concerned, the music of life was dead. I was a walking zombie, unable to feel anything but the pain. Apathy saturated my life. I fought numerous colds and viruses as my immune system was weakened by the grief. It seemed I would never move on from this plateau. When asked, "How are you?" I responded in the only way I knew to truthfully answer without unloading on them, "I'm holding on, thank you."

Those close to me continued to encourage me and undergirded my wobbly faith. "God is a good God, Renee. He is not going to desert you in the middle of this trial," Linda assured me. She continued to admonish me as she said, "In spite of what you're feeling right now, don't let go of what you know it true." She spoke with such conviction, so certain of what she was saying. Her words struck the chord of truth buried deep within me. Though emotionally I was falling apart, I knew what she was saying was true. Her words slipped into the soil of my heart and began to take root.

No matter what the circumstances and regardless of the facts, death inevitably brings an emotional ride on the Tilt-a-Whirl of guilt. We blame ourselves, thinking somehow our loved one's death is our fault. We can't help but look inside our hearts to ask, *What could I have done that I didn't do?*

Before the Lord, I knew I had done everything I possibly could to help Chuck's recovery. I was at the hospital every time they allowed visitors. I prayed more than I've ever prayed in my entire life. I had the whole town praying for him. I tried to work with the medical personnel in any way possible to give them any information that might be helpful. But the bottom line was: It wasn't enough. Somehow I have failed. I tried every way I knew to assure Chuck of my love and commitment to him. Yet, my love for him, even the girls love for him, wasn't enough to give him a reason to live. Guilt, whether legitimate or illegitimate, seeks to invade the deep recesses of our minds during the grieving process. It is one of Satan's greatest tactics to destroy those left behind. Guilt is another tool the accuser of the brethren uses as he actively plots to ruin the survivors. We must recognize it for what it is and give it no place in our hearts. Illegitimate guilt (guilt which is unjustified) must be renounced as unfounded and then discarded. Legitimate guilt (guilt caused by valid reasons, genuine failure or neglect on our part) must be confessed so that we can experience forgiveness. Then we can put it behind us and determine to learn from that circumstance. Thankfully, I learned very quickly how to get off this emotional roller coaster.

I didn't recognize it at first. As I walked through my grief, I discovered that I needed to go back by myself to the places that had been a part of our life as a couple. It was a necessary part of my own healing. Of course, I was immediately confronted with our last house, our church and community, and the hospital that I must drive by every day. I needed to face these places alone and let the memories run through my mind. Yes, the anguish was excruciating. It was unbearable torture to remember "how it used to be," but I needed to take the lid off all these thoughts and emotions racing through my mind. To neglect this would only postpone my grieving.

The torment continued when the dreadful day came to clean out Chuck's office at the church. Shelves of books were stacked from the floor to the ceiling. Oh, how he loved to read and study! Where would I put all of them? Even though we had a room designated as "the study" in our new home, there was no way all of these books would fit. With painstaking love, I sorted through them all, looking at his personal notes and highlights, letting my tears flow freely. Some of the books were too meaningful to part with—the one given to him when he was ordained into the ministry at Frostproof, the Bible presented to him by the deacons of the church just a few months earlier when he graduated, and books filled with his own illustrations and comments he had used with the youth as a study course. They contained so much of him! *The girls have to see this when they're older,* I thought. I packed to sell the ones that were not as personal. Several weeks later, I left the girls with a friend and drove to the seminary in New Orleans. I set up shop in the cafeteria and put up a "For Sale" sign. Some of the professors who knew me expressed their sympathy. (A few years later one of them told me, "It broke my heart to see you sitting in the cafeteria trying to sell Chuck's books.")

Most of the student body had no idea of the reason for this book sale. I remember one young man saying, "Oh, your husband must have graduated and doesn't need these books now."

I replied, "Yes, he did." No, it wasn't an intentional lie. Chuck had graduated—from life on this earthly terrain to his heavenly home. It was too much to explain. I would only have shocked this unsuspecting man to have tried to tell him all the facts.

As the lunch hours ended, one man who had been observing me learned the real story. He walked over and said, "How about $50.00 for the remainder of these books?"

"Sold!" I replied. I was well aware of the fact that this was an act of kindness to me on his part. He probably didn't really care about the books. Perhaps he was stretching his finances to spend $50 in one shot. (How well I knew that money is tight for most seminary students!) But because of his sympathy towards me and desire to encourage me, he bought the books.

It took three years after Chuck's death for me to conclude my pilgrimage of the places that had been so meaningful in our relationship—without him. I returned to South Florida in May, 1990. When I stepped off the plane, my hostess asked, "What would you like to see first?"

Without hesitation, I replied, "I want to see our former campus."

We soon arrived and my journey back in time began. As I walked through the halls and rooms that now looked so different, my mind's eye saw a different picture. "This is the place where we first met," I told her. "Here is the room where I received my first kiss. . . . This was our first apartment."

I couldn't hold back the tears. It saddened me to relive those days. I tried to retain my composure, but a great sense of loss and aloneness overwhelmed me. At that moment, it didn't matter that I had been trying to work through my grief for three years. It was as fresh and painful as it was the day Chuck died.

The outpouring of love and support I received from numerous friends and acquaintances during my time of sorrow brought some balance to my emotional roller coaster ride. I am still humbled as I think of the self-sacrificing ways in which so many people gave of themselves to comfort me and the girls. My closest friends, a small group from our ladies' Bible study, let out all the stops as they came to my side. I wish all who grieve could be blessed with such wonderful support.

Unfortunately, not everyone I encountered was as wise, understanding, or patient as these friends. Though I'm sure they meant well, there were many times I was crushed by both the advice and actions of others. I'll never forget one friend who casually said to me, "When are you going to take down all these pictures of Chuck?"

I didn't say what I was thinking. I gave a simple answer, "Oh, I'll do it sometime." But I really wanted to scream at her, "I'll take them down when I'm good and ready! You act like I should try to hide this part of my life as if you want me to forget that this was my husband for ten years! I can't just erase Chuck's memory from my life and pretend he didn't exist!"

Another person once said, "You know, now that it's just you and the girls, you don't need that big house. Why don't you sell it and get a small apartment? It will be a lot less work for you."

"That's probably true," I replied with a "thanks for the advice" smile. But inside, I was ticked! I wanted to tell her, "You don't understand what this house means to me. This is 'home,' and you have no concept of the comfort and security I find by being in this place. So much of my world has already been torn from me. You're suggesting I give up even more? Besides, I don't want to live in a small apartment. I happen to like this house, thank you very much. And I'm willing to do the work needed for the privilege of living in it!"

Still others said things like, "I don't know how you can stand to live in that house. I couldn't take being confronted with all the memories every day. Doesn't it upset you?"

No, it didn't. I found a great sense of peace in the rooms of that house. I can't explain it, but it seemed that God wanted me to be there. That may not be the case for some people. For them, it may be best to move to a new place, but for me, it was best to stay. We err when we think there is only one right answer for every person facing grief. What is right for some may not be right for others. We are all different people and we all handle our pain in different ways. We must not condemn someone who chooses a different route than we think we would take if we were confronted with the same circumstances.

Many people expected me to up and move back to North Carolina to be with my parents. For a number of reasons, I didn't believe that was the best course of action for me or the girls. In spite of my clear and rational explanations for my decision to stay, some people were unable to comprehend them. It hurt me to know they thought I was being foolish, stubborn, and even stupid not to move. A few were so bold as to tell me straight out what they thought. "I can't believe you're staying down here. If it were me, I'd put the 'For Sale' sign up and be gone. You're crazy to stay here when you could be in North Carolina."

How easily words of advice come from some who have never had to walk that road. Regardless of their opinions, I knew I must do what I believed was right for our family. But their insensitivity and lack of respect for my opinion did nothing to ease my sorrow.

My emotions and interactions with others took me up and down on a roller coaster ride that was unpredictable and fluctuated from one day to the next. "Singing the Blues" became my theme song for months on end. Some days I was pleasantly surprised to have a good day, free from the presence of the trio of grief, sorrow and depression that so often accompanied me. *Maybe we're getting back to normal,* I hoped against hope. The very next day, however, usually found me falling from the top to the bottom, as depression, sorrow and grief's hideous laughs echoed in my mind. *I thought I was beginning to get over this. I thought the worst was behind me. Now I see I haven't really gone anywhere. I'm right back at square one.*

I concluded, *I must be the lowest slime and a terrible Christian!*

The disillusionment of realizing the continued magnitude of my pain only added to my despondency. "I'll never get over this. The pain is here to stay," I slowly sighed.

I can't count the number of times I've had people say to me, "You shouldn't feel like that!" as I ventured to open my hurting heart to them. I know they meant well. They didn't want me to hurt, but quite honestly, that response only added to my grief. I concluded, *If I shouldn't feel this way, then there must be something wrong with me... because I do feel this way! I must be the lowest slime and a terrible Christian!*

I felt so angry! I wanted to scream at them, "How can you tell me what I should or shouldn't be feeling!?! Did your husband commit suicide? Do you have any clue what my daughters and I face now? You have absolutely no right to talk to me like this! Don't you think I know these emotions are uncomfortable? I'm trying to deal with them the best I can. Give me a break!"

Pretending these feelings of hurt, shame, anger, fear, and loneliness didn't exist didn't make them go away. And thoughtless remarks from others didn't resolve them and comfort me. They only increased the pain.

Yes, I've been on all the emotional rides available as a result of death's invasion of my world. It was good for me to learn that what I experienced was normal. Reading books on the subject of "grief work" confirmed that what I was feeling was OK. As I talked with others who had gone through the grief experience, I saw I wasn't the only one who had felt that way before. I realized, *I'm not weird! I'm not the only one to experience these emotions. They felt the same way, too.*

No, I wasn't going crazy. No, I wasn't being unspiritual. I was being human; one who felt the lingering consequences of sin's entrance into the universe; one whose spirit longed for my heavenly home; but who must live today in a world marred by sin; one whose mourning touched her—physically, emotionally, mentally, socially, and spiritually. My humanity needed to walk through these feelings and face the pain and sorrow in all it's fury in order to get through the storm to the other side. I've heard it said, "The way out is through," and I've found it to be true.

The way *out* of pain is to walk *through* the pain. If I were ever going to recover the capacity to truly live again, I must confront the past head on, experience the great sorrow, and then release it to God. Denying it ("No, it doesn't really hurt."), postponing it ("I'll deal with that later. I'm too busy right now to think about it, I've got work to do."), seeking a quick replacement of our lost loved one ("I just need to find somebody new."), trying to minimize the loss ("It's not really that bad."), or acting like the brave, strong one ("I'm spiritual enough that I can take it. I don't need to cry. That would be a sign of weakness."). None of these responses bring the relief our souls crave! The time of weeping and mourning (Ecclesiastes 3:4) that we all want to avoid is actually the vehicle that brings about the healing we truly need and desire.

I know what it is to "Sing the Blues" because I sang them for a number of years. In fact, at that point, I thought it was the only song I'd ever sing anymore. Sometimes, even today, the song returns unexpectedly, and once again I must sing this song of the night. But now I know that its presence is only temporary, and that it will depart. Now I know that although I may find myself suddenly thrown onto that emotional roller coaster once more, eventually I will get off. I know how to bring the ride to a halt. It won't last forever, like at first I thought it would. Just as there is a time for mourning, there is also "a time to laugh" and "a time to dance."

At that point in my life, that time wasn't too far off. Just around the bend. Bits and pieces of the sweetness of life's musical refrain began to drift into my days. Little by little, one phrase at a time, very softly, I began to hear excerpts of the music I used to know. Could that mean the song of restoration isn't far behind?

> Does Jesus care when my heart is pained
> too deeply for mirth and song?
> As the burdens press and the cares distress,
> And the way grows weary and long?
> O yes, He cares; I know He cares.
> His heart is touched with my grief.
> When the days are weary, the long nights dreary,
> I know my Savior cares.

Lyrics to the hymn, "Does Jesus Care?" by Frank E. Graeff

8

How Do You Keep the Music Playing?
Death's Impact on Relationships

The lyrics of a popular song written in the early 1980's asks the question, "How do you keep the music play ing? How do you make it last? How do you keep the song from fading too fast?"[1] Good question, especially when the chaos you're currently facing has upset the rhythm of life to the point you don't know which end is up! How do you maintain current friendships when death's intrusion has removed one of the key players of the game? Is it possible to keep these relationships from fading into oblivion, or will they eventually die, too?

Little did I know that the dark stain of death would affect this area of my life, also, as it seeped into every nook and cranny of my world. I was unprepared for the numerous changes death's violation would bring. Slowly I began to realize that not only had I lost Chuck, but the majority of our previous relationships would be changed—and yes, some of them would be lost. Was there no limit to how far death's impact would go? Would death ever be satisfied and say "Enough!" or would I continuously find other ways it sought to steal what was left of my life?

Let me quickly clarify that a number of my dear friends have stood by me through thick and thin. They were a great source of comfort and support for me during the dark days of losing Chuck. They would be here in a flash if I called for help this moment. I thank God for these people. Because of their care, concern, and encouragement, I have been able to survive the storm.

Yet when a couple is dismantled, there is a normal and profound impact on relationships with other couples who have been friends. Each couple has a unique personality as a unit. When that unit ceases to exist, a different personality is presented to other couples, changing the way they relate to one another. Their interactions and activities are all thrown off balance. Confusion often reigns as they all try to regroup. The women can no longer sit and talk of their own interests while the men are watching football. Someone is left out. Someone is left alone. Even with good intentions to try to keep things the same, the former balance among the players in this relationship is gone. The equilibrium has changed. Some are never able to make adjustments for these changes, and the relationship slowly ebbs.

I have personally found this scenario to be the case with many of the couples who were close to Chuck and me. An odd number, such as three, doesn't work well in our society. Though I have retained my friendships with most of the women in these pairs, Chuck's death affected my relationships with the couples. The majority of the time now, when together as a "threesome," the husband sooner or later excuses himself for his own activities while his wife and I visit. I've found I now receive many more invitations for lunch with the girls than Friday night dinner with the couples!

Because I saw how these friendships were affected by the loss of my mate, and perhaps due to my own feelings of conspicuousness, I chose to stop participating in our church's "Super Supper Six" program which was designed to encourage couples to get to know one another. Three couples sign up to have dinner together once a month, with each couple taking a turn as the host. Chuck and I had enjoyed becoming better acquainted with others in our church through this activity. After his death, I chose not to continue. I didn't fit. I didn't have a mate, and I found it awkward to be in an event planned for "couples." Some people may argue that I should have continued, but I felt relieved not to face the pressure of knowing I didn't really belong there. It would only have magnified the fact of my loss, compounded my pain, and thrown me in a position in which I felt totally out of place.

While the death of a loved one causes some relationships to die slowly, others change instantaneously. It was a rude awakening for me to see "good friends" suddenly withdraw from me. People that Chuck worked very closely with and who were an integral part of our church family in key leadership positions no longer had anything to do with me. They chose to avoid me completely. Though I never said a word, I couldn't help but think, *I thought you were a true friend. I thought you cared about both of us. Now you and your family never call to say 'hi,' never invite me and the*

*girls over, and barely speak when we pass in the hall at church.
If you were truly Chuck's friend, wouldn't you show some concern
for his widow and his children? Why are you acting like this? Is
it easier for you to have no contact with me? What did I do to make
you treat me like this? Are you angry at me? Do you blame me for
Chuck's death?*

Perhaps they were unable to face death's harshness head on.
Could seeing me be a reminder of their own immortality and
vulnerability to death's clutches? It's still a mystery to me why
death can cause people to react in this way.

It was obvious almost immediately that some old friends chose
to avoid me because they didn't know what to say. The awkwardness and stigma associated with suicide were more than they
could handle. It was easier to avoid contact with me so they
wouldn't have to struggle to find the right words. They didn't
know what to say, so they went out of their way to avoid me and
said nothing. There are times when no words are appropriate
and the mere presence of a friend says everything. That's not
what I'm referring to. I'm speaking of the times when their
noticeable silence makes us all uncomfortable, when the *absence
of words* says more than words could ever say, the times when
they see you coming down the hall and suddenly turn to go the
other way. I wish they'd say something. A simple "I'm so sorry"
would do! Anything. . . instead of treating me like I had the
plague!

Others had the courage to call or visit, but they tried to ignore
any mention of Chuck or the terrible ordeal I was experiencing.
They may have said to each other, "Let's not say anything that
will remind Renee of him, and maybe she'll feel better. Let's not
talk about it. Don't mention his name. Keep the conversation on
other things."

Walking on these eggshells merely added to the awkwardness
we all faced. As hard as they tried to avoid mentioning Chuck's
name, the fact of his death hung over our heads like a dark cloud.
Seeking to avoid the obvious was not the solution. Trying to act
like Chuck never lived or never committed suicide and avoiding
all references to him seemed very superficial to me. I wanted to
say, "Don't try to sugar coat this for me. Please be real with me!
These are the facts I must acknowledge and deal with. To avoid
the subject offers me no help in any way. I can't erase the twelve
years of my life with Chuck. Give me the freedom to talk about
him. Let me talk with you! Don't you understand I have a great

need to talk about this entire ordeal?"

Thankfully, there were numerous times when wise friends lovingly sat and listened as I "got it all out." They didn't condemn me as I rambled, repeated the same thing over and over, searched for the right words, and tried to put all the fragmented pieces together in my very confused and slow-functioning mind. Time and time again they graciously listened to me tell the story— "just one more time." This was an essential part of my own healing process. An "ostrich with his head in the sand" position may have been the only way some people knew to handle this death. Perhaps their effort to avoid any reference to Chuck's life or death was more for their own benefit than mine.

And then there have been the times when I'd walk up to a group and all of a sudden the conversation stopped as everyone stared at me! Or I'd enter the room, and immediately I saw people begin to whisper. I knew what they were saying. My mind filled in the blanks. "Please don't treat me like I'm the villain!" I wanted to beg. I was a "public widow" because my story was known throughout the area. Everyone knew everything (or so they thought). Any privacy I had previously known was gone. My own paranoia increased when I thought that the entire community was talking about my husband's death.

I knew I must be careful not to become overly dependant on my loving friends. When Chuck died, I could never have made it without them. They were lifesavers for me—my only link to life! But as I began to recover, instinctively I knew that I must guard against being "smothered" by their love and concern. It took some time, but eventually even among my closest friends I began to see how our relationships were changing. They continued to welcome me in their homes with open arms, but I was the one who began to be uncomfortable with this arrangement. *They have their own families, their own kids, and husbands to take care of. You're intruding on their family time, and you need to back off,* my mind told me. *You can't be so dependant on them. You're going to have to get a life of your own!*

Weekends were the worst. I knew my friends would be busy with their families. I didn't want to bother them and "wear out my welcome," but I greatly needed to feel like I was part of a family. Frantically, I looked for something to keep us busy. The quietness and aloneness of just the three of us in our home alone was too hard to handle. I made a concerted effort to see that the girls and I had some activity planned for Fridays and Saturdays.

I had to find something to do: go to the Mall, shop at Wal-Mart, or take a walk. Otherwise I knew I'd only sit home and cry.

The times when we couldn't find anything to do were the times I got on the phone to call friends in other states. I didn't care what the phone bill was (very unlike my normal, conservative nature). I had a desperate need to "reach out and touch someone," if only over the phone. *I've got to talk with someone, just so I don't feel like I'm alone in this world,* I said to myself.

Time and time again they graciously listened to me tell the story. This was an essential part of my own healing process.

I fought the same battle every Sunday after the morning service. I realized, *Everybody else will be gathering together for a family dinner while I go home alone with my two babies.* If we were going out to eat after church, I often asked another family to join us just so we wouldn't be eating alone. But many times, they declined and we ate by ourselves, feeling very conspicuous and out of place. Somehow, a young widow with two small little girls didn't fit into the former relationships like we previously did. I was the fifth wheel, and unfortunately there's usually only a need for four!

I still laugh about the fact that some women began to see me as a threat to their marriages. "You've got to be kidding," was my first response when someone pointed out that one lady was worried about her husband doing odd jobs for me at the house. The thought never entered my mind that another woman might be jealous of me! "Jealous of what?" I asked with bewilderment. But now that I was "available," their view of me changed. An unattached woman is often seen as a potential threat to many married women. I soon learned to always include the wife any time her husband might be assisting me in some job I was incapable of handling alone.

Some people want to rescue a hurting person by trying to "fix" the situation. They miss the "old you," the one they knew before grief took over. Their own need fuels their desire to hurry you along in the grieving process. That proved to be true among some of my own friends. More than once I was told, "You just need a good man to take care of you, Renee. You need a husband, and those babies need a daddy. Who can we fix you up with?" After mulling this over in their heads, they'd suddenly announce, "I've got someone I want you to meet, Renee," as if just replacing Chuck as soon as possible would make everything all right again!

Though I wanted the girls to have a father, I had no desire for a husband. At that point I was certain I'd never love again. Didn't they understand I wasn't ready for another relationship? Didn't they know I must do the needed grief work from losing Chuck before I had anything to give to someone else? Trying to make everything right by simply replacing the missing part doesn't usually work when it comes to relationships. Even with the intense sorrow I carried, I had enough sense to know that my circumstances could not be "fixed" by a hurried remarriage. In fact, it would only make things worse to enter a new relationship before I recovered from grieving the loss of this one.

On the other hand, the majority of my friends have been overly protective of me. They never want me to be involved with any man ever again unless he comes riding up on a white stallion and has a kingdom of riches and prestige in the neighboring land! They told me about particular men who were pointed out by others, "He's not good enough for you, Renee! You must be careful and realize how vulnerable you are. You're a great catch, and you'd better watch out that some charlatan doesn't come by to take advantage of you." By their standards, no one will ever pass the test or meet their approval!

As I had learned in so many ways before, it soon became apparent to me that I must seek the Lord and follow His leading. If I try to listen to all the voices around me, I only become confused and frustrated. It didn't take long for me to see that everybody had their own opinion of what I should do and what was best for me! Regardless of which way I go, or what I decide, someone is going to think I'm doing the wrong thing. That's why I've got to seek the Lord's leading. I will never be able to please everyone, but I can please God if I obey his voice.

I've had to guard against being overprotective with my girls. When death quickly steals one we cherish, we tend to go overboard in guarding the survivors from any possible danger or loss. My heart's attitude was, *I lost Chuck to death. I'm going to do everything I possibly can to make sure I don't lose you girls, too.* How easy it is to permit our fears to run rampant and drive us to cling to them in an unnatural way. *Loosen up, Renee!* I reflected. *You've got to give them the freedom to live a normal life. You're going to have to trust that God is taking care of them. All of your over-protection is ruining both you and them.*

There is also a temptation to put survivors into roles and responsibilities they are not able to bear. Little boys feel they must be "the man of the house" now that Daddy's gone. Little girls may try to mother the mother! I've seen my Nicole slip into that role a few times. I must admit, it felt good to have someone trying to take care of me. But thank God, I quickly realized this was inappropriate.

"She's a little girl, Renee," the Lord whispered. "Don't allow her to overload herself with roles she is too young to fulfill. She must complete her childhood roles before she will be able to function effectively in the ones to come."

As I grasped the situation, I firmly but lovingly said, "Nicole, we don't need two Mama's in this house. I'm the Mom, and I can take care of this very well, thank you." After several occasions of my taking control in this way, Nicole has learned "Mom's got it under control." She doesn't have to try to be something she's not, but she can be secure in knowing the authority figure in her life will function in that capacity. This allows Nicole to enjoy being a little girl and continue her normal growth and development.

Any time there is a loss, the vacancy will be filled again in a different way. I've seen this happen in relationships. Please don't misunderstand: many close friends during my days as Chuck's wife are still dear, cherished friends. Yet by virtue of the change in my status and responsibilities, friendships have also changed.

I fought it for three years, but I finally broke down and attended a "singles" function. My own incorrect, preconceived ideas of this category of people only added to my distaste for becoming a part of such a group. "That's like walking into a meat market with everyone there eyeing one another, seeing who's available. I'm not into that!" I defiantly stated to my friend who suggested I might enjoy being with others who were "single again."

Even with all my efforts to fight against it, I finally broke down and took the first step by attending a local church singles function. It actually came about because of the intense loneliness I felt one Saturday. I was depressed all afternoon. Then, while talking with my friend, Faye, (married with three kids) on the phone, she suggested, "Why don't you call that big church in town and see when they're having their Singles Christmas Party? You might enjoy it, Renee."

Out of desperation, I said, "OK. I'll find out when it is."

At 4:30 that Saturday afternoon, I placed a call to the minister of education. Carroll had been a fellow seminary student with Chuck and had often invited me to come to the singles events at his church. Until now, I had always declined. I didn't get an answer at his home, so I dialed the church number. I thought to myself, *Big chance that he's at his office on a Saturday afternoon!*

But suddenly I heard someone say, "Hello." Carroll himself answered the phone. I couldn't believe it!

With hesitation and a faltering voice I said, "Carroll, it's Renee Scheidt. I was just wondering when the singles were having their Christmas Party. I thought about coming."

He quickly replied, "It's tonight at 6:30. Come on, girl!"

"But Carroll," I said haltingly. "I don't know a soul there. You've got to take care of me!"

"Don't worry about a thing, Renee," he assured me. "You come on, and we'll take good care of you. We've even got a nursery for your girls. I promise we'll make you feel very welcome!"

With fear and trembling, two hours later I stepped into the church building. To my astonishment, I found I had more in common with this group than I previously wanted to admit! In fact, it wasn't nearly as bad as I had played it out to be in my mind! I discovered it was good to talk with other men and women also trying to raise their children as single parents! It was good to meet others who knew the pain of losing a mate (whether by

There is One, however, who never changes, who never disappoints or fails us.

death or divorce) and grappled with the reality of loneliness and the total responsibility of keeping everything going! No, I didn't feel out of place or like a fifth wheel as I did with my married friends. To my surprise, I found a great deal of support among these "single again" folks. *This is what you've needed, Renee,* my heart gently spoke. *They are facing many of the same problems you are. You might have gotten here by a different route than most, but you're all in the same boat now. You can encourage each other. In many ways, your situations are very similar.*

From that shaky start, I began to develop friendships with some of these people. Though I had been very reluctant, I finally came to accept my "single again" status. I was ready now to join the group and their activities. I've made wonderful friends with men and women through this association. Oh, I could have continued to fight against the tide, but once I gave in and took the plunge, I discovered an oasis of refreshment in numerous ways! The relationships I've made have enriched and influenced my life tremendously. I wasn't willing to give this opportunity a chance for a long time, but I would have missed out on so much if I had refused to give it a try! The vacuum created by the loss of past relationships was now filled with people who understood and cared.

And so once again, death brought more changes into my life, including changes in my relationships. Some of the changes have been painful, and I didn't want to face them. Reluctantly, I have had to "let them go." But other changes brought great joy and healing to my broken heart. I'm learning that there are two sides to most everything we encounter. In this world, not many things are either all good or all bad. To every up, there's a down. For every minus, there's a plus. Following every mountain top is a valley. The tares grow with the wheat (Matthew 13:24-30). Author and speaker, Ron Dunn, stated, "Good and evil run on parallel tracks and usually arrive about the same time!"[2] But one thing is certain: nothing will remain the same. Change is the name of the game. We must constantly make adjustments and move with the flow. To refuse to move on with the changing times only results in our own emotional death.

Though I didn't ask for or initiate changes in my relationships, they came. Probably more than most, I've been blessed with an abundance of unusually strong friendships. The support I've received in my time of grief has been incredible. Yet I've also been hurt and disappointed by some friendships. The fact is: some people will let us down. I don't say this with condemnation. I don't set myself up as judge, because I'm guilty as well. I admit I've failed others many times. Though I wanted to keep the music of all our relationships playing as it previously had, I couldn't. That song was for another time and place. I haven't been able to make the music last in every case. Some tunes have faded away, and some died very quickly. But new songs have grown and sprung to life for a new day, a different place and time.

There is One, however, who never changes, who never disappoints or fails us. His presence and love are constant, unaffected by changes in the rhythm of life. He's the One we can always count on, the friend of all friends. Even death can't separate us from His love! Isn't it good to realize that death can't destroy this relationship?! It won't change whether we live or die! "If we live, we live for the Lord, or if we die, we die for the Lord; therefore whether we live or die, we are the Lord's!" (Romans 14:8, NASB)

To make certain that we got the message, Paul spelled it out and covered all the bases. He obviously wanted to give us the full assurance that regardless of what we may encounter, nothing can separate us from God's love.

"Who shall separate us from the love of Christ? Shall tribulation, or distress or persecution, or famine, or nakedness, or peril or sword?. . . For I am convinced that neither death, nor life, nor angels, nor principalities, nor things present, nor things to come, nor powers, nor height or depth, nor any other created thing, shall be able to separate us from the love of God, which is in Christ Jesus our Lord" (Romans 8:35, 38-39, NASB).

The old hymn said it well:

> Earthly friends may prove untrue, Doubts and fears assail.
> One still loves and cares for you: Jesus never fails.
> Jesus never fails; Jesus never fails.
> Heav'n and earth may pass away
> But Jesus never fails.

Lyrics to the hymn "Jesus Never Fails" by Arthur A. Luther

9

New Melody and Lyrics
Starting Over

For many months after Chuck's death, I went around in a daze. Oh, I somehow managed to do the work I needed to do. Responsibilities were not left undone. But there wasn't much life left in me. I remember the first Christmas after Chuck died. *Who cares about decorating a tree? I wondered. Or buying gifts for people?* I wished we could have skipped the whole month! I knew, however, I couldn't deprive my little girls of what was supposed to be a joyous season. For their sakes, I went through the motions to celebrate the Savior's birth. Outwardly, I did the right things. Inwardly however, it was all a forced effort.

As time passed, certain verses from the Bible seemed to jump out at me as I read. In particular I recall reading Isaiah 61. Jesus quoted verse one as a reference to Himself during His earthly ministry (Luke 4:18-20). It said that He came to "bind up the brokenhearted." I most definitely qualified in that category. Verse three of Isaiah 61 went on to say that he came to comfort those that mourn. "Hey, God, that's me. Do you see me over here in my little corner of the world? Could you comfort me?" I sobbed.

The verse continued by saying that He could give beauty in place of the ashes, the oil of joy instead of sorrow, a garment of praise for the spirit of heaviness. I began to wonder if He could do this in my life. "Lord," I prayed, "I feel like sorrow and heaviness will be my continual companions the rest of my earthly days! But You said You could replace those dark emotions with joy and praise. Could You do that for me, God? I don't want to just survive. I don't want to just exist! Would You let me truly live again? Could meaning and joy once again be a part of my life instead of just trying to survive each cruel day?! David asked You to 'restore unto me the joy of my salvation' (Psalm 51:12). I need You to do that for me, too, Lord! Please rebuild the ruins of my life. Please have mercy upon me and heal my broken heart and wounded spirit!" I begged.

I recalled the promise of Joel 2:25, "I will restore to you the years that the locust have eaten." I wanted to say, "Lord, they've come through and stripped this piece of ground. There's not one green, living thing left! I know that You are Jehovah Rapha, the God who heals. Does that include these damaged emotions? Could You heal a heart that has been shattered into millions of pieces?"

"Lord," I prayed, "I'd rather come out on the other side still affirming Your goodness and faithfulness instead of being negative and critical.

The thought of restoration was in my mind now, but I still wasn't certain it could ever happen to me. Just knowing that God was in the reconstruction business was good news, especially since I needed it so badly. Could God's soothing balm reach down deep enough to help someone who hurt as much as I did? I knew that there were many others, either currently living or in times past, who suffered much more than I could ever imagine. Some of them seemed to emerge from the fiery furnace with a sweeter, more radiant countenance, more love for the Lord, and a greater testimony to His faithfulness in spite of their hard times. Others, who perhaps had not suffered as great a trial, came forth with a sour look on their faces, always expecting the worst, griping about everything under the sun, and impossible to please. I wondered what made the difference. Why were some able to deal with the hard times in a positive manner, even letting God use it to their benefit in the long run, while others' lives seemed ruined because of a certain event?

One lady in particular came to my mind. She had suffered several severe storms. Her life had also been invaded by death's unwelcome presence. She lost two children in tragic, sudden circumstances, and afterwards, she always griped and complained. Even when she answered the phone, she sounded like gloom and doom! God used her as an example in my life of what could happen to me. The Spirit gently whispered, "Give yourself a little time, Renee, and you'll be just like her. Look on down the road at what you'll become if you don't deal with this pain the right way."

"If I have a choice in the matter, Lord," I prayed, "I'd rather come out on the other side still affirming Your goodness and faithfulness instead of being negative and critical. But just how do I get there from here?"

I realized that the different outcomes are determined by different perspectives on the tragedy. The issue is not: "Will we encounter pain?" That is a given! We live in a fallen, sin-cursed world, and we all suffer in different ways, at different times, and in different degrees. No one had to convince me of that fact! I knew it only too well. Romans 8:21-22 tells us that even the creation groans and travails in pain, waiting for the redemption. When pain comes knocking on our door, we can choose how to handle it. The right choices help us to move forward instead of getting stuck in the mire of bitterness and self-pity. We can either cooperate with God in the recovery process and be refined by our trials, or we can go our own way and let the wounds stay open, preventing healing from taking place. Author James Martin states, "A man may emerge from the experience of suffering the better for his experience. But there is no guarantee that he will. . . . It is the attitude a man adopts to his suffering that is the determinative factor."[1]

Just how do we work with God to aid the healing procedure? As I see it, it all boils down to two options. Either we believe God and trust that He will do what He said, or we renounce His words and let the bitterness build inside. We can choose the way of faith and refuse to give a place to anger, bitterness, and resentment. I was familiar with the warning found in the book of Hebrews concerning the negative consequences bitterness can produce in our lives: "See to it that no one misses the grace of God and that no bitter root grows up to cause trouble and defile many" (Hebrews 12:15 NIV). The choice to let bitterness have root in our hearts will only trouble us, and many others will be adversely affected by it. I surely didn't need that! I had enough problems without creating more because of the wrong attitude! Bitterness, anger, and resentment can't be put in one nice, neat little compartment of our hearts. If we try to contain them, these painful emotions will slowly seep out of the box to take over our entire lives. They will color all that we do and say. It reminds me of a spider weaving her web. Little by little, one strand at a time, the web is woven. If we don't break the strands when they initially surround us, we soon find ourselves tangled in the web, wondering how we got in this place! We can't allow ourselves the luxury of holding on to our hurts by refusing to let them go. The price is too high. We wind up being the victims of our own wrongful attitudes, and we destroy our lives and condemn ourselves to a critical, negative, doomsday existence. Again I quote from James Martin, "The reaction of resentful rebellion achieves nothing except to aggravate the distress of our situation and to make our ultimate defeat more sure."[2]

On the other hand, we can choose to deal with our pain by means of faith. Beginning with Abraham in the Book of Genesis, we see that faith was required of those who follow the Lord. "Abraham believed God and it was counted to him for righteousness" (Romans 4:3 KJV, see also Genesis 15:6). Faith is the means of entering the family of God. It is by grace we are saved through faith (Ephesians 2:8). Once we are born again, we continue to "walk by faith, not by sight" (II Corinthians 5:8). Colossians 2:6 says that in the same way we received Christ (by faith), we also walk in him. It was Jesus Himself who asked the question, "When the Son of man comes, will he find faith on the earth? (Luke 18:8 NASB).

"Help me God," I pleaded. "I don't want to let bitterness take root in my heart and just make things worse! Please help me to keep my attitude right. I want to trust You. I'm trying to believe You, Lord, but it's not always easy. I know the right way, but now I need You to help me make it real in my life today," I prayed.

I found this emphasis on the necessity of faith reiterated in the book of Habakkuk, one of the minor prophets. Habakkuk is a short book, but its truth made my head spin! Habakkuk was confused by the fact that God was using ungodly people to chasten His own children of Israel. How could God do this? God's only answer to Habakkuk was "walk by faith" (Habakkuk 2:4). Habakkuk never got the answer he sought! In chapter one, we find him asking, "How long, O Lord, will I call for help and thou wilt not hear?" (Habakkuk 1:2 NASB). But by the end of the book, we see a complete turn around in his attitude. His situation hadn't changed. The circumstances were still the same, but chapter three concludes with one of the most amazing statements of faith in the Bible. "Although the fig tree shall not blossom, neither shall fruit be in the vines; the labor of the olive shall fail, and the fields shall yield no food; the flock shall be cut off from the fold, and there shall be no herd in the stalls; yet will I rejoice in the Lord, I will joy in the God of my salvation. The Lord God is my strength, and he will make my feet like hinds' feet, and he will make me walk upon mine high places" (Habakkuk 3:17-19, KJV).

Habakkuk decided that no matter what happened (including his whole world falling apart), he would still believe God. In the midst of the good times and the bad, he would still rejoice in the Lord. Job repeated this perception when he said, "Naked came I out of my mother's womb, and naked shall I return there. The LORD gave and the LORD hath taken away; blessed be the name of the LORD" (Job 1:21, KJV). Just a few verses later Job said to his wife, "Shall we receive good at the hand of God, and shall we not receive evil?" (Job 2:9, KJV) Job attributed the good and bad alike as coming from the hand of God. The ultimate display of faith is shown when Job stated, "Though he slay me, yet will I trust in him" (Job 13:15, KJV).

As I viewed the example of these Old Testament saints, the message pierced deep into my own heart: *What about you, Renee? What will your choice be? You aren't the only one who has suffered down through the ages. You aren't the first one to lose a loved one to death. How will you handle the pain? It's up to you to decide.*

The faith I saw exhibited in these men was incredible to me! This is "the trust of the unexplained." This is trusting our Father even without knowing the answers. This is faith not dependent on what is happening. Better yet, this is faith *in spite of* what is happening! Isn't that what faith actually is? Hebrews 11:1 gives us the definition of faith as "the substance of things hoped for, the evidence of things not seen." Isn't faith believing God when we can't see how things will work out, when nothing makes sense? Why would we need faith if we knew it all or could understand all? It is precisely at those times we are called upon to exercise faith!

Isaiah focused on this same truth when he said, "Who is among you that feareth the Lord. . . that walketh in darkness and hath no light? Let him trust in the name of the Lord, and stay upon his God" (Isaiah 50:10, KJV). How well Isaiah described my own situation. The lights were out, and I was groping in the darkness trying to find my way. It seemed every way I turned I found God asking the same question of me, "Will you trust me, Renee?"

Faith's Hall of Fame in Hebrews chapter eleven had always been one of my favorite passages. The triumph of believers has been a motivating force to keep me keeping on. Yet quite honestly, it was the last few verses of the chapter that now captured my attention. After listing a multitude of people who escaped harm and overcame great obstacles, the writer concludes with this statement:

". . . Others were tortured and refused to be released, so that they might gain a better resurrection. Some faced jeers and flogging, while still others were chained and put in prison. They were stoned; they were sawn in two; they were put to death by the sword. They went about in sheepskins and goatskins, destitute, persecuted and mistreated—the world was not worthy of them. They wandered in deserts and mountains, and in caves and holes in the ground. These were all commended for their faith, yet none of them received what had been promised. God had planned something better for us so that only together with us would they be made perfect" (Hebrews 11:35-40, NIV).

"Here's where I fit in, Lord," I sighed. "I'm part of the 'and others,' those whose faith didn't spare them from the hard times, those who didn't experience the miraculous, desired deliverance. If I could choose, I'd prefer my name to be in the first part of Hebrews eleven! I want to be ranked with those whose circumstances were changed because of their faith, those who got their miracle." Unfortunately, God didn't ask me where I'd like my name to fit in. The choice was not mine to make.

Was there something wrong with the faith of these Christians that they were not "victorious" as we hear so often today? No, not at all! Their faith was in a loving Heavenly Father, not dependant on what life might throw at them. Let me quote Philip Yancy's book, *Disappointment With God*, "We tend to think life should be fair because God is fair. But God is not life. And if I confuse God with the physical reality of life—by expecting constant good health, for example—then I set myself up for a crushing disappointment."[3]

Habakkuk, Job, and the "others" listed in the latter verses of Hebrews eleven were committed to God, period. In the good and the bad. They didn't follow the Lord for the personal benefits; they followed because they loved Him. Their display of faith made me painfully aware of how shallow my own commitment had been. It forced me to face the hard question, "Will I be faithful even when the music begins to play in a minor key? What if the music stops altogether? Or is my commitment only good when I can sing the peppy, up-beat songs?"

Just what was it that God wanted from me now? And not only me, but each of His children, whether in the good times or the hard times? The answer was clear: He wants us to trust Him. "Without faith it is impossible to please him," we read in Hebrews 11:6a. How can I please God today when I am dazed, broken, and distressed by my tragedy? How can I please Him when my heart is broken, the music has died, and I'm just about to go down for the last time? The answer is: believe Him. "Believe that He still is and that he is a rewarder of them that diligently seek Him" (Hebrews 11:6b). As Philip Yancy has well stated, "Faith is believing in advance what only makes sense in reverse."[4] Faith is not always the absence of questions and doubts. Instead, it is continuing to do what you know is right in spite of the questions and doubts!

The bottom line question God asks me today is: "Will you trust Me, Renee?" Will you trust Me when you feel like I've abandoned you? Will you trust Me in spite of all the questions and doubts you battle in your heart and mind? Will you trust Me when Chuck's death makes no sense to you? Will you trust Me that I have a master plan?. You aren't a mouse in a maze. I will keep My word to you. Will you trust Me to take care of you and your precious girls? Will you trust Me, Renee?"

With all my heart I want to say, "Yes Lord, I trust You! I still don't understand. The questions remain unanswered, and I'm still off balance from this death blow. But I want to believe You and know that You're with me, guiding each step I take." For me this is the only viable option. To use a phrase coined by the saints of old, I was "shut up to faith." God put me in a corner where I had no other choice but hold on to Him. Ron Dunn has often said that we won't trust God until we have to. That's where I found myself: No tricks up my sleeve, no aces in the hole. I was put in a position where I was forced to rely on the Lord. It was all or nothing at all.

I wouldn't want you to be under the wrong impression that I have always had great faith to believe God and His promises. More times than I want to admit, my faith has been weak—and sometimes almost non-existent. Sometimes I have had to cry out as the father of the demon possessed boy did in Mark 9:24, "I believe, help thou mine unbelief" (KJV). I have often struggled to rest in God's hands. But praise God that He is always faithful to me, even when I'm unfaithful to Him! Ron Dunn's statement in his book, *Faith That Will Not Fail*, has given me insight into this area. I quote, "That's what faith is—resting on God's faithfulness. 'But,' you say, 'my faith is so weak.' Yes, but your God is so strong. Which are you going to trust—your weak faith or your strong God?"[5] It's not the amount of faith that's crucial. Jesus said just a little bit, the size of a mustard seed, could move a mountain. (Matthew 17:20). It's the object of our faith, the Lord God Almighty, that counts.

It's not the amount of faith that's crucial. It's the object of our faith, the Lord God Almighty, that counts.

One day I will cross over to Heaven's shore. There I will be able to see the big picture! The puzzle will be finished, every piece in place. As I look back on my life on earth, I will see how God's hand led me all the way. My understanding will be complete. I'll then know totally what I now only know in part. I can imagine myself saying, "I see it now, God! You were right! So You were in it after all! It's so clear to me now, Lord. How could I have missed it? Now I see that You have done what was best and right!" But the mirror that I currently am looking in is all fogged up and blurry. It's dark and prevents me from seeing very well. Many times it's hard for me to determine just what I'm looking at. The shapes are hard to define.

This is what Paul meant when he said, "For now we see in a mirror darkly, but then, face to face; now I know in part, but then shall I know even as also I am known" (I Corinthians 13:12, NASB). The Lord asks, "Will you trust Me in the darkness, Renee? With just the little bit of information you have, will you trust Me?"

As I have struggled with these truths, I found it helpful to write the following lyrics based on Isaiah 50:10. I've entitled it "Dark Night of My Soul." Perhaps you can identify with these feelings.

> Lord, I see no light as I walk along this road.
> I cry to You and wonder where You are.
> It seems I am alone to face life on my own.
> How I need You now to guide my stormy way.

Chorus:
Help me lean on You, Lord, in the dark night of my soul.
Help me find the strength that only You can give.
Help me choose to trust in You when all I see tells me
    not to.
And know You'll pull me through the dark night of my
    soul.

I will not stop walking through this darkness, Lord.
I know the light will shine again one day.
I will not stop calling, calling on Your name.
You are faithful and will bring me through this pain.

Many years ago while I was in college, I cross-stitched two of my favorite verses to hang on the wall of my home. At the time I had no idea how much I would need to turn to these verses for comfort in the days ahead. These verses still hang on the wall in my family room. I still refer to them as I face the challenges of each day: "Trust in the Lord with all thine heart and lean not unto thine own understanding. In all thy ways acknowledge him, and he shall direct thy paths (Proverbs 3:5,6, KJV).

I don't have to understand all that the Father is doing. I am simply to obey, one step at a time, one day at a time, trusting that God is with me each step of the way. "Be still and know that I am God," (Psalms 46:10a, KJV), the Holy Spirit reminds me. By choosing to depend on God, trust in His Word, and refuse to let bitterness and anger take over in my life, I then open myself up to the healing touch of the Great Physician. I have cried as Jeremiah, the weeping prophet did, "Heal me, O Lord, and I shall be healed; save me, and I shall be saved; for thou art my praise" (Jeremiah 17:14 KJV).

There is still a balm in Gilead for all who will come. Those who mourn and grieve their loss can still find the promise: "The days of thy mourning shall be ended" (Isaiah 60:20b KJV). "How?" you ask. "How do we get there?" Take the road of faith. It will lead you there.

At this point in my journey, I think I started to faintly hear the melody of a song I once knew. I thought the song had died. Somehow it sounds a little different than before. The harmonies have been altered. The tempo is a little slower. But if my ears serve me correctly, the lyrics seem to be saying,

Every joy or trial falleth from above
Traced upon our dial by the Son of Love.
We may trust Him fully all for us to do.
They who trust him wholly find him wholly true.
Stayed upon Jehovah hearts are fully blessed
finding as He promised perfect peace and rest.

Lyrics to the hymn "Like A River Glorious" by Frances Haveral

10

A Song for Mourning
Experiencing God's Comfort

People who experience loss need to grieve. In fact, failure to go through the grief process cripples recovery from emotional traumas. The only way out of the Land of Grief and Sorrow is through it. William Cowper, who wrote many of our beloved hymns, said, "Grief is itself a medicine." Author Doug Manning wrote in his book, *Don't Take Away My Grief*, "Grieving is as natural as crying when you are hurt, sleeping when you are tired, eating when you are hungry, or sneezing when your nose itches. It is nature's way of healing a broken heart."[1] The Mourning Song must be sung if we are ever to recover our capacity to find life worth living once again.

The one who claims to be a child of God is not "unspiritual" or "weak" because he mourns losses. Paul acknowledged that Christians sorrow, but not as those who have no hope. He then encouraged us to "comfort one another with these words" (I Thessalonians 4:13, 18, KJV). I am offended by those who come to funerals with their "praise God, hallelujah" masks. "Glory to God, our loved one is now in Heaven!" they piously exclaim. Yes, that's true, but that's not what mourners need to hear at that moment. No doubt, those who have passed over to the other side are much better off than those of us left behind, but great loss must not be treated so glibly. I have to fight the urge to tell these superficial people, "Would you get real? Do you not understand what people feel when they have lost a parent, child, spouse, or friend? This is not the time or place for your zippidy-do-dah song. If you have nothing better than this to offer, please just go home!"

As we experience and express our emotions, the soothing comfort of God will eventually pour over our hearts like a balm.

His consolations reach down deeper than our pain. He has promised that no matter how great the pain, His comfort is deeper still (see II Corinthians 1:5 and 7). Jesus promised that those who mourn "shall be comforted" (Matthew 5:4). We need to give one another the permission to mourn so we can experience this comfort.

For many years, I knew the passage in the first chapter of II Corinthians which speaks about the comfort of God. Paul addresses God as "the Father of mercies, and the God of all comfort, who comforts us in all our afflictions so that we may be able to comfort those who are in any affliction with the comfort with which we ourselves are comforted by God" (II Corinthians 1:3,4, NASB).

"That sounds real good, Lord," I honestly said. "But how is this real in my life today when it is all I can do to make myself get out of bed and take care of my babies? Where is this comfort I so desperately need? How can this be a reality and not just some beautiful words I read out of the Bible? Lord, I need You to comfort me this day! I don't know what all this means, or how You do it, but I'm asking You, please, in mercy and love, pour Your comfort into me. If You don't, I don't think I can go on," I sobbed to my Heavenly Father.

I look back upon my own grief experience, and I realize there were particular ways I was comforted. Perhaps none of these ways are new to you. You may have heard them all before. Sometimes, however, it is good to remind ourselves of truths we already know. My time of sorrow was made more bearable by focusing on these truths. If they helped me, I believe they can help others as well. These applications, however, shouldn't be limited to grieving the death of a loved one. Any trial or affliction can be lightened as we experience the comfort of God.

Through His Word

Romans 15:4 says, "For whatever things were written in earlier times were written for our learning, that we, through patience and comfort of the scriptures might have hope" (KJV). We receive comfort from God's Word, which is the only fully objective means we have of knowing God. It is the standard by which the subjective aspects of our faith are lined up. What precious promises would we have to hold on to apart from His Word? For years I've sung the old hymn, "Standing On the Promises." These promises become an anchor for our souls

(Hebrews 6:19), during the stormy seasons of life when we find ourselves being tossed about. We can cling to them! Our spiritual well-being depends upon it! Take God's word for it! He is the One who cannot lie and will do what He says. In Psalm 119:50 we read, "My comfort in my suffering is this: Your promise preserves my life."

"Lord, I need You to comfort me this day! If You don't, I don't think I can go on"

The importance of memorizing God's Word, hiding it in our hearts, was made clear to me during my time of grief. Certain verses popped into my mind as I groped with the harsh realities of Chuck's death. The first night I went to bed alone following Chuck's death, the following verse kept running through my mind, "Cast thy burden upon the Lord, and He shall sustain thee" (Psalm 55:22). I had learned that verse in church when I was a child. It was part of the worship service we used each week. Now, many years later when tragedy struck, this verse came to mind. The chorus of the hymn, "God Will Take Care of You," played over and over in my thoughts. I firmly believe this was God's word to me at that time. Because I had stored His word in my heart, the Holy Spirit could bring these words to my mind and pour comfort into my aching soul. What if I hadn't stored these verses away prior to my time of crisis? If these promises hadn't been deposited in me, there would have been nothing there for the Spirit to bring to mind. It's similar to making deposits into my account at the bank. How many times have I gotten in trouble because I tried to withdraw what wasn't there! I must first make the deposit if I want to make a withdrawal later. I can't withdraw what I haven't put in, and the benefits of withdrawing money are dependant on what has been deposited. The application for our spiritual lives works in the same manner. Make the necessary deposits so that when you need to make a withdrawal, the spiritual "funds" are available. Memorize the promises of God. Hide them in your heart. You will find them to be your anchor in the midst of the storm. You will experience God's comfort through knowing His Word.

Through His Spirit

God comforts us through the Holy Spirit. The Holy Spirit dwells in all believers. In fact, one of the names of the Holy Spirit is "The Comforter," which means "the one called alongside to help, a consoler." The disciples were alarmed when Jesus announced that he was leaving. He quickly sought to relieve their fears by stating, "I will pray the Father, and he shall give you another Comforter, that he may abide with you forever; even the spirit of truth. . . I will not leave you comfortless; I will come to you (John 14:16-18, KJV). God now lives within us. The Holy Spirit works in us to give us the desire and power to do His will (Philippines 2:13). Paul attributed his anticipated deliverance from prison partially to "the supply of the Spirit" (Philippines 1:19). He orders our steps, and directs our ways which often are unknown to us at the time (Proverbs 16:9; 20:24).

I believe I was directed by the Spirit of God the morning of Chuck's death. There was one point after Chuck went to lie down in the bed and I went into the master bathroom to finish dressing, that I grabbed a load of clothes to take to the washer. As my hand reached for the door, the thought came to me, "Why don't you first put in your contacts so you won't have to come back and do that later?" I changed my course of action, dropped the dirty clothes, and put in the contacts. Then I walked out of the bathroom and discovered Chuck was no longer in the bed. In retrospect, I believe the Holy Spirit directed me to change my mind. I believe if I had walked out of the bathroom as I first planned, I would have come face to face with my husband holding a gun in his hand. In his deranged mental state, he could have hurt me as well as himself. It is my belief that God protected me by His Spirit and worked through my thought processes to change my mind.

When I went outside to look for Chuck, I stepped on a nail and had to return to the house. As I look back, I am convinced that God appointed that nail to protect me from finding Chuck's body. I was headed straight across the road where he lay with a gun shot wound to his head. Stepping on that nail prevented me from continuing in that direction. Even in the middle of the trauma, God's goodness was displayed by His leading me—by the sharp point of a discarded nail.

One of the ministries of the Holy Spirit is to comfort us in our sorrows. He strengthens us and gives encouragement to our downcast hearts in the midst of the trial. In Him, we find power to carry on, power which is not of ourselves but that which is given to us by the Spirit of God as we yield to Him. So many times I've looked back and wondered, *How in the world did I make it? How did I get through the storm?* My only answer is, "By the strength and grace of the Lord given to me by His Spirit."

I am fully aware that it is not my strength that has brought me through the valley, but by strength given to me from above. When you find the burden being lifted, and you know it's not because of anything you did or didn't do, you can then give credit to the Holy Spirit. He comforts us in ways we don't understand, and we receive the benefits of His work in our wounded lives.

Through His People

God has chosen to work through His people, the church, to meet the needs of others. We are His hands and His feet, extensions of God to a hurting world. He is "fleshed out" to others through His body, the Church. If He wanted, God could rain down manna from Heaven to feed the hungry just as He did with the Israelites in the Wilderness. But so far, I haven't seen any laying on the ground. In our case, He expects His people to care for the needs of one another. Jesus made this point when He criticized people for not caring for others. He said, "I was hungry and you gave Me nothing to eat; I was thirsty and you gave Me nothing to drink; I was a stranger, and you did not invite Me in; naked and you did not clothe Me; sick, and in prison, and you did not visit me. Then they themselves also will answer saying, 'Lord, when did we see you hungry, or thirsty, or a stranger, or naked, or sick, or in prison, and did not take care of You?'" (Matt 25:42-44 NASB).

I can hear the protests, "Lord, now come on! You know if we had known You were hungry or thirsty or sick, we would have been there for You! You know we'd take care of You! We just didn't know, Jesus!"

The reply of our Lord pierces deep within: "Then He will answer them saying, 'Truly I say to you, to the extent that you did not do it to one of the least of these, you did not do it to Me'" (Matthew 25:45-46, NASB).

Clearly, we have a responsibility to one another—especially during a crisis. Those who have been comforted by God are to pass on the consolation they have received to others in need (II Corinthians 1:4). When our world is laying in pieces before our very eyes, and the breath is knocked out of us, we need someone to lend a hand of comfort and strength in our behalf. Our brothers and sisters in Christ can ease the pain during this time and administer God's consolation to us.

My own church family came to my side in a variety of ways. One of the reasons I chose to stay in Louisiana after Chuck's death was because of the support my spiritual family gave me. I needed their help to get back on my feet again. In many practical, thoughtful ways, they took care of me until I could recover from the tremendous blow. So many times people will sincerely say, "If there's anything I can do, let me know." But most hurting people are reluctant to ask for help. I'd like to suggest some ways that the church can bring comfort to those facing traumatic situations. I've been the recipient of all of these. I know how much it meant to me, and I believe others can find comfort through these actions as well.

• **Encouraging Words**—Words have the ability to "minister grace to the hearer" (Ephesians 4:29) and edify those who are downcast. This can be in written form, spoken face to face, or over the telephone. Who doesn't appreciate receiving a written note reminding us somebody cares and that we aren't forgotten in our struggle? Isn't it encouraging to get a real letter in the mailbox instead of just junk mail and bills!

The many cards and letters I received after Chuck's death are still very precious to me. To this day, I can still recall one card in particular whose message comforted me in a special way. This hand-written note was more meaningful to me than any expensive, fancy card.

Take the time to place the phone call to say, "I've been thinking of you today, and I wanted to see how you're doing." Speak to those you pass in the hall at church or work. Your kind words may be the encouragement a heavy heart needs to hear.

Perhaps you're thinking, "But I don't always know what to say!" That's all right. Sometimes there are no words that are adequate. I know how awkward many of our church family felt after Chuck's suicide. I know they were at a loss for words and didn't really know what to say to me. "I'm so sorry" is always appropriate for such times. Please don't give sermons telling the afflicted person: "In everything give thanks, for this is the will of God in Christ Jesus concerning you," (I Thessalonians 5:18) or "All things work together for good" (Romans 8:28). I would have probably slapped anyone who dared to lecture me in that way! The heart-felt sympathy expressed by a card, a spoken word, even a caring look or hug says what needs to be said: "I care about you, and I'm so sorry you have suffered this loss."

• **Physical Presence**—During the hard times, it is comforting to have a friend by your side. The tragedy being faced somehow seems to grow even larger when you find yourself alone.

There were times after Chuck's death I probably would have started to climb the walls had it not been for the presence of one of my Christian friends. They even set up shifts and made sure someone was with me all hours of the day! "Linda will be here from 9:00 to noon, then Trish is coming from noon to 3:30. Karen will stay till 9:00 that evening." I couldn't have made it without them! They didn't try to keep a running conversation going. I needed them just to "be there." But when I was ready to talk, they were ready to listen. Their presence in my home showed me I was not alone. That helped tremendously. After three weeks of this arrangement, my pastor's daughter, Beth, a college student living at home at the time, moved in with me for a month. These people's presence during the initial shock of losing Chuck helped me begin to cope with my situation.

We see this same point illustrated in the life of Job. After hearing of his tragedies, three friends came to his side. They did well for the first seven days. During this time, they simply sat by his side and didn't say a word. It was only when they opened their mouths with their pious explanations of his suffering that they messed up!

I didn't think of it at the time, but the minute I stepped out into the public eye after Chuck's death, I needed a friend with me. I remember the first time I went to the mall after Chuck's death (at my friend's insistence that I "get out of the house"). I had no desire to go to the mall. As my dad would say, "I ain't lost nothing out there!" But my friends insisted I go, so Joy and I took off while Linda kept the girls. How do you think I felt when I saw people in our community whispering to one another when we passed? I could almost hear the words, "That's the wife of that preacher that just killed himself a few weeks ago. Boy, I'd like to know what was really going on in that house." I didn't want to face this sort of gossip! I needed Joy by my side to encourage me to hold my head up and keep walking.

In many of our evangelical churches today, an invitation is given at the close of the service to "come forward and accept Christ as Savior." Don't we employ this same principle as we sit by one who has never trusted the Lord and say to them, "Would you like me to go with you?" The physical presence of another person can give the encouragement and comfort needed to move forward with our decision.

When your friend is hurting, just be there. Don't worry about what to say. Just go to her side. You probably underestimate how much your presence means to one trying to keep her head above water.

• **Physical Help**—The variety of ways to offer physical assistance is limited only by our imaginations. Let me share with you some of the ways my church family helped that were particularly meaningful to me.

Bringing food. Even as a child I remember my mom taking food to someone's home during a death or other tragedy. Only when my own life was shattered did I understand the value of this deed to the hurting heart. Cooking is one of my least favorite activities. Even when I'm feeling great, I still hate to cook! After Chuck's death, do you think I cared about what we were going to have for supper that evening? If it had been left to me, we would probably have had a can of vegetable soup every night. Here again, my church family filled in the gap. Under Linda's direction, people signed up to bring us evening meals. . . for three months! You can imagine how spoiled I became! What a relief not to have to worry late in the afternoon, *What am I going to fix tonight for the girls?* There's nothing like a good home-cooked meal. This is a wonderful opportunity to comfort someone being tossed about on the sea of affliction.

Household chores. When pain is knocking on our door, who cares when the kitchen floor was last mopped? Does it matter the last time the sheets were changed when every extra minute is spent at the bedside of a sick friend or family member? Wouldn't it be a great way to offer comfort to a hurting friend by saying, "Look, I know you've really had a lot on you lately. Why don't you give me your house key? Jan and I will come over Friday morning and clean. We can vacuum, dust, mop the kitchen floor, change the sheets, and clean the bathrooms. Then you can come home to a clean house."

Tell me one person who wouldn't feel better coming home to a clean house instead of a dirty one! Tell me one person who wouldn't be encouraged by such an act of love! Not everyone can afford to hire a housecleaner. Wouldn't this be a wonderful ministry to those in difficult situations? I know how much this meant to me after Tara was born when I was unable to clean in preparation for the company who would soon arrive for Chuck's graduation. So join with a friend and make the offer to help. It might seem trivial to you, but this is definitely a way of comforting those who are hurting.

Baby-sitting. For those with small children in the home, it is a treat to get out of the house for an hour or two without packing the diaper bag and bottles and putting babies in car seats! Wouldn't it be a wonderful way to encourage a downcast friend by saying, "I'll keep the children, you go on and have some free time. Go to the mall, visit a friend without worrying, 'Oh no, what is my child into now?!', buy groceries with no kids hanging out the cart crying, 'I want this!', run errands. . . whatever you want to do! We'll be fine. Just have a good time."

Many women who have left a professional job to stay home with the children during the preschool years face quite an adjustment. They often miss the adult conversations and feel out of touch with other adults. The whole family can benefit from letting Mama have a few hours to herself. Again, not everyone can afford baby-sitters or Mother's Day Out programs. Why not offer to keep the kids and give Mom a break? The whole family will benefit from giving a mother some time for herself. After all, there's a lot of truth to the statement: "If Mama ain't happy, ain't *nobody* happy!"

This is a wonderful ministry for senior adults who no longer have children in the home, and perhaps have no grandchildren close by. For many years after Chuck's death, there were two couples in our town that we adopted as our "Louisiana grandparents." They brought a sense of security and safety to both myself and the girls. We needed them, and hopefully, they received a blessing from being involved in our lives. Pick up the phone and make the offer to watch the children. You don't know how that just might make somebody's day!

Other ideas. There are a host of other actions that you can do to comfort those who are hurting. Perhaps you have professional skills such as accounting, and you could offer to help with the checkbook or file income taxes. Our church financial secretary was a great blessing to me in this way after Chuck died.

Maybe you are a hair stylist or do nails. What women doesn't feel better after going to the beauty shop? I still consider it a treat to have my hair done! Offer to pick up something at the grocery store and bring it by on your way home. Help address thank you notes that need to be mailed. This seemed too big a project to tackle after losing Chuck. I needed to write a mountain of cards! Though I wanted to express my gratitude for the numerous kindnesses to me and the girls, I didn't have the strength to start. Trish offered to give me a hand and even bring the stamps and cards with her! Working together made the job much easier for me to handle.

As simple a thing as answering the phone can be a great relief to a person in pain. My phone seemed to ring off the hook following Chuck's death. I remember thinking, *If that phone rings one more time, I'll yank it out of the wall! Please don't make me repeat this story again!* It was such a help for my friends to answer the phone and relieve me of unnecessary repetition.

Take note of the "special days" and make sure your hurting friend is not alone during these times. Birthdays, anniversaries, and holidays can be especially difficult. Often, the anticipation of the soon coming "special day" is worse than the reality, and fear may produce more torment than the actual day itself. Why not invite your friend to join your family for dinner? Take her to lunch on her birthday. Let her know she isn't alone or forgotten. Let her know you remember and care about her.

My birthday came five months after Chuck's death. About a dozen friends gathered at Linda's to give me a party. You don't know how much that meant to me! When my girls' birthdays rolled around, Tara's on May 1st, and Nicole's September 19th (the one year mark of Chuck's death), my friends were there again. I needed their support during this time, and they didn't fail me. What could easily have been a very sad time turned out to be a good day because my friends made a special effort to be there for us.

Giving a book is a good idea. "I got so much from reading this book, and I thought you might enjoy it, too." If they don't like to read, give them a cassette tape to listen to. I spent many hours at night the first year after Chuck died listening to tapes by some of my favorite speakers. I even took notes and tried to fill my mind with truth, hoping to eventually bring my raw emotions into alignment. These speakers will never know how much they ministered to me in this way.

One very difficult task I dreaded after my husband's death was cleaning out his clothes closet. We shared a walk-in closet, and each time I went to find my own clothes, I was stung again with the fact that Chuck was gone. I hated going in the closet to find something to wear. Mignonne, one of my close friends from our church in Livingston, drove down to help me pack Chuck's things. I would never have been able to do it by myself. Together, we cried as we packed the shirts, pants, and coats we had seen Chuck wear so often. I kept some items for Nicole and Tara which I thought they might find meaningful as they got older. We even went through some of my clothes and put them away. I knew I could no longer wear certain outfits and lingerie that were part of "us" as a couple. The memory was too painful. Seeing them only made me cry; it was another harsh reminder that Chuck was dead. These things must be put out of sight. Mignonne loaded everything in her car and gave them to friends and needy people in Livingston.

Our bedroom was one of the hardest rooms for me to go in following Chuck's death. This had been the room where we had known each other as husband and wife. Instinctively, I knew I couldn't handle keeping this room as it was. Though I had no idea what kind of income I would have, I determined to redo this room. I would go in debt if necessary, but the room had to be changed! Men from our church came and painted the walls a new color. Linda and Karen went with me to New Orleans to buy a new bedroom set. Joy made new curtains and throw pillows. It helped me tremendously to walk into a "new" room, and it was worth every penny spent to make these changes. This may not be something everyone needs to do, but I believe it was a healing factor for me.

There are some jobs that a woman is not accustomed to doing that can really be a source of frustration. Changing the oil in the car, and checking the tire pressure was something new for me. I knew nothing about keeping the tires rotated, trimming bushes, or cleaning the filter on the push lawn mower! Needless to say, I am experienced in most all of these areas now. I am thankful for the men in our church who helped me in these areas till I could get back on my feet again. I still hate having to be responsible for these things, but at least I now know what needs to be done!

Any number of "menial" jobs are just waiting for those who truly desire to help someone whose world has been shaken. What may seem trivial to you, a simple task to be completed in a short amount of time, can be overwhelming to those thrown off balance from the storms of life. Use your imagination to discover even more opportunities to comfort those who are hurting. You'll find your own heart being blessed as you give of your talents and time.

I have no doubt that one of the reasons we have been able to pick up the pieces of our shattered world is because many people across the country prayed for us.

Prayer. We often try every possible thing we know to do, and then give a deep sigh as we say, "Well, there's nothing else we can do. I guess we'll just have to pray." Though we might not want to admit it, prayer is often the last resort instead of our first response! We cheat ourselves by this lack of prayer. Paul acknowledged that it was the prayers of others which helped him out of tough situations. "You also joined in helping us through your prayers. . . favor [was] bestowed upon us through the prayers of many" (II Corinthians 1:11, NASB). He wrote from his prison cell: "I know that this shall turn out for my deliverance through your prayer" (Philippines 1:19, NASB). We often underestimate the power of praying for others, but it is actually the greatest single action we can take to help one who is hurting.

Following Chuck's death, many people said to me, "Let me know if there's anything we can do."

I quickly learned to respond, "Would you please commit to pray for me and the girls? Would you put our name on your prayer list and daily lift us up before the throne of the Heavenly Father?" I have no doubt that one of the reasons we have been able to pick up the pieces of our shattered world is because many people across the country prayed for us. God answered their prayers, and we received the benefits. It is my testimony that God has carried us through the tumultuous times on the wings of prayer, many from people I have never met.

I have heard people say before, "I knew you were praying for me. I could feel it." I wondered if perhaps there was something wrong with my spiritual life since I couldn't honestly say I had ever "felt" the prayers of others. My first experience with this was about three weeks after Chuck's death. It was a Wednesday night, another day of excessive grief and sorrow. I was still stunned by all that had happened. We were finished with supper, and I walked into my small music room. From out of nowhere a song began to spring forth in my heart. A glimmer of joy sparked in my mind. I couldn't explain why the great pain lessoned for a brief time. *Where is this coming from?* I asked myself. I glanced at my watch, and then I knew. It was 7:15 p.m.—prayer meeting time for many churches. God's people were holding me up before Him to ask Him to comfort me in the midst of my pain. God worked in my life in response to their prayers.

People can receive comfort and strength from the Lord by our praying for them. On this side of Eternity, we may never know just how much the load was lightened because of our prayers. I attribute much of my own recovery to the prayers offered in my behalf by God's people. "Pray for one another. . . . The effective prayer of a righteous man can accomplish much" (James 5:16b. NASB).

As we journey through the death of our dreams and hopes, we will find God's comfort seeping into our lives in various forms. It may be through His Word to us, through the power of His Spirit within us, or through His body, the church, as it extends itself to us in His behalf. Experiencing God's comfort in the dark night of our souls allows us to sing the Mourning Song. Though no one wants to sing this song, the Mourning Song must be part of our repertoire in order for our Book of Songs to be complete. He will hold true to His promise to comfort us. "Comfort, O comfort my people, says your God" (Isaiah 40:1, NASB). "For I will turn their mourning into joy, and will comfort them and give them joy for their sorrow" (Jeremiah 31:13b, NASB).

We will then be able to say, not only because of the teaching of God's Word but from personal experience, "Earth has no sorrow that Heaven cannot heal."

Be still my soul: the Lord is on thy side;
Bear patiently the cross of grief or pain;
Leave to thy God to order and provide;
In every change He faithful will remain.
Be still my soul: thy best, thy heav'nly Friend
Thro' thorny ways leads to a joyful end.

Lyrics to the hymn "Be Still My Soul" by Katharina Von Schlegel—from Psalm 46

11

A Song for Wilderness Wanderings
Surviving Tough Times

Life goes on. In spite of my wanting time to stop, it marched forward. Sometimes I felt like screaming as I saw people in their daily routines, "How can you carry on as if nothing has happened?! Don't you know my husband just died? Don't you understand what I now must face?"

I identified with the writer of Psalm 137. He found himself in a strange country far from home and remembered "how it used to be." He wrote, "By the rivers of Babylon we sat and wept when we remembered Zion. There on the poplars we hung our harps, for there our captors asked us for songs, our tormentors demanded songs of joy; they said, 'Sing us one of the songs of Zion!' How can we sing the songs of the Lord while in a foreign land?" (Psalm 137:1-4, NIV). The same question resonated through my mind, "How can I sing the song of the Lord while in this foreign land, this barren wilderness?" I too had "hung up my harp," and I believed the music was gone. In His grace and mercy, however, God can still give a "song in the night" (Psalm 77:6). Chuck's sudden, shocking death threw me into the wilderness. I knew I could wander around in this desert for forty years as the children of Israel did, walking in circles, going nowhere. During the initial shock of losing Chuck, I didn't even care if I wandered for the rest of my life. As I began to regain my balance from this crushing blow, however, God planted within my heart a desire to deal with my hurt so I could get out of the dry, dusty land. I prayed, "Take me to the green pastures and quiet waters, dear Shepherd. I've spent enough time in the valley of the shadow. I don't want to stay in this barren land forever." I wish I could give you a nice, neat formula that leads from the wilderness to the land of milk and honey. I wish the scriptures had a precise, easy prescription for dealing with pain. No doubt we are given gems from God's Word here and there, but the pat answers I prefer are strangely missing. In his book, *Journey Through Grief*, Robert Williams makes this observation:

> We still wonder why there are no distinct prescriptions for the handling of grief. When we reflect, however, upon what God is wanting to make of us, we are almost persuaded to believe that their absence is intentional. We must not depend upon rules, pat answers, or even solutions that someone outside ourselves might supply for us. God is putting down into the cavernous recesses of our beings the inner resources with which to experience life. The principles that He asks us to adopt are inner mandates that make us into bulwarks of Christ-likeness. His life is being galvanized into us. His presence is being made the sentry over every heartbeat. The power of that Life and Presence will not only produce life in us; it will be adequate to face the onslaughts that would destroy that life.[1]

If I were dealing with an alcohol abuse problem, I could attend an AA meeting and begin the twelve steps to get back on track. They have found that putting certain principles into action and aggressively facing the problem can put a person on the road to recovery.

I can't find a step-by-step process in God's Word for the wilderness wanderings. I can glean biblical principles that can begin to lead us out of the desert. As we trod this path one step at a time, we can take positive actions to keep from getting stuck in a rut. Over a period of time, we'll make progress. It's possible to pick up the pieces of a shattered life and start to build one more time. There are no "quick fixes" and no short-cuts. If there were, believe me, I would have found them! But choosing to employ the right ingredients will gradually help us to find meaning in life once more. Death's striking blow doesn't have to incapacitate us for the rest of our lives.

The following suggestions are by no means comprehensive. These are key elements however, that have been tremendously helpful to me; and hopefully, you will find them beneficial when you find yourself wandering in the wilderness and need a song in the night.

Truth: It is essential that we fill our minds with truth! What is truth, you may ask just as Pilate asked when he questioned Jesus (John 18:38). Jesus clearly stated in His prayer to the Father, "Thy word is truth" (John 17:17, KJV). Much of what we encounter in our society is contrary to the Word of God. We need to ask, "What does the Bible say?" in order to have the proper mind-set. How else will we be able to distinguish a lie from the truth? Romans 12:1 speaks of the renewing of our minds which enables us to resist the fiery darts of the devil and our own confused emotions.

Paul encourages us in Philippines 4:8, "Whatever is true, honorable, right, pure, lovely, of good repute, if there is any excellence and anything worthy of praise, let your mind dwell on these things." As an act of our will, we can choose to think on the right things, for "as he thinketh in his heart, so is he" (Proverbs 23:7 KJV).

In our modern society, computers are a necessity in the working world. Yet as wonderful and effective as a computer may be, it can't print out what has not been put into it! This principle is true in our personal lives as well. To have the proper emotional response, we must keep our minds focused on the right things. Dwell on the negatives, and you'll be negative. Focus on the positive, claim God's truth, and healing can begin. Recite Scripture, listen to good teaching tapes, and sing songs that emphasize the truth—especially when emotions are telling you the opposite! Author Margaret Clarkson says, "Feeling, in fact, has nothing to do with it; we cling to naked truth and stake our all on that. We repeat these truths, blindly believing with a faith that refuses to be daunted, until one day we discover, often to our own surprise, that there is no longer any shadow of doubt in our hearts—we know the truths to which we have been clinging so desperately."[2]

Like a sponge which soaks up water, saturate your mind with God's truth. This affirmative action leads to faith and resists the negative elements around us.

Imaginations: You can literally drive yourself crazy by letting your imagination run rampant. "If only" and "what if" are the wrong things to dwell on because they only lead downward to the pit of despair. I know, because I battled this problem for a long time. *What if* I had come out of the bathroom sooner? *What if* someone had driven by as Chuck was walking across the front yard? *If only* the hospital had returned our call sooner. *If only* they had listened to me when I told them he wasn't ready to be released. We need to avoid speculations. Don't keep hitting the "Rewind" button to play that same old song over and over again. Push the "Eject" button and refuse to play those tapes! Replace them with ones that will build you up and strengthen you instead of defeating you. II Corinthians 10:5 says, "casting down imaginations and every lofty thought that raises itself up against the knowledge of Christ, taking every thought captive to the obedience of Christ." Refuse to entertain vain speculations. Get rid of wrong thoughts by replacing them with right thoughts based on truth.

Acceptance: Sooner or later we need to accept the reality of our situation. Until we do, we continue to bang our heads against the wall and make the situation worse. Missionary to India, Amy Carmichael, has said, "In acceptance lieth peace." As long as we continue to refuse to accept the current situation, peace will evade us. Robert Williams states, "No amount of tears and sorrow will change the fact of loss. Our only real option is to change our attitude toward it. Accordingly, we must place our best effort in that direction."[3]

I believe it is here that the question of "why" must come to rest. We need to move from "why" to "what now."

We can learn to play the cards dealt to us. If the situation can be changed, then change it! (I'm not speaking of passive resignation here!) But if it is unchangeable, acceptance is the first step to moving on. Everything you have encountered has been allowed by the sovereign hand of God, "filtered through fingers of love" as speaker and writer Kay Arthur says. The Serenity Prayer, written by the German theologian Reinhold Nieburhr, is so appropriate for these times: "God grant me the serenity to accept the things I cannot change, courage to change the things I can, and wisdom to know the difference." Again, I quote Margaret Clarkson who so aptly states, "We must accept the worst and then hope, and trust, and work for the best."[4]

I believe it is here that the question of "why" must come to rest. We need to move from "why" to "what now." Our lack of knowing "why" often makes our struggle even more intense. We think, *If I only knew why, I could handle this.* However, knowing "why" wouldn't change the situation and if we knew "why", we might not like the answer, and we might not be able to comprehend it. At this point, we are called to put our faith into action. "Lord, help me trust You." The Psalmist wrote, "Commit your way to the Lord, trust also in Him, and He will do it" (Psalm 37:5 NASB). Acceptance of the situation is necessary if you are going to take the next step forward.

Prayer: Pour out your heart to God; be honest with Him about your emotions. He already knows what you're thinking and feeling so you might as well 'fess up to it! Acknowledge your emotions and experience them so you can deal with them appropriately and bring about the desired change. Denial and suppression are not the answer. Again, I speak from my own experience. I used to think, *I know that it's wrong for a Christian to be angry, especially with God. I want to be a good Christian, so no, I'm not angry!* Recognize your frustrations. Instead of denying them, admit them to the Lord. Then change can begin to take place. When I read the Psalms, I see how honest David was with God. Every imaginable emotion is acknowledged, from loftiest praise to deepest despair. David was called "a man after God's own heart," and he encouraged us to "trust in him at all times, ye people; pour out your heart before him. God is a refuge for us" (Psalm 62:8). He also wrote, "The Lord is nigh unto all those who call upon him, to all who call upon him in truth" (Psalm 145:18). David is a good example to us of admitting our feelings to the Lord—including the painful ones—to keep from becoming bound by them. This step is essential if we are to make progress in our grief recovery work.

Time: Give yourself the gift of time. Remember that recovery from the hard knocks of life is a process. Healing of damaged emotions takes time, just as physical healing takes time (barring a direct intervention of God). There is no "time limit" for getting back on track when we've been knocked off the road. Different people travel at different rates of speed. People heal of physical wounds in different amounts of time, and the same is true of our emotions. It is terribly insensitive of others to ask questions such as, "Aren't you over this yet?" If we were able to be "over it," don't they think we would be?!

The parable of the fig tree in Luke 13 shows that time is a

necessary element for growth to occur. Though the landowner was ready to destroy the tree because it hadn't produced fruit in three years, the gardener persuaded him to give it another year. "Let it along sir for this year, too, until I dig around it and put in fertilizer; and if it bears fruit next year fine; but if not, cut it down" (Luke 13:8-9 NASB). Along with pruning and nurturing, time was needed to see if the tree would produce. When we deal with the hard times, we also need time and attention so that we can bear fruit. This need for patience is contrary to the "instant society" that we are accustomed to today. Fax machines, microwaves, E-mail, cellular phones, jet planes, and a host of push-button conveniences all serve to encourage us to "want it now!" But God's way is often more time-consuming. He isn't interested in the "quick fix." He wants us to experience the long-term transformation that occurs over time. Let me be quick to add that time in and of itself doesn't necessary bring healing. Undoubtedly, there are some wounds that only time can heal. But to assert that "Time heals all wounds" is untrue and has been proven false over and over again. In fact, I've known people (and I'm sure you have too) who just got worse as time passed! "She never got over it!" tragically describes many people who have suffered great losses. The wound must be properly treated, or the infection will grow and fester, spread further, and do more damage.

Both of my girls love to play outside. They often run bare-foot around our home (it's in our blood from our country ways!). More times than I like, I've had to remove splinters from little feet and hands. Now that my girls are bigger, they understand that Mama must take the splinter out so the wound can heal. When they were younger, they viewed my efforts to remove the small piece of wood as an action that only caused them more pain. "No, Mama, please, leave it alone!" they wailed, but I knew it must be removed—in spite of the current pain—for the healing to begin. Though it hurt my own heart to hear their cries, I still acted in their best interests.

Our time of grief will prove to be redemptive only if the necessary steps are taken in the process of healing. If our wounds are left unattended, however, time will only allow the wound to fester.

People: John Donne said, "No man is an island." This truth is magnified during the crisis times of our lives. People need people! I can hear some protest, "No, not if you're really spiritual. You only need the Lord." That's not the way God made us however. We have a natural need for relationships, being made as relational beings. One author has written: "It is a basic human need. God created us with a hunger for relationship—for relationship with him and with our fellow people. At our very core, we are relational beings"[5] The writer continues, "The foundation of existence lies in relationship, for it is the way God exists. . . . Since we are created in his likeness, relationship is our most fundamental need, the very foundation of who we are. Without relationship, without attachment to God and others, we can't be our true selves."[6]

Isn't it ironic that when we are hurting the most, we tend to isolate ourselves from others and our source of help? We shouldn't be too proud to admit we are hurting and have a problem! Building a support system is imperative for those who grieve.

I must confess that there was an element of embarrassment for Chuck and me when he first admitted himself to a psychiatric hospital. My initial reaction was, "Let's keep this quiet! Don't let the church know what is really going on! This will ruin our reputations, and it may cost us our jobs!" But on that Wednesday evening as I was preparing to go to prayer meeting, the thought popped into my mind, *If I can't tell my brothers and sisters in Christ, then who can I tell? What is the church for, anyway? Isn't this what the church is about, "bearing one another's burdens"?*

When I swallowed my pride and shared my husband's struggle, our church rallied to our side. The burden was made more bearable because I wasn't carrying it alone. Many encouraged me, empathized with me, and even opened up and shared their own experiences they had kept secret for so long. It is certainly much easier to handle the hard times with the support of good friends. I believe this is what Paul meant when he wrote, "Rejoice with those who rejoice, and weep with those who weep" (Romans 12:15 NASB). Truly "a friend loves at all times, and a brother is born for adversity" (Proverbs 17:17).

Seasons: Remember that your current hardship may be devastating, but it is only temporary—"for a season," as Peter reminded suffering believers (I Peter 1:6) Some seasons seem to last longer than others! We are all familiar with the phrase, "This too shall pass." In the midst of our pain however, we tend to lose sight of this fact and feel the immediate trial will never be resolved. But as surely as the sun rises and sets each day, so too the seasons change. Spring always comes. Though the darkness falls, the sun will shine again. The night doesn't last forever.

Each season has it's own purposes in our lives. One author suggests that "our growth has different 'seasons.' Some seasons are for planting (spring), some for nourishing (summer), some for harvesting (fall), and some for dying (winter)."[7] While I'd prefer it always to be harvest time, the fact of the matter is, all seasons are needed for growth to take place.

Growing up in the country allowed me to see this truth exhibited in the physical world. My daddy has worked farm land for as long as I can remember. As a child, I even had my own cotton patch. I've watched my dad get on the tractor and prepare the soil, plowing and disking it to make it ready for planting. At just the right time, he planted the seeds. Some time later, he put out the fertilizer, and he prayed for rain as the seeds began to grow. Then we waited. I couldn't hurry the growing process. We simply had to wait. If we had a good season, the crop came up and produced. At harvest time, we were out in the field to gather in the crop. As the year continued and the weather turned cold, the old plants died away. Once again Dad plowed the dead stalks under and waited for spring to return to start the cycle over again.

These principles of agriculture are also true in our lives. We need to experience all the various seasons of life if we are to be mature and complete.

The words of the Preacher from Ecclesiastes 3 present this truth in eloquent form:"To everything there is a season, and a time to every purpose under Heaven. A time to be born, and a time to die; a time to plant, and a time to pluck up that which is planted; a time to kill and a time to heal; a time to break down, and a time to build up; a time to weep and a time to laugh; a time to mourn and a time to dance; a time to cast away stones and a time to gather stones together; a time to embrace, and a time to refrain from embracing; a time to get and a time to lose; a time to keep and a time to cast away; a time to tear and a time to sew; a time to keep silence, and a time to speak; a time to love and a time to hate; a time of war and a time of peace" (Ecclesiastes 3:1-8, KJV).

Though my girls are still very young, I have already seen this principle at work in our lives. When Nicole and Tara were in the preschool years, sometimes it seemed like I'd never get away from having a child underfoot! I thought, *Wouldn't it be nice to go somewhere without a diaper bag and baby bottles? And don't forget the pacifier or no one will be happy!* But time passed, and suddenly my Tara marched off to first grade. For the first time in eight years, I no longer had a little girl at home with me during the day. That season of my life is over. A new season has arrived. Now I am beginning to understand when others tell me, "They grow up so fast!" I'm sure I'll turn around, and they'll be gone, walking out the door with babes of their own as the song says! Nothing stays the same. The seasons change. Yours will as well.

Laughter: It's been said that "laughter is the best medicine," and guess what? It's free, free for the taking! It doesn't cost a dime! There are no big medical bills or insurance forms to fill out to receive this prescription! Laughter is good for your whole body, and brings healing. Some have called it "internal jogging." Others have viewed laughter as a safety valve which releases inner pressures. Modern medicine is now proving the reality of what the Bible stated years ago, "A joyful heart is good medicine, but a broken spirit dries up the bones" (Proverbs 17:22). *Anatomy of an Illness*, written by Norman Cousins, gives substantial evidence of the medicinal benefits of laughter. When we laugh, endorphins are released from the brain that increase the body's capacity to fight inflammation and relieve pain. He states, "Ten minutes of genuine belly laughter had an anesthetic effect" on the cancer he fought, producing "at least two hours of pain-free sleep."[8]

Jerry Dahmen reports in his book, *I Love Life In Spite Of It All*, "A hearty laugh can give you a 'runner's high,' releasing endocrines, the body's natural pain-killers. A research study by a Yale University medical team proved that laughter clears the respiratory system, provides a healthy emotional outlet, combats boredom, and gives one a better self-image. Beyond that, a good laugh helps us enjoy life far more than when we frown."[9]

But what if you don't feel like laughing? What if the effort is just too great? That's how I felt after first losing Chuck, but two little lives were dependant on me alone now. I wanted to protect Nicole and Tara by doing anything I could to help ease their pain. I remember forcing myself to get down on the floor with them and tickle their little tummies. They rolled in delight. I tossed them in the air as high as my arms could throw them, and I watched their faces shine with glee. Though this was a forced action for me, it actually proved to work for my benefit as well as my girls.

One of my dearest friends, Brenda, is a nut! I've never met anyone with such a sense of humor. She also happens to be my hairdresser. Many times after Chuck's death, I'd call and make an appointment to have my hair trimmed whether it needed it or not just so I could be around Brenda. I knew she would make me laugh, and I knew I'd feel better after being in her presence.

So go ahead and put forth the effort to make yourself laugh! Spend time with folks who enjoy living, watch a funny movie, or read a comical book. The temporary diversion is needful for more reasons than one! From my own experience, I confirm the teaching of the Proverbs which say, "A joyful heart makes a cheerful face" and "a cheerful heart has a continual feast" (Proverbs 15:13a, 15a).

Hope: Hope is the life blood of the human race. Author and speaker, Hal Lindsey, wrote, "Man can live about forty days without food, about three days without water, about eight minutes without air, but only about one second without hope."[10] As long as a person has hope, the human spirit can endure most anything. But when hope has been crushed, despair and depression grip our hearts. The scripture says, "Hope deferred makes the heart sick, but desire fulfilled is a tree of life" (Proverbs 13:12 NASB). Hope is always available for the child of God. He is "the God on whom we have set our hope" (II Corinthians 1:10, KJV), the One who can take all the broken pieces of our hearts and bind them together again. The promises of God's Word give us hope. As we keep our focus on these truths, hope begins to blossom forth in our hearts.

For a time after Chuck's death, I lost all hope and resigned myself to a life of sorrow and pain. I thought joy would only come to me after I died and reached Heaven and that it was gone forever on Planet Earth. Then I came across the verse that says, "I had fainted unless I had believed to see the goodness of the Lord in the land of the living" (Psalm 27:13, KJV). The truth of that verse hit me upside the head! I prayed, "Lord, do You mean to say there is more of Your goodness for me in this life? I'm still in the land of the living—even though I feel like I'm half dead. But You're telling me that there is still good that I can enjoy here and now? It's not just for after I leave this life?"

Psalm 23:6 states, "Surely goodness and mercy shall follow me all the days of my life." God has promised that though "weeping make endure for the night, joy comes in the morning" (Psalm 126:5). As I contemplated these truths, the seed of hope started to grow in me. Though I knew it was a long shot, I began to hope that perhaps I too could know goodness, mercy, and joy in this life again. The words of the psalmist from Psalm 42:5 became my own cry, "Why are you in despair O my soul? And why have you become disturbed within me? Hope in God, for I shall again praise Him, for the help of his presence."

Let the seed of hope take root in your heart. It will help you face the days to come and give you a reason to live.

Action: During my wilderness wanderings, I didn't have the luxury of quitting like I so often wanted to do. I had to keep going for my girls. Only God's grace and strength enabled me to keep moving when I only wanted to curl up and die. I was forced to take action, often in spite of my desires and emotions. I had to keep doing what I knew was right in spite of how I felt. In reality, this was one of the best things I could have done to begin the journey out of the desert.

The model of a train engine, coal car, and caboose, Fact—Faith—Feelings, is helpful. Remind yourself of the facts, then by faith begin to implement actions that will move toward your goal. Feelings are the caboose that will eventually follow. We need to resist the tendency to let our feelings (which are so often painful) be the engine of this train. I would accomplish very little if I let my feelings lead me! It is rare that I "feel" like cooking supper or "feel" like getting up in the morning! But once I have initiated the action, the good feelings usually (but not always) follow. How true it is that it is easier to act your way into a feeling than to feel your way into an action!

In the last few months, I've started jogging. For a long time, I've known exercise would be good for me, but I haven't had the motivation. That motivation strangely appeared when I recently found I couldn't fit into some of my clothes! I have to admit to you that 90% of the time, I don't feel like jogging. It would be fine with me just to forget it. The facts are, however, that I'm spreading out in the wrong places! Unless I want it to get worse, I'd better take action! Jogging will help me get back in shape. So regardless of how I feel, I take off down the track. By the time it's over, I'm glad I endured the discipline, and actually, I feel better.

If you behave the way you would like to be, you will become

that! Popular speaker and author Mamie McCullough, has a little phrase which goes like this, "Fake it till you make it!" By God's strength, we can take the right actions which will lead to the right feelings. Paul stated this principle when he wrote, "I buffet my body and make it my slave" (I Corinthians 9:27a, NASB). I like the way the King James version puts it, "I bring it [my body] into subjection." You may feel like you're getting nowhere, but if you refuse to quit, you'll eventually see progress, and growth will occur. "Trust in the Lord and do good" (Psalm 37:3, KJV). Keep sowing the good seed, and you will reap a bountiful crop, because "a man reaps what he sows" (Gal 6:7 NIV). Take action, and you will reap the benefits.

The quality of life that lay ahead would be determined by the choices I made each day.

All of these principles help us keep the right attitude, and "attitude determines altitude." My attitude and responses to the tragedy in my life held the key for dooming the future or propelling me to growth and strength. For many years, I had heard the saying, "It's not so much what happens to you, but how you respond to what happens to you that determines whether you'll be defeated or victorious." Now I realized the truth of those words: The choices I made during those dark days were setting the course for the future.

Yes, I couldn't undo the past, and some people said I had a right to accept a "poor me," victim mentality. This choice, however, would result in my own death—my own slow, emotional suicide. I was responsible for my life. The choices I faced were a road that would eventually lead me out of the wilderness. The quality of life that lay ahead would be determined by the choices I made each day. It reminds me of an old saying I'd often heard: "Life is like a piano. What you get out of it depends on how you play it!"

"Which way are you going to go, Renee?" the Spirit whispered. "How are you going to play it? You have a choice. Why don't you choose life, faith, and love? It's a much better way than the alternative." Focusing on God's truths reinforced this choice for me.

Maybe you're saying, "I've tried all of those things Renee, and it didn't work for me. I'm tired of all this positive-thinking hype."

I understand. I didn't immediately begin to employ all of this either. What if nothing works? What if you're doing everything you know to do, and you're still stuck in a rut? I've felt like that before. Let me offer a few suggestions:

- Accept your humanity. God does! It's comforting for me to realize: "Just as a father has compassion on his children, so the Lord has compassion on those who fear Him. For He Himself knows our frame; He is mindful that we are but dust" (Psalm 103:13,14, NASB).

  Don't put unrealistic expectations on yourself. Don't demand more of yourself than God does. Allow room for your humanity as you continue striving to recover from the harsh blow you've encountered.

- Call for prayer support. You don't have to fight this battle alone. Let your intercessory prayer warriors stand in the gap when you're too weak. God will work in your life in response to their prayers! Paul wrote the believers in Corinth, "You joined in helping us through your prayers. . . . favor was bestowed upon us through the prayers of many" (II Corinthians 1:11, NASB). Send out the call for prayer! Bring in the reinforcements!

- Recall God's faithfulness. Remembering what He has done in the past can give you faith and hope for today. He is the God who cannot lie; He is faithful and true. And He is still faithful to me in spite of my unfaithfulness to Him! "If we are faithless, He remains faithful; for He cannot deny Himself" (II Timothy 2:13, NASB).

- Start Again. You don't know how close you may be to stepping into the light. It may be just around the bend! So keep on keeping on! What if Naaman, the captain of the Syrian army who suffered from leprosy, had dipped in the Jordan only four, five, or six times instead of seven as Elisha instructed (II Kings 5:1-14). He wouldn't have been healed because he would have quit too soon! Or what if Elijah's servant got tired after looking for the rain cloud five times instead of seven as he was told? (See I Kings 18:41-46.) We must be persistent and stand firm until the end! The apostle Paul encourages us, "Let us not be weary in well doing; for in due season we shall reap, if we faint not" (Gal 6:9 KJV). Tomorrow is a new day, a chance to begin once more.

Sometimes it's best just to go to bed when we are physically and emotionally drained. A new day will bring a new beginning and a rested body. Even Elijah, the great prophet of God, needed a time to rest after the battle on Mount Carmel! The psalmist wrote, "It is vain for you to rise up early, to sit up late, to eat the bread of sorrows; for so he giveth his beloved sleep" (Psalm 127:2, KJV). Paul admonishes us, "Having done everything, stand firm" (Ephesians 6:13, NASB). "Let us not be weary in well doing; for in due season we shall reap, if we faint not" (Galatians 6:9). Each new day brings a fresh start and a new opportunity to try one more time.

I don't know about you, but it didn't take long for me to know the wilderness was not where I wanted to stay! Putting these principles into action has worked to move me on down the road toward greener pastures. Often, it wasn't easy. Often, it wasn't what I really wanted to do. There have been times when I took one step forward only to take two steps backward!

Initially, I was surprised to discover that I could sing the Lord's song in a foreign land, but singing sure has made the journey easier to bear. The Wilderness Song wasn't one I would have chosen to sing, but I now know it has it's place. Anything else wouldn't have been right. The "zippidy-do-dah" tunes I had so often sung before aren't appropriate by the waters of Babylon. The Song for Wilderness Wanderings is the song designed for those who hurt in the deserts of life. It brings healing and relief as only it can. Even death can't prevent this song of the night from seeping forth from my broken heart.

> Some thro' the waters, some thro'; the flood;
> Some thro' the fire, but all thro' the blood;
> Some thro' great sorrow, but God gives a song,
> In the night season and all the day long.

Chorus of the hymn "God Leads Us Along" by G.A. Young

12

A Richer Melody Emerges
The Benefits of Hard Times

I recorded a song on my second project entitled, "Hard Times," written by my friend Gary Driskell. I've had plenty of first-hand experience in dealing with the hard times. After experiencing the devastating effects of Chuck's death, I should be an expert in handling difficult times. I should be able to breeze through any trial, but I still struggle just like everyone else. I've learned that we only finish one battle to begin another. As long as we live, we must fight the good fight of faith. The battle is not over until we see the Lord face to face. Who hasn't had to deal with the hard times of life? The Bible says our trials and temptations are "common to all" (I Corinthians 10:13). No one is immune, no one is exempt. It goes with the territory.

Though I love the whole song Gary wrote, the chorus keeps swirling around in my mind. It says: when our world is torn to pieces during hard times, we are forced to hold on to Christ. During this time, we actually see the strength of our faith.[1]

This perspective reminds me of suddenly realizing your house is on fire, and you have just minutes to save yourself. As you flee from the flames, there's only time to grab the one thing that is most precious to you. That's how it is when our world is turned upside down. When the music dies, when there's nothing left to hold on to, we're forced to hold on to Jesus. Everything else has been torn to pieces. When our lives are stripped of so many other "things," our eyes are opened to what is of real value in our lives. Jesus is still there even when everything else is gone. In his book, *Trusting God Even When Life Hurts*, Jerry Bridges summed up this point very well when he wrote,

God uses adversity to loosen our grip on those things that are not true fruit. A severe illness or the death of someone dear to us, the loss of material substance or the tarnishing of our reputation, the turning aside of friends or the dashing of our cherished dreams on the rocks of failure, cause us to think about what is really important in life. Position or possessions or even reputation no longer seem so important. We begin to relinquish our desires and expectations—even good ones—to the sovereign will of God. We come more and more to depend on God and to desire only that which will count for eternity.[2]

Through the corridors of time, many who have experienced severe heartache have said, "When Jesus was all I had, I realized He was all I needed."

Why would God allow His children to go through these hard times? Why doesn't He shield and protect us from every pain? It is not my purpose to write a book on the "why's of suffering." Many good books already expound that subject and are readily available. But I want to offer a few insights that have helped me cope with this issue. These perspectives help me understand how God can turn the difficulties—even the death of one we thought we could not live without—into a positive factor for us.

James Martin stated, "Given our cooperation, God can transform our mistakes and our accidents. He can make even our suffering a means of blessing and enrichment."[3] The music of life can be enriched, with a richer melody than ever before because of the hard times.

Dr. John Claypool lost a young daughter to leukemia. He wrote, "But if we are willing, the experience of grief can deepen and widen our ability to participate in life. We can become more grateful for the gifts we have been given, more open-handed in our handling of the events of life, more sensitive to the whole mysterious process of life, and more trusting in our adventure with God."[4]

"More grateful, more open-handed, more sensitive, more trusting." These are the words Dr. Claypool uses to express how the times of adversity and sorrow can broaden our ability to really live! Perhaps this was one of the reasons James, the half brother of our Lord, wrote, "Consider it all joy, my brethren, when you encounter various trials, knowing that the testing of your faith produces endurance. And let endurance have its perfect result, that you may be perfect and complete, lacking in nothing" (James 1:2-4 NASB).

I don't know about you, but my first reaction when facing a

difficult time is not generally one of "joy." In my limited way of thinking, it's hard for me to equate joy and trials in the same thought! They seem so contrary to one another, exact opposites. How is it possible to put them on the same level?

Only when I consider the big picture and not my immediate adversity can I "count it all joy." The reason for joy is not the trial but the good that it can produce. I need to remind myself to look at the results of having my faith tested! If I choose to bear my pain God's way, the way of faith, then the Scripture teaches that I can be "complete, lacking in nothing." What more could a person want? What else would one desire? Isn't this what Paul meant when he said, "as having nothing, and yet possessing all things" (II Corinthians 6:10).

"When Jesus was all I had, I realized He was all I needed."

I found this same emphasis of joy during the hard times in Romans 5:3-5. Again, Paul wrote, "We exult in our tribulations, knowing that tribulation brings about perseverance; and perseverance, proven character, and proven character, hope; and hope does not disappoint." The "tribulations" weren't the basis for rejoicing. No one enjoys the pain! No one wants to hurt! Especially me! I'd prefer "the comfort zone," thank you. Let me take the easy way out. But after making such a statement, the harsh reality of what that really means slaps me in the face: comfort means more to me than character. My selfish human nature wants to breeze through on smooth seas and sunny skies. How accurately Dr. Paul Brand and Philip Yancey noted this truth when they titled their book, *Pain, The Gift Nobody Wants*.

But the fruit of going through the trial makes the pain worth the gain! The benefits outweigh the suffering. As it is often said in the athletic world, "No pain, no gain." The principle applies to our spiritual and emotional lives as well. Short-term pain equals long-term gain! By struggling, going through the fire, walking through the valley of the shadow of death, our lives can be enriched to a new dimension we never imagined. Though it can be tormenting and anguishing, suffering can be the means to a more meaningful life on earth as well as eternal rewards. "Our suffering has meaning and purpose in God's eternal plan, and He brings or allows to come into our lives only that which is for His glory and our good." [5]

God loves me too much to leave me alone to my own selfish devices. Adversity is one of the means He uses to help me grow and develop. "God does not delight in our sufferings. He brings only that which is necessary, but He does not shrink from that which will help us grow."[6]

I have seen this truth illustrated in many examples in the world of nature. My girls love to chase butterflies. . . and sometimes even catch them! What beautiful creatures designed by God! But butterflies weren't always so lovely. At one time the beautiful butterfly was an ugly caterpillar! What brought about the change? How does a creepy caterpillar become a gorgeous butterfly, free to spread its wings and fly through the sky? The transformation takes place by the caterpillar spinning its self into a chrysalis. Inside this protective shell, the amazing changes occur. Inside the chrysalis, the newly formed butterfly must free itself by pushing and pulling, fighting and struggling to emerge. I have to resist the urge to help this small insect in it's struggle because my intervention would only cripple the butterfly by preventing it from gaining strength through the struggle. The effort to break forth from the chrysalis is *absolutely necessary* in order for the development of the butterfly's strength. The butterfly would never be free to fly if it didn't struggle.

The lesson to me is obvious: My struggles are necessary for me to be all that God created me to be. Going through the hard times can actually be the key that frees me from the bondage of my own selfishness and immaturity. My development is more important to God than letting me remain comfortable. He desires that I grow up to a mature person, reflecting Him in all that I do and say, being "conformed to the image of His son" (Romans 8:29). Adversity is one of the tools God uses to accomplish this purpose. Robert Wise aptly states, "Our painful experiences that close around us like a tomb, become the mold in which our wings are formed. What seems to be so hindering may be the very strength that allows us to fly. These times. . . may be the times we are completing our personhood."[7]

Sometimes I've wondered if Paul and James discussed these thoughts with Peter because he, too, equates suffering with rejoicing. Let me quote his words, "In this you greatly rejoice, even though now for a little while, if necessary, you have been distressed by various trials, that the proof of your faith, being more precious than gold which is perishable, even though tested by fire, may be found to result in praise and glory and honor at the revelation of Jesus Christ" (I Peter 1:5-7, NASB).

Peter uses the phrase, "the proof of your faith." It takes me back to the chorus of the song "Hard Times," which says, "There's no other way to know the strength of your faith, but in the hard times." How can I know the strength of my faith? How can my faith be proved to be genuine? How do I know my faith isn't just all hype but not lived in the trenches of adversity? By putting it to the test of hard times. An army can sit in camp all day long, bragging about its ability to defeat any enemy. "OK, prove it!" someone says. "Quit talking about it, and let's see how strong you really are. Let's see what you've got!" It is only in the midst of the battle that the strength of the army is displayed. That's where their strength is measured!

In the same manner, our faith is put to the test. Ron Dunn has said, "Mark it well: faith never escapes testing. . . . Faith must be tested. An untried faith is an untrustworthy faith, because until it is put to the test we can never be sure if what we are calling faith is really faith." [8] Faith isn't tested by prosperity, but only in the hard times.

Peter put a high premium on the testing of our faith. "The proof of your faith [is] more precious than gold, which is perishable" (I Peter 1:7 NASB). In our world today, gold is considered one of the most valuable metals and a mark of wealth to those who possess it. Nations use it as a form of international money. Investors seek to include gold in their investment portfolios. This precious metal is often used to make jewelry which many women love to wear, including me! When I'm trying to look my best, I always bring out my favorite pieces of gold jewelry. (Though I must admit, most of mine are fake!) From earrings, necklaces, bracelets and rings, I use gold to dress up my outfit. It is the crowning touch to the entire look I am trying to achieve.

The lovely gold used to make fine jewelry didn't come out of the earth looking that way! Quite a process is involved to reach this final state. The gold ore taken from the earth must be crushed to a pulp, reground, filtered, and finally put into a fiery furnace where all the impurities are removed. It is the crushing, grinding, filtering, and fire that finally produce the desired final product.

As lovely and precious as gold may be to some people, it doesn't compare to a tested and proven faith. In the final analysis, gold won't be that valuable at all. In fact, in Heaven gold is so common that the streets are paved with it! From God's perspective, the development of my faith through the fires of adversity is more precious than gold. Once again I'm faced with the harsh reality of my twisted, warped value system. What is really important anyway? Will I be like Esau, only looking to immediate gratification and selling myself short (see Genesis 25:28-34), or will I have the wisdom to see beyond the short-term pain to keep going for the long-term gain?

I see the same principle at work when I admire a sparkling, brilliant diamond. Again, they are considered one of the most prized possessions in a woman's jewelry collection because of their great beauty and value. Their rarity increases their value. It has been said that "diamonds are a girl's best friend," and most young ladies receive a diamond ring when they are engaged. Because money was so tight when Chuck and I were married, I never got my diamond. But do you realize that what we see today as a precious jewel was at one time a worthless chunk of carbon? How did the transformation take place? Time and pressure, time and pressure, time and pressure!

Does this have any application for me? Yes, it does! Just as the caterpillar has to go through the struggle, gold must go through the fire, and diamonds are only formed by great pressure over thousands of years, the principle applies to me as well! I can't develop as I should without struggling, without the fiery furnaces of affliction, and without facing the pressures life brings my way. If I want to be free to fly and shine forth as gold, brilliant as a diamond, I must go through the painful process. In this way, our tragedies can truly be transformed into triumphs.

I have discovered during the "dark night of my soul" that my eyes are opened to new truths and insights that cannot be found in the bright light of day. There are some things that can only be revealed in the nighttime. Let me quote again from Robert Wise, "The empty times can bring a profound depth of insight and understanding that can be found nowhere else. These riddles in our daily experience are critical to our personal development. And, in the end, they help us to walk in total confidence, not only by what we can see but also by what we believe."[9]

As a young girl growing up in the country, I remember many nights when my daddy took me outside to look at the stars. We looked for the Big Dipper, the Little Dipper, the bright North Star, and we hoped to see a falling star. In the last few years, my understanding of a simple truth of stargazing has blossomed: You can only see the stars in the nighttime when it's dark. Though they are still shining during the daylight hours, they are unnoticed by the human eye. It's got to be dark for us to see the stars. Annie Dillard states this truth very clearly, "You do not have to sit outside in the dark. If, however, you want to look at the stars, you will find that darkness is required."[10]

I can hear you saying, "The girl is real slow! Everybody knows it has to be dark to see the stars!" Sure, I've known that for years, but somehow I hadn't connected this physical reality to my spiritual and emotional development. The same truth that applies in the physical world has application to our inner lives as well.

"But I don't like the dark Lord." I plead in my child-like way. "I want to walk in the bright sunshine! Why do I have to go through the night? Can't we cut this part short, Father?"

"No, Renee," my Father replies. "The evening is necessary. It's just as important as the daylight. In fact, it is essential for your total development," He gently whispers to me.

Yes, I know that all sunshine makes a desert. I know that if it never rained, then I'd never grow. But my fallen human nature still wants to resist the path that leads through the valley of the shadow of death.

As I struggle with the tough times, it is encouraging to me to look at the example of Jesus. He understands my battle because he too had to deal with these emotions that I face when I encounter difficult circumstances. Hebrews 4:15 says, "For we do not have a high priest who cannot sympathize with our weaknesses, but one who has been tempted in all things as we are, yet without sin." The writer goes on to admonish us to "look unto Jesus, the author and finisher of our faith, who for the joy that was set before him endured the cross, despising the shame" (Hebrews 12:2 NASB). My attention is drawn to the very same words used together once again that seem so contrary to one another from a human viewpoint: joy and endurance.

In his humanity, our Lord struggled with going to the cross. It caused Him so much anguish in the Garden of Gethsemane, He asked, "If it be possible, let this cup pass from me" (Matthew 26:39 KJV). "Isn't there another way, Father?" He was asking! Three times He prayed the same words! Luke records that His agony was so great that He sweat "great drops of blood falling down to the ground" (Luke 22:44 KJV) and was strengthened by an angel from Heaven. But He was committed to the Father's will, not His own. "Nevertheless, not my will, but thine be done" (Luke 22:42 KJV). He submitted to the Heavenly Father and endured the short-term pain for our long-term gain. He was able to endure the immediate suffering because He looked ahead to the results it would bring.

The principle is clear: Keep the total perspective in view to endure the current conflict. If Jesus applied this principle, then I believe I would do well to follow suit. Moses put this same truth into action. Hebrews says he chose to suffer affliction with the people of God rather than enjoy the pleasures of sin for a season, because he was looking for the reward (Hebrews 11:24-26).

Keep the total perspective in view to endure the current conflict.

You and I have the advantage of these witnesses serving as our models. God calls me as well to keep the proper perspective on my situation. I'm in this fight for the long-haul. No short-term stint for me! Sometimes it may appear that I'm losing this part of the war. That's how I felt the day Chuck died. I'm sure that's how it looked to all those who saw Jesus die on the cross on Friday! But praise God, it's not over! I may lose the battle but still win the war. No one says it better than popular writer Tony Campolo, "That's Friday, but Sunday's coming!" Leo Tolstoy's epic novel, *War and Peace*, has a scene which dramatically illustrates this truth. The movie version of this great piece of literature shows the young Prince Andre talking with his father, the Czar of Russia, about the pending battle with the French the coming day. The young boy asks, "Will we win the battle tomorrow?"

His father, full of wisdom gained through the years, replies, "I think not."

Alarmed and frightened by this answer, Prince Andre cries, "Lose the battle!? But what if we do lose this battle? What will become of us?"

The czar answers with words of wisdom that I need to remember, too. "We don't count all the battles. We only count the last battle. The last battle is the only one that really matters."

"The complete purpose of today's problems is known only when tomorrow arrives. When the sun rises again, the shadow will disappear."[11] As this truth seeps into my heart, I begin to pray, "Help me, Father, to resist the tendency to focus on my immediate crisis. Remind me that what I see now is not all there is. Thank You for using the hard times to open my eyes to what is of real value in this life. Thank You for what You are working to accomplish in me that will actually be for my good when it's all said and done. I don't like the process, Lord. I cry as Jesus did, 'If it be possible, let there be another way!' Yet I choose to submit to You just as He did, knowing that You only do what is for my best."

Please understand. The anguish and heartbreak I have experienced through the death of my husband genuinely has been eased as I have grown to see these truths, but I continue to face great loss which is still very painful at times. Realization of these truths helps, but grief is still necessary—and it still hurts. Suffering changes us—for the better if we deal with it the proper way. But it still hurts! At times, it has almost been more than I could handle. "Lord, I know You said You won't give me more than I can bear, and You will make a way of escape so that I can endure it (I Corinthians 10:13). But I don't like this 'enduring' part! Why can't You just fix everything instantly? Just beam me on out of this mess! I'm holding on by a fingernail now. One more piece of cargo on this ship and we're sunk. I can't take anymore!" My suffering makes me conscious of the fact that this is not Heaven. I'm not home yet. Pain and suffering are part of our fallen world.

The strains of music that once disappeared from my life were slowly but surely resurrected, gently drifting into my ears and penetrating deep into my heart. The music now is more complex than before. Everything's not the simple major chord structure I used to hear all the time. Simply using the tonic, sub-dominant, and dominant-seventh chords somehow seem very glib and trite now. The Master Musician has chosen to weave minor and diminished chords into the musical structure. At first I didn't want them. But little by little, I'm beginning to see that the use of these darker chords adds a richness to the music that was missing before.

I never dreamed that the use of these tones could enhance the music like it has! From my point of view, it initially seemed so wrong, so dissonant! However, I'm beginning to hear a new dimension to the music that I previously didn't hear. I guess that's why it's always best for this student musician to yield to the Master Musician's touch.

> God hath not promised skies always blue,
> flower strewn pathways all our lives through;
> God hath not promised sun without rain,
> Joy without sorrow, peace without pain
> But God hath promised strength for the day,
> Rest for the labor, light for the way,
> Grace for the trials, help from above,
> Unfailing sympathy, undying love.

Lyrics to the hymn "What God Hath Promised" by Annie J. Flint

13

And the Song Plays On
Delayed Effects

N ever the same again. No, I won't be the same again."
That's a line from a song I sang during my college
days. Today I am many years removed from those
carefree days of school, but I sing those words to describe death's
sudden, unanticipated intrusion into my life. I faced this in-
vader, and I am forever changed. I not only suffered the major
loss of my husband (Wouldn't that be more than enough?) but
numerous "secondary losses" as well. Death has left its indelible
mark upon me, and these marks color each day of my life. Who
can face this enemy face to face without being different than
before?

The lingering effects of death have produced a bittersweet
melody with both positive and negative marks, major and minor
tunes. Most assuredly, the intense sorrow and torturing agony
I have suffered through the death of my husband have taken a
toll on me in many ways. Physically, mentally, and emotionally—I have endured the stress and strain of the death blow.
Some people seem to age very quickly after losing a loved one.
Had I? I remember the first time I returned to central Florida
after Chuck's death, to visit friends I hadn't seen in over four
years. I couldn't help but think, *I wonder how I will appear to
them? Have I noticeably aged because of all the stress I've
endured? I know I've been through the mill, but will they think I
look like it, too?*

As death ripped away my husband and my girls' father, I found
myself confused about my own identity. Chuck wasn't the only
one who died that Friday morning. Part of me died, too. The man
to whom I had been joined as one for ten years was suddenly

yanked from my life. Half of "the two who became one" was abruptly removed. During our married years, I grew accustomed to being introduced as "Chuck's wife, Renee." That role had become part of my identity, who I was and what I did. Without warning, in just a matter of seconds, that role ceased to exist. It was now no longer "we" but "I." I questioned, "How do I function as a single in a world where I'm used to being part of a couple?" Each time I had to fill out an application or information sheet, the grief rose within me as I faced this change in my identity. I wondered, *Do I check the "widow" box, or "single" or "Mrs."?* I qualified in all three categories. This simple task suddenly became complex.

The change of my status and identity within the church was difficult to face. For the past eight years, we had been a part of "the inner circle"—the ministerial staff and their wives. Suddenly, I was no longer "the wife of one of the ministers." This fact was made strikingly clear to me when our church had their annual deacon and staff banquet a few months after Chuck's death. For the first time in eight years, I wasn't a part of this event. I sat home alone that Saturday evening thinking of those with whom we had worked so closely all gathered together for an evening of fellowship. I told a friend, "It doesn't seem right for me not to be there. It makes me wonder, 'Who am I now?' I'm confused about my own identity. I still feel married, but I'm single. I still feel like a wife, but I don't have a husband. I feel like I should be with all of our friends tonight at the banquet, but I'm left out. I don't belong there anymore. I'm no longer part of that circle."

Things had changed. I was no longer married and no longer the wife of a minister. Quite honestly, at that point I wasn't sure who I was or where I fit in. I felt like the misfit, searching to find my place in society.

For a while, some of the singles in their mid-twenties from our church tried to spend time with me, but I didn't feel like I belonged with them either. I couldn't take off at 10:00 p.m. to get pizza. I had two little girls in the bed. I couldn't drop what I was doing and head for the movies. I needed to find a baby-sitter first. No, it didn't seem there was a place for me anywhere.

Even at church, I debated which Sunday School class to attend. Yes, I was a widow, but I was too young to join that class! Yes, I was single, but I had kids to take care of, and there was no "single again" class. And why would I want to join that group even if there were one available? Wasn't "single again" for those who were divorced, those whose marriages failed? I didn't want to be a part of "those people!" No, I wasn't a married co-ed, but at least these people were my age with children the ages of my girls. I decided to stay in my same class even though I didn't officially meet the designation of "Co-Ed." Thankfully, no one ever told me I was in the wrong class or tried to get me to move to another one. Had they done that, I probably would have stopped coming to Sunday School altogether.

Over time, I accepted my change of status. It's no longer uncomfortable for me to say, "I'm widowed," or "I'm single again." I knew that I had made great progress in this area when one of Chuck's relatives once introduced me by saying, "This is Chuck's wife." Though I knew what he meant to say, the thought raced through my mind, "No, not anymore. I was his wife for ten years, but that was another time and place." I finally came to accept a new identity apart from my former relationship with Chuck.

Death's entrance radically changed the rhythm of our family life. Our entire definition of "family" changed, and we were thrown off balance by the sudden departure of our husband and father. How does a family survive the loss of this key player? When the head of the house and chief breadwinner is no longer there, the other family members stagger as they try to restore the equilibrium they so desperately need. In addition to continuing to care for my home and children and my part-time work, I was now responsible for the roles Chuck had filled: home maintenance, car repair and up-keep, financial choices, income-production, and decisions on parenting. Everything was thrown in my lap! Total responsibility. No one to ask, "Honey, what do you think?" to help balance my thoughts. No one to ask, "Would you watch the girls while I run to the store?" (Either we all go or no one goes!)

So many things about which I knew nothing were now up to me! *This is a man's job!* I told myself as I ventured out into a new arena! Yet the bottom line was, there was no man to do it. It was now my job, and I must take care of it. I'm the only woman in my neighborhood who mows the yard, trims the bushes, checks the air pressure in the tires, and climbs up on the roof to cover the chimney! But either I have to do it or get someone else. My responsibilities have increased and changed because of the death of my mate.

Because of the tender ages of my girls, they were unable to lend a helping hand in the extra work load. As they have grown, however, they now contribute by completing chores appropriate for their ages. They realize, "We're all in this family, and we all need to do our part." Even with their help, it still can be an overwhelming task to try to keep everything going. It seems there's never enough time to get everything done that needs to be. I constantly fight emotional and physical overload. Single parenting has to be one of the most demanding roles a person is called upon to fulfill. This too is part of the change in our lives since Chuck's death.

Separation anxiety is a very real issue.

These changes in my identity and role responsibilities are not the only changes I've had to face. I've also had to bury dreams I had for the future. Death shattered those dreams into billions of pieces, never to be put together again. My dreams of joy, laughter, and purpose in living with my husband died when he died. I will never see Chuck teaching the girls to play basketball or ride a bike. We won't attend their graduation together as proud parents and watch our girls receive their diplomas. They will never have their daddy walk them down the aisle on their wedding day. Chuck and I won't sit together in our rockers as we grow old. Nicole and Tara's children have been robbed of the grandpa they should have had. Those dreams and expectations were buried with Chuck.

My girls are faced with the fact that they are "different" because they have no daddy. Just this week at school my Nicole was asked to draw her family tree. She didn't know what to do about her father. Tears of sorrow began to roll down her face as she realized—again—that her daddy was dead. The teacher wisely allowed her to be excused from class to wash her face. The family tree should have grown to fulfillment, but it was chopped off in it's prime. Death changed all of that.

Family traditions and routines that were an integral part of our lives have been altered because of Chuck's death. I have tried to keep the ones that I could, but that wasn't possible with all of them. The "sheet rides" and "wheelbarrow rides" their Dad used to give the girls are over. Daddy won't put them on his shoulders to place the angel on top of the Christmas tree anymore. Other simple things that we did together, like family walks after dinner, are gone. The girls and I have established new traditions which are absolutely necessary in readjusting to the changes. But saying good-bye to the old ones hasn't been easy.

When a child suddenly loses a parent, he become fearful that the other parent might also leave. Separation anxiety is a very real issue that death produces in children whose parent is now gone. How could Nicole help but think, *Am I going to come home again one day and find that Mommy is gone, too? That's what happened with Daddy.*

I have worked overtime to restore the stability in my girls' lives that was drastically shaken with the sudden removal of their father. In fact, I wouldn't leave them with a baby-sitter for months after Chuck's death because I knew how fearful it would make them. Nine months after losing Chuck, while visiting my family, I left the girls with Mamma and Pawpaw for the evening to attend my high school reunion. Of all people they would be comfortable with, it's Mamma and Pawpaw! But as I started to leave, Nicole began to cry, "Please don't go, Mama! Please stay here!"

"I'll be back in a few hours, Baby. You'll have fun with Mamma and Pawpaw," I said to give her some reassurance. But it didn't work. I drove down the driveway knowing my child was crying for me. She was scared that Mama might not come back.

Sometimes without warning and when I least expect it, something triggers my mind and causes it to flash back to "the way we were." There have been occasions when I've had a double-take when I saw someone. I thought, *That looks just like Chuck!* Or I'll hear a hearty laugh, and I'm reminded of how he loved to laugh! A song will come on the radio that had special meaning to us. It sends me back in time, but this time it is accompanied by the pain of my loss.

An innocent comment by someone has the capacity to send me whirling downward. Three years after Chuck's death, I went to get information about a school I was considering for Nicole to attend as a first grader. After talking with the administrator and being shown the facilities, she said to me, "Go home and talk it over with your husband."

Her words totally caught me off guard. Before I had time to think through how I should answer, the words tumbled from my lips as the tears suddenly ran down my checks, "I have no husband to ask." I quickly left with no further comments. *Why should such a simple statement upset you so much, Renee? I reasoned. I've dealt with the fact that I have no husband for three years. Why, all of a sudden, does this bother you so much?*

Even I was surprised at my reaction. Why? Because it took me back to the entire painful experience. It was a fresh reminder that things were drastically different now for me and the girls. It vividly pointed out that our family was different. The instant flashbacks of that simple statement sent me spinning.

This same type of episode happened almost six years after Chuck died when I sold the car we bought two days before his death. I really had given it no thought, and I was happy about the new car I was purchasing. But when the time came to transfer the title, the notary said, "Renee, the title is in Chuck's name. I need the succession papers to complete this."

"No problem," I replied. "I'll get them to you later today." But that brief conversation started the ball rolling and sent me back to the pain once more. The rest of the day was overshadowed by death's lingering sting, as I realized I was giving up yet another piece of my life with Chuck.

I've come to see that at any time I am susceptible to a wave of grief which—without notice or warning—may come crashing down, sending me to the bottom emotionally. Thankfully, as time has passed, these occasions are less frequent, and I don't stay down as long. But the reality is, even with a life that is currently overflowing with God's goodness, even with the healing of my broken heart, I know my capacity to relive the sorrow—any time, any place. I will always be susceptible to sorrow coming upon me unexpectedly. No, I won't be the same again since encountering death.

Though I have made conscious efforts to keep the proper mindset, I haven't been able to control what goes on subconsciously. The experience of traumatic situations stirs subconscious thoughts which come to the forefront during the night in our dreams. For years after losing Chuck, I had a recurring dream concerning his death. It still comes from time to time when some event in my day stirs the muddy waters.

Financially, death has also dealt a great blow. All of our married life, we worked diligently to gain the necessary degrees to be fully equipped for the job and receive good remuneration for our work. These goals motivated us to sacrifice and live on a very small income. We believed that the end results would be worth it. It seems ironic that at the very point when we thought we could begin to enjoy some of the financial fruit of our labor, Chuck died. What did it matter then that he had a doctorate degree? What were all the years of "just getting by" for now? The anticipated financial gain from all the schooling never came. With Chuck's death, the income level of our family dropped tremendously.

As a result of death's intrusion, I fought the temptation to put up a wall of self-protection around my heart. I told my heart, *It's too painful to give yourself totally to someone else when you wind up losing them. Don't let yourself be that vulnerable again. It hurts too much. Hold back and protect yourself!*

Wouldn't it be easier and safer to live like a turtle in a self-protective shell? Then I could avoid the risks. I could stick my neck out from time to time, but I could get back inside quickly. Anyone who has suffered the loss of a close relationship needs to deal with this very real (and in some ways, very appealing) option. But I've learned I'm only cheating myself if I choose to avoid relating to others.

There is no such thing as "painless love." If we are to experience the ecstasy of a truly loving relationship, we can't hold back. To choose to love is to take the risk of being hurt. It is impossible to know love in it's fullness without giving all of your heart. If I seek to reserve part of it, I lose part of the joy. I then settle for much less in the relationship, and I am the loser. To know the fullness of the joy, I must be willing to take the risk of being hurt.

Since death entered my life, I've developed a greater capacity to care for other hurting people. New depths of compassion have been forged deep into my soul, increasing my sensitivity for others. As people share their painful situations with me, the tears well up in my eyes. Encountering their grief reminds me of my own grief. I find myself crying with and for them because I know their anguish. I know the hard road that lies ahead. I know the battle they will fight as they confront the questions, doubts, and emotions that run through every part of their being. I don't have to work up sympathy anymore. It comes without effort, and I find myself weeping with those who weep. More than just sympathizing, I now empathize with them as their pain is projected into my own heart and soul.

There's a new longing in my heart now for my heavenly home. Oh, before Chuck died, I knew it would be glorious when we all got to Heaven. But quite honestly, life on earth was good enough for me! There were so many things I wanted to do before I said good-bye. I wasn't in any hurry to leave! Yes, I wanted to see the Lord, but I wasn't praying for His speedy return. My childish mind thought, *Please wait, Lord, until my girls are grown before You come to take us home. I want to see my grandchildren, Lord.*

No longer do I ask the Lord to wait. I'm ready to go. God has put a new longing in my heart. Now I pray, "Even so, come Lord Jesus." I now realize that even the best this life has to offer is far short of the wonders awaiting us in Heaven. We're just eating the crumbs from the banquet meal we will feast on there! The goodness of life that we currently enjoy is just the appetizer for what's coming. Yet so often we want to hold on to what we've got, satisfied with much less because it's safer to keep clutching to the known. I've discovered I'm living way below my standards. I see this now in a way I didn't before Chuck died. Now I know what Paul was saying when he wrote, "For we know that the whole creation groans and suffers the pains of childbirth together until now. And not only this, but also we ourselves, having the first fruits of the Spirit, even we ourselves groan within ourselves, waiting eagerly for our adoption as sons, the redemption of our body" (Romans 8:22-23 NASB).

During my speaking and singing engagements, I'm often asked, "How long did it take for you to get over it and back to normal?"

I wish I could say, "Oh, about a year and a half. Then everything was just great again. God has completely taken away the pain, and I never cry over Chuck's death or miss him anymore. And Nicole and Tara never hurt because they don't have a daddy. We're over it."

But the answer I must honestly give is not the one they want to hear. It is, however, the truth. I tell them, "In some ways, you never get over it. Even now, over seven years later, if I allow myself to reflect on the situation, I fight the tears. I can still feel the grip of grief moving across my heart, bringing sorrow with it. Every time I recount the story of my life with Chuck, I face the pain again. There will always be permission to express appropriate grief over Chuck's death. It is not all-encompassing or totally consuming as it initially was, but it will always have it's place. But after experiencing the sorrow, I can move on. It no longer prevents me from reinvesting myself in the game of life. I discovered I can laugh again, and that I still have a future. The fact that I sometimes still grieve my loss doesn't mean I'm not happy or content today. I am! What it means is that I have accepted his death, accepted my current situation, and can go on with the business of living. I'm no longer trying to hold on to life as it was with Chuck. I've released it. I can let go and give myself to what lies ahead. In many ways, my life has never been better! Much of the reason for today's joy is because I've learned valuable lessons about life. But I would be lying if I said it never hurts, or I'm never saddened about what has happened to us, or if I put on a plastic 'praise God' mask. To tell you I never mourn Chuck's death anymore would be untrue." This is an honest statement of what life is about in a world overrun by sin, pain and sorrow. It's acknowledging my humanness. It doesn't mean I'm carnal or unspiritual because I can still hurt over my loss. It's being real.

Even with these minor tones that have colored my world as a result of death's effects on me, it is still true: "In every loss, there is a gain." I couldn't have said that for a long time after Chuck died. I simply didn't believe it. But God has worked deeply in my heart to show me He is good and gracious. The laws of His kingdom (which are so contrary to those we currently see) say that in losing, we win; in giving, we gain; in dying, we live! The reality is that I've gained more from experiencing death's effects than I've lost. Death has taught me some lessons that have made my life more meaningful. I would *never* have volunteered for this class if given the option! But since I have been forced to walk this path, it has made my life richer, more fulfilling, and more satisfying than ever before. I wouldn't have known this dimension if I had not encountered death. Though it came to destroy, life sprang up from the ruins death left behind. I would never have learned to sing The Resurrection Song without first experiencing the death of the song. The lushness and richness of the melody of the new song I now sing would have gone undiscovered.

Out of necessity, I have found new strengths and skills that would have remained dormant had I not been forced to draw upon them. Initially, these were unwelcome changes, but they have resulted in my spiritual and emotional growth. Even just a few years ago, I would never have dreamed that I would be a speaker or writer. An entirely new ministry—much different than the one I envisioned—has risen for me from the ashes of death. In 1989, I realized that other people could benefit from hearing what happened to me. If they heard my story, perhaps they wouldn't make some of the same mistakes I made, and maybe they could experience some of the comfort I have felt. I prayed and talked to my closest friends about this idea. They encouraged me to begin Renee Music Ministries, Inc.

My first recording was completed in 1990, and it contained a very special song I wrote to Nicole and Tara, "Father to the Fatherless." This song tells my two precious girls that God promises to be their Father in a unique way because their earthly father is gone.

Now that Daddy's gone,
In our heart there is a yearning.
If only I could take away your pain,
But God has clearly said He's our comfort and our
   healing.
You are safe in His keeping.
You have found His special care.
As you children grow,
It's so good to know. . .

Chorus:
He's a father to the fatherless.
He'll meet your every need.
When you're longing for a father's touch,
His love will intercede.
When the world seems cold and hard,
Remember you are His delight.
He's a father to the fatherless.
You are precious in His sight.

God is always true.
You can rest upon His promise.
He will not fail to do just as He said.
You can call on Him;
His name is "Abba, Father."
Loving arms will surround you;
Gentle peace you will know.
As you go along,
He will make you strong.
(Repeat the chorus again.)[1]

Opportunities began to come my way to share my story through singing and speaking in local churches. Slowly, my boundaries expanded, and I was asked to go to churches outside our city to lead seminars. I was even asked to be the "keynote speaker" for some conferences! My new ministry blossomed, and I found it difficult to continue to work at my church and keep up with this new ministry. So in the Fall of 1993, I resigned the position I had held at our church for eight years, and I devoted all my energies to Renee Music Ministries. By 1994, my second recording, "All for the Good," which is based on God's promise in Romans 8:28, was finished. As I have traveled and performed, many people asked me to write my story so they could read it and share it with friends. This book is the expression of my heart and my attempt to meet these requests. As I look back at these last few years of ministry, my heart is thrilled to see how God has used Chuck's life as well as his death to bring encouragement to others and glory to Himself.

A pastor's wife who recently heard me speak and sing and who had previously known me many years ago as "Chuck's wife" recently commented to me, "Who would have ever thought, Renee, that you'd be the one on the platform? I watched you stand by Chuck's side. He was the one out in front, but now it's you. I can't help but wonder if you'd be doing what you are now if Chuck were still living." No, I wouldn't be doing this if Chuck were still alive, and frankly, I'd much rather have my husband and be a quiet housewife. But God can bring light out of darkness and meaning out of tragedy.

Death has made me painfully aware that life is fleeting. You might ask me, "Didn't you know that before Chuck died, Renee?"

Of course I did. I could quote verses about this truth. "As for man, his days are like grass; As a flower of the field, so he flourishes. When the wind has passed over it, it is no more; and its place acknowledges it no longer" (Psalm 103:15-16, NASB). But until Chuck died, this was just another heady, theological truth. Suddenly on September 18th, 1987, the truth became reality for me. "Now I see, Lord. Now I know from experience what this verse really means!" I cried. Death has taught me all too well that life is short. Anyone at any time can be snatched from me. Before, it always happened to "someone else." Now the "someone else" was me.

Just this evening, my heart was gripped with the fleeting nature of life as I received a phone call that a US Air plane crashed outside Pittsburgh leaving no survivors. All one hundred and thirty one people on board were dead. Panic raced in me as I grabbed the phone to call my only sister, who is a flight attendant with US Air. Was Sherry working that flight? I had no idea of her schedule, but I knew she often flew in and out of Pittsburgh. There was no answer. Next, I called Mom and Dad. *They'll know her schedule. They can tell me she is safe,* I told my heart. But again, no answer. It was about an hour before I finally heard from Sherry. Yes, my loved one was safe. But what about the families of the one hundred and thirty one people who weren't? Our enemy, death, sometimes strikes very suddenly in the most horrendous ways.

As I realize that life is truly brief, I count every day with someone I love as a gift. We must cherish the moments we are given, be thankful for each day and not take it for granted. The reality is: no one has any guarantee he will see tomorrow. We often put off till tomorrow things that we should do and say today; but for some, tomorrow never comes. "Make this time count, Renee. Make the most of this moment, "the Spirit gently whispers.

This truth is magnified when death suddenly takes one you love. It's too late to go back and take the vacation to the beach that you just never got around to. There is no more time to spend curled up together on the couch watching an old movie. It's as if the bell rings to announce, "Time's up. The game's over!"

"No! Not yet!" I want to protest. "There's still so much I meant to do! I intended to...." But those opportunities are gone forever. After Chuck died, I regretted that we always worked so hard and didn't take more time to play and enjoy fun things together. We were so busy studying for the up-coming test, working at our jobs, trying to make a living... trying to get ready to *really* live. But we never got the chance. None of those things mattered much when he was dead. "If I could only go back and do it one more time, I'd be sure that I...." But you can't. It's all over.

Death also taught me to focus on what's really important. We clutter our lives with so much trivia that there is no place left for what actually matters. The "tyranny of the urgent" reigns over the real matters of significance. We spend much of our physical and emotional energy playing "trivial pursuit," then we offer the left-overs to those we love the most. This society runs a mile a minute, and we need to learn to say "No" to what is insignificant so we can focus on the truly vital matters. We need to ask ourselves, "When it's all said and done, will it be more important that I kept the house spotless or that I read a nighttime story to my little girl? If I knew this was my last week with my husband (or parent or child or friend), would I run to as many committee meetings that take away my time with him? If God somehow let me know that in three months he would be gone, would I spend so much time in front of the TV, or more time doing things together? What's really important anyway?" Death has helped me learn to say "no" to things that have very little consequence in order that I might focus on what is really important.

So death has changed me, and it has changed the way I now relate to others. It made me focus more on making today count and living so there are no regrets, with as little unfinished business as possible to work through after my loved one is gone. Hopefully, my girls and others I love are benefiting from these lessons death has taught me. I would like to think that my relationships with them are better because of what I've experi-

---

Would I spend so much time in front of the TV, or more time doing things together? What's really important anyway?

---

enced by meeting death face to face. I've learned to avoid leaving angry. Instead, I want to somehow communicate the message: "I love you!" Each time we go our separate ways, it could be the last time we see each other on this side of eternity. Anything could happen to any of us. I wouldn't want to live with the guilt or regrets of knowing that things were not right between us when my loved one died. Sometimes I forget, but my daughters and I usually leave each other with the words, "I love you with all my heart. You're the best!" If they never see me alive again, I want to know that those were the final words spoken between us.

This truth was emphasized when my grandmother recently died. We had a special relationship since I was the first grandchild in our family. Grandma kept me during my preschool years while Mama worked, and that only served to strengthen our bond. She had been in declining health the last few years, but she was still able to live in her own home just across the road from the house in which I was raised. I always made it a point to "go see Grandma" when I returned to North Carolina, because I knew she might not be there the next time we came home. I made certain Nicole and Tara also visited her, and we didn't leave without saying good-bye. I told them, "Girls, Great-Grandma is getting really old. Her body is wearing out. We don't know if she'll still be living the next time we're here, so let's be sure to spend some time with her now." You don't know how glad I was that I made this a habit, because seven weeks after we returned to Louisiana from Christmas holidays, the phone call came informing us of her fall and hospitalization. Only two days later, Grandma died. My lips uttered, "Thank You, Lord, that I took the girls over to say 'Good-bye' before we drove away. Grandma knew we loved her." Once again, the truth was stressed to me by Death's shadow, "Life is short, so make each moment count. Focus on what's really important."

I faced death in all the cruelty and pain it could bring, and I discovered that, in reality, I have nothing to fear. What a paradox that death broke the bondage of our fear of death! Hebrews 2:14-15 says, "Through death he [Jesus] destroyed him that had the power of death. . . the devil; and delivered them who through fear of death were all their lifetime subject to bondage" (KJV). The death of Jesus took away death's sting and freed us from its bondage. Like a boomerang, death brought about its own destruction by means of the death of Christ! That's why Paul can boldly proclaim, "Death is swallowed up in victory. O Death, where is your sting? O grave, where is your victory? . . . Thanks be to God who gives us the victory through our Lord Jesus Christ" (I Corinthians 15:54b, 55, 57 KJV). John Donne, one of England's greatest poets and preachers of the 1600's, wrote in his famous poem, "Death be not proud, though some have called thee mighty and dreadful, for thou art not so. For those whom thou think'st thou dost overthrow die not, poor death, nor canst thou kill me. . . . One short sleep past we wake eternally and death shall be no more. Death, thou shalt die."

Death has taught me that no one is truly prepared to live until they are prepared to die. It would be depressing to think that the grave is the final end. Who would not be in a state of despair to stand by the casket of a loved one and hear the minister say, "Ashes to ashes, dust to dust." If that's all there is, why live? What's it all about anyway?

Our belief in the Resurrection of the dead, as evidenced by

Christ's victory over sin, death, and the grave, gives us hope and strength to carry on. There is more to life than what we currently see! Paul firmly declared this truth when he wrote, "If we have only hoped in Christ in this life, we are of all men most to be pitied. But now Christ has been raised from the dead, the first fruits of those who are asleep. For since by a man came death [Adam], by a man also came the resurrection of the dead [Jesus]" (I Corinthians 15:19-21 NASB).

Jesus said, "Because I live, you shall live also" (John 14:19 NASB). Jesus tried to convey this message to Martha as she stood weeping over the death of her brother Lazarus. He said, "I am the Resurrection and the life; he who believes in Me shall live even if he dies" (John 11: 25 NASB).

Though we sorrow when we lose one precious to us, believers in Jesus Christ have the assurance that our life continues in a better place. A place where God "shall wipe away every tear from their eyes; and there shall no longer be any death; there shall no longer be any mourning, or crying, or pain; for the first things have passed away" (Revelation 21:4 NASB); a place where God will trample all of his enemies under His feet, and "the last enemy that will be abolished is death" (I Corinthians 15:26 NASB).

Death turns out to be the biggest loser of all! "The joke's on you!" I want to shout! "You thought you had won by robbing us of one we dearly loved. What you didn't realize was that the game wasn't over! Now you lose, Big Time! For my Lord Jesus holds the keys to death (Rev. 1:17-18), not you!" For those who die in Christ, death is merely the passageway to glory, the dark tunnel that leads to the everlasting light!

And so the song goes on. . . sometimes in the minor mode. Areas of my life clearly reveal death's stain, and the effects linger in many, many ways. Yes, some of them are negative, but now the positive far outweighs the negative. And just knowing that there is coming a day when death shall die and be destroyed gives me courage to walk on. You see, I know the final score! And we win!

Death's sure defeat is clearly portrayed in a poem by an unknown writer entitled "Just Think," It goes like this,

Just think. . .
Of stepping on shore and finding it Heaven;
Of taking hold of a hand and finding it God's,
Of breathing a new air and finding it Celestial;
Of feeling invigorated and finding it immortality;
Of passing from storm and Tempest to an unbroken
    calm;
Of waking up—and finding it Home!

14

A Song of Resurrection
Singing a New Song!

As I write these words, it has been almost eight years since Chuck died. Initially I felt, "I'll never sing again! The voice that once lifted beautiful songs to the Lord no longer exists. The music is gone forever." Anyone who has been deeply hurt by death's presence—or who grieves a loss of any kind—experiences these thoughts. "No matter how good life may be in the days to come, it will never be as good as it was because of _____ (fill in the blank with the traumatic event or loss in your life)."

I know the feeling. I was convinced that life would never be good again or have any meaning. I resigned myself simply to exist. We have a God, however, who is still in the miracle-working business! He still performs the miracle of resurrecting dead dreams, reviving broken hearts, and restoring destroyed emotions. He has given us the promise: "The Sun of righteousness shall arise with healing in his wings" (Malachi 4:2a). As a demonstration of His grace and goodness, God desires to take our shattered lives and make them a living example of how He rewrites the song and resurrects the voice to bring forth a more beautiful melody than the previous one. By His strength and mercy, the song that died in my heart has been resurrected.

"I can sing again!" I want to shout from the mountain tops. It's a new song, something very different from the former songs I sang. Admittedly, it's been a hard song to learn. The melody and lyrics are the most difficult I've ever tried to sing. This new song is on a different plane, a dimension I didn't even know existed before! Walking through the dark places made me realize the value and depth of this new music.

I survived what I thought would kill me, but more than just surviving, I was surprised to discover the capacity to know joy and satisfaction again. Instead of continually looking backward to the past, I gradually began to look to the future and anticipate good things. Releasing Chuck took time and effort (It's called "grief work" because it is work!). Often I felt as if I were making no progress at all. Other times, I even regressed! But that's all part of the healing process. Releasing doesn't mean forgetting. I'll never forget all Chuck and I shared. He will always hold a special place in my heart, but I can move forward and accept the changes life has brought. I've stopped fighting to hold on to my past. That's what it means to "let it go." It is not an act of disloyalty, or betrayal, or an indication of how much I loved him, but I have to acknowledge the inescapable facts and respond to them in the best possible way.

We have a God, however, who is still in the miracle-working business! He still performs the miracle of resurrecting dead dreams, reviving broken hearts, and restoring destroyed emotions.

Many words are used to describe this process: healing, renewal, restoration, integration, reorganization, resolution, recreation, reinvestment. They all communicate the same message: the capacity to live again still exists. Adjustment to a new life is possible. The equilibrium that was thrown totally off balance can be restored. Life can be meaningful once again. Emotional energies can be rechanneled in new directions. The energy level that was totally depleted at the beginning of your crisis can be revitalized. The continual burden and sorrow that enveloped you for so long need not be permanent. The point is clear: there's still a lot of living to do!

Of course, I still bear the scars of my heartaches. They haven't disappeared, but they don't hurt like they once did, either. I've chosen to think of them as my "Ebenezer, a stone of help." This is what Samuel called the stone he raised to remember the Israelites victory over the Philistines. He proclaimed, "Thus far the LORD has helped us" (I Samuel 7:12, NASB). As I gaze upon my scars, my Ebenezer, they all remind me of God's faithfulness in the past and how He proved himself to be true in the midst of the storm. They are also a symbol of hope as I look to the future; no matter what may come, God won't desert me. Together we can face tomorrow.

Jacob struggled with the Lord at Peniel (Genesis 32:24-32) and told Him, "I will not let you go unless you bless me." Jacob was put in a position where he had no choice but to wrestle with his assailant who came upon him suddenly in the night. But as a result of the struggle, God blessed him and then changed his name from "Jacob" (trickster) to "Israel" (prince of God)! In his book, *When Heaven is Silent*, Ron Dunn points out: "The very thing I'm wrestling against may be the thing God wants to use to bless me."[1] But please notice: Jacob walked with a limp for the rest of his earthly life! The scar and limp which remained, however, were considered a small price to pay for the multitude of blessings that were derived from the fight.

I too walk with a limp. I've struggled with the Lord and the events He has allowed to take place in my life. In some respects, I will always bear the marks of these traumas, but I'm beginning to see just a small glimpse of the immense value of the struggle. Even my pain has been allowed by God "to do good for you in the end" (Deuteronomy 8:16, NASB).

I'm the first to admit that the song I'm singing now is not one I wanted to sing. Left to myself and my own plans, I would have kept everything very simple, a nice, neat tidy little package. As I've walked life's highway, I've found the easy road is not necessarily the best road. To reach our goal of becoming mature in Christ and grow up in all aspects in Him (Ephesians 4:13,15), we need to incorporate songs of different styles and from different areas of life. Our repertoire needs the darker tones and richness which only emerge in the wilderness wanderings. How else could we know God's comfort if we didn't sing The Mourning Song? How would we know God has a more beautiful chord arrangement than our simple structure unless we allowed Him to replace what seemed to be best to us with His own chord selection? We would never be able to sing The Resurrection Song without first experiencing the death of the former song. We must trust The Master Musician and yield our lives to the touch of His skilled hand. When we do, I'm convinced that one day we will find ourselves surprised at the beauty of the music. One day we will awake to hear the music reentering our world, and before we even realize it, we will discover we're *singing again!*

Musical Coda

When I was a child, students had to master "The Three R's" of reading, 'riting, and 'rithmatic if they were to do well in school. Now that I'm older I've learned that knowing "The Three R's" is still essential to graduate from the school of Hard Knocks. But "The Three R's" are no longer reading, 'riting, and 'rithmatic. The school of Hard Knocks and The University of Adversity has redefined them. I am indebted to Ron Dunn for teaching me these new definitions which have been a great source of help to me as I've tried to pass the graduate class on Hard Times and Sorrow. I think you might find them helpful, too.

The Three R's for dealing with adversity are these: always remember that no matter what happens in this life time, God has: 1) a right; 2) a reason, and 3) a reward. Let me explain.

God has a right because of
Who He is and What He has done.

We owe our very existence to God. We would not be here apart from the fact that He created us. He is the Creator; we are the creation. He is the Master; we are the servants. He is the Potter; we are the clay. Because of Who He is, the Lord God Almighty, we have no right to say, "What do You think You're doing?" As the Sovereign Lord of the Universe, He can do whatever He pleases. . . and do it very well!

Jeremiah uses the illustration of the potter and the clay to emphasize this point, "'Can I not. . . deal with you as this potter does?' declares the Lord. 'Behold, like the clay in the potter's hand, so are you in my hand'" (Jeremiah 18:6, NASB). Isaiah strongly states the case, "Woe to him who quarrels with his Maker. . . . Does the clay say to the potter, What are you making?" (Isaiah 45:9, NIV).

For years I have taught private music lessons in my home. I am of the old school that believes the teacher is the authority and the student is to obey. Recently I asked a piano student to play a piece for me, but she replied, "No."

Wrong answer! Not the right thing to say! I quickly realized. With a smile on my face, I firmly replied, "Let's remember that I am the teacher, and you are the student. The student does not tell the teacher 'No.' So we'll try again, and start with the first measure of this song." Because she knew I meant business, my student obeyed.

We are overstepping our bounds when we think we can demand an explanation from God because we believe our "rights" have been violated. The truth is that He has a right—by virtue of Who He is—to do as He deems best.

God not only has a right because of who He is, but also because of what He has done as our Redeemer. Much more than merely creating us, He bought us back. He has purchased us by the shed blood of Jesus upon the cross. No greater price could ever be paid than the one God paid to redeem you and me. Quite honestly, it baffles my mind that God thought I was of such value to pay that kind of price for me. Had the decision been mine, I probably would have replied, "The cost is too great. It's not worth it." Praise God that He didn't think the price was too high to pay!

I once heard a story that makes this point crystal clear. A little boy was given a piece of driftwood by his father for his birthday. He decided to carve a boat out of the wood. After spending many hours on the tedious work, the boat was finished. He put on a bright coat of paint and carved his initials on the bottom. Finally, it was time to take the boat to the little stream down below his house. Carefully the young lad placed the boat in the still water. "It's floating!" he exclaimed. "It's doing what I made it to do!" Thrilled with delight, he walked along the edge of the stream as the boat began to move with the current. How exciting to see his accomplishment! As they continued, however, the water began to move more quickly. His eyes looked up, and he saw a fork in the stream ahead. His little boat began to drift toward that side, and he watched in anguish as the rushing water pushed his boat out of his reach. "No!" he yelled. "Come back this way!" But it was too late. Unable to stop it, the boy watched his precious boat sail away on the other side of the stream. Tears filled his eyes as he realized his boat was gone, lost forever.

Heartbroken, the little boy returned home empty-handed. A few weeks later, this young boy walked down the streets of his small town. As he passed one of the shops and glanced in the window, something caught his eye. *That boat in the window sure does look a lot like the one I made!* he thought to himself. As he moved to get a closer look, he was amazed at how similar it appeared! *I've got to check this out!*

He went into the store and removed the boat from the display shelf. "There they are! My initials on the bottom! Mr. Store-keeper, Mr. Storekeeper, this is my boat! My daddy gave me the wood for my birthday! I carved it, and I even have my initials on the bottom. See?" he said with excitement. He was convinced that this was a miracle for sure!

But to the boy's dismay, the storekeeper replied, "I don't know about that, Sonny. I paid good money for this boat. If you want it, you'll have to buy it."

Without hesitation, the young boy bounded from the store, yelling, "I'll be right back! Hold it for me!" He rushed home, broke open his piggy bank and took every cent. He didn't care what the price tag was. No price was too great to pay to buy back his boat. Hurrying back to the store, he ran in and gave the man his money. Clutching the boat in his arms as he left, the storekeeper heard him say, "Now you're twice mine, little boat, because I made you and I bought you back!"

Dear friends, do you not see that in the same way, we are the Lord's twice, by double ownership? He made us, and He bought us back! Paid for by the blood of Jesus! We belong to Him, not ourselves. That's what Paul meant when he wrote, "Do you not know. . . that you are not your own? For you have been bought with a price: therefore glorify God in your body" (I Corinthians 6:19-20 NASB).

Let us not forget that indeed, because of Who He is and What He has done, God has a right.

God Has a Reason

As a little girl, I must have driven my mom and dad half crazy always asking "Why?" I wanted a reason for everything! It's natural for a child to ask "Why?" My parents often took the time to try to explain, but to me, their explanations usually made no sense! We seemed to see things very differently! Now as a mother of two young girls, I know the frustration my parents must have felt. Nicole and Tara bring the same questions to me! Doesn't it please you as a parent when your child does what you ask her to do without having to know why? Isn't it music to our ears when they simply reply, "Yes ma'am."

I've often gone to my Heavenly Father asking "Why?" I thought that knowing the reason for the seemingly senseless situation might help me. I have lain in my bed alone, begging God to explain the reasons for Chuck's death to me, and why He seemed to shut His ears to our desperate cries. I've met other people who have told me how God revealed to them the answers and reasons they longed for in dreams or through the words of another believer. For me, it hasn't happened that way. My big question, "Why?" remains unanswered.

But my heart is strengthened to know that even though it may be unknown to me, God has a reason. I may not get the answer to my question until I reach Heaven's shore, but I feel a little better to realize I am not alone in this matter. In fact, I'm in very good company! The Bible doesn't record that God ever told Job the reason he suffered the things he did. We don't find God explaining to Joseph all the reasons why he was treated so unfairly for so long! Why God chose to deliver Peter from prison but allowed James to be killed by the sword is not given (see Acts 12). Yet faith calls me to believe that there *is* a reason. For me, it is enough to believe that there is a master plan. I am not a mouse in a maze. If I need to, I can wait and trust in my Father's love and mercy until the day the reasons are clear to me.

Though I love the contemporary praise and worship songs, the old hymns of the faith hold a special place in my heart. One summarizes what I've tried to convey here:

> Trials dark on every hand and we cannot understand
> All the ways that God would lead us to that blessed
>   promised land;
> But He'll guide us with His eye and we'll follow till we
>   die;
> We will understand it better by and by
> By and by, when the morning comes
> When the saints of God are gathered home,
> We will tell the story how we've overcome;
> We will understand it better by and by.

Lyrics to the hymn "When the Morning Comes" by Charles Tindley

God may not reveal to you the reason for your painful circumstance. You may never know the purpose in your loved one's death. However, I encourage you to hold tight to the truth that He has a reason. And you know what? It's probably something better and far greater than you or I could ever imagine!

God Has a Reward

The Scripture promises that "there is a reward for the righteous" (Psalm 58:11, KJV). "God is a rewarder of them that diligently seek Him" (Hebrews 11:6b, KJV). As believers, we will receive rewards when we stand before the Judgment Seat of Christ (II Corinthians 5:10). The works we have done that withstand the testing of fire will be rewarded. "He shall receive a reward" (I Corinthians 3:14). Our efforts are not in vain in the Lord. That's the promise of I Corinthians 15:58: "You know that your labor is not in vain in the Lord."

My first reaction to hearing this is, "That's great, but do I have to wait until I die to enjoy any of the fruit of my labor? Can't I have some reward now, while I'm still living, struggling with trying to make it today?" The answer is Yes! God also rewards His children here and now in this life time. It's not only "pie in the sky in the sweet by and by," but also for the "nasty here and now!" Our work in the Lord will not go unrewarded. I've discussed some of the rewards we experience in some of the previous chapters. There is life abundant for those who walk with the Lord (John 10:10). As I've gotten a little older and have walked through more valleys, I've realized, however, that the best gift of all that God gives us is the gift of Himself. He is better than any reward or gift I might receive. His words to Abraham were "I am thy exceeding great reward" (Genesis 15:1, KJV). Knowing that He is with me—whatever may come—is of more value than any material possession or spiritual blessing He might give me.

How do you think it makes the Lord feel when we prefer "things" instead of Him? Am I seeking what God can give me, His outstretched Hand and what it holds? Or have I come to the place where I realize His presence in my life is more valuable than any possession or pleasure I might receive from Him?

My girls are still of such a young age they can't go out and buy gifts for Mom like they want to. Every Mother's Day, they work diligently to make me the prettiest card they possibly can and a present they have made. While I cherish these gifts, I'm always quick to add, "But *you* are the best gift of all! Having you as my girls is the best Mother's Day present ever!"

Don't you think that God is waiting to hear those words from our lips? Yes, He rewards us with many blessings here and now and in eternity. Yet He Himself is the best reward we could ever receive. Only by growing out of our childish ways and moving toward the goal of being mature believers do we come to this realization. And we only grow out of our childish ways into responsible, mature Christians by walking through the hard times.

Sometimes I've wished I could sit down with some of the saints of old for an interview. Wouldn't it be great if we could ask them a few questions! I guess the one that immediately comes to my mind is, "Was it worth it? If you had the chance to do it all over again, would you still follow the Lord? Now that it's all said and done, what do you think?" What would be their responses? Let your imagination run with mine as we consider this scenario.

"Was it worth it Paul? I mean, you were considered a Hebrew of Hebrews, a Pharisee of Pharisees! You studied under the most esteemed teachers of your time and were considered blameless as far as keeping the law was concerned. Yet you gave it all up! In fact, you went so far as to say that though you suffered the loss of all things, you counted it as dung that you might win Christ! You became a fool for Christ and even suffered execution under the hands of Nero for your faith! Was it worth it Paul?"

Knowing that He is with me—whatever may come—is of more value than any material possession or spiritual blessing He might give me.

"What about you, John the Baptist? Do you think it was worth it? Don't you realize that you shouldn't have been so bold? Didn't you know it wasn't the smart thing to do to tell the king he was living in adultery? Why didn't you keep your mouth shut and your head on! It's obvious that you never read *How To Win Friends and Influence People*. Was it worth it John?"

"Stephen, you were the first martyr for the church. You had so much potential, yet because of your boldness in telling the Jews that the one they just crucified was the promised Messiah, they stoned you! Was it worth it Stephen?"

"Habakkuk, you saw God allow your nation to be destroyed by a heathen people with no regard for God. But you said if everything was destroyed and taken from you, you would still rejoice in the God of your salvation (Habakkuk 3:18). You asked God for an answer, but didn't receive the answer you sought! Now that it's all said and done, was it worth it?"

"Job, how I've longed to talk with you! You lost everything and never knew why! You've suffered more than probably any other member of the human race! Yet you said that even if God killed you, you would trust Him (Job 13:15). Now be honest. Do you really think it was worth it Job?" Peter, you were crucified upside down because you said you weren't worthy to be crucified in the same way as your Lord. John the Apostle, they tried to kill you by throwing you in a pot of boiling oil. When that didn't work, they banished you to a lonely island to keep you quiet. Was it worth it, guys?"

Unanimously they all stand and reply without delay, "Yes, most definitely yes."

I quickly ask, "Well, then, could you give me some advice on how I can make it, too, as I walk toward my heavenly home? Sometimes the going gets real rough, as I'm sure you remember. The temptation to quit, and forget it all can seem very appealing."

Their answer penetrates deep into the depths of my heart. Paul acts as spokesman for the entire group and says, "Don't be shortsighted, only looking at your present condition. Keep the eternal perspective in mind. Remember that your present, light affliction is just for a moment in view of eternity. It's working for you an exceeding, eternal weight of glory. And don't look at what you see, because that's only temporary. Look through eyes of faith at the things you don't see, because that's eternal! I assure you that what you're going through right now, your current suffering, is not even worthy to be compared with the glory that's waiting for you! And one more thing, keep looking to Jesus, the author and finisher of our faith. He endured the shame of the cross because of the joy that was set before Him. Let him be your example to follow. Yes, it was worth it all, and yes I'd do it again if given the chance, with an even firmer conviction than before" (II Corinthians 4:17, 18; Romans 8:18; Hebrews 12:2).

Suddenly, as if conducted by a director that I can't see, they all begin to sing in unison a song I've heard before! "This is for you, Renee, and for all the others journeying to the other side. Keep these words in your heart, and it will give you strength for the journey and hope for your hurting heart:"

It will be worth it all when we see Jesus.
Life's trials will seem so small when we see Christ.
One look at his dear face all sorrow will erase.
So bravely run the race till we see Christ.

Lyrics to the hymn "When We See Christ" by Ester Rusthoi

I sit in silence as I contemplate this imaginary interview, convicted of the smallness of my faith and humbled before the greatness of our God. I regret I ever doubted Him. My heart is stirred with a new determination to trust and obey, encouraged by the words I have just heard.

Perhaps you too have found yourself groping in darkness, as you grieve loss in your own life. Your song has disappeared, and you think it will never return. Pain is knocking at your front door, about to tear it down, invading your heart, permeating each moment of every day. Somehow pain, death, and sorrow find their way to each one of our homes at one time or another. They've got my number, and I'm sure they have yours, too. I'd be foolish to think that just because they invaded my life once in a major way, they'll never return. I know they'll be back. Next time, I'll be more prepared for their invasion.

Pain has many faces and comes in many forms. Death, divorce, broken relationships, prodigal children, disease, lost jobs, accidents that cause permanent physical disability, marriages that fall far short of what you thought they would be—all of these are different ways it may appear at your door.

So come on and sing along! The Master Musician is waiting for you.

I'm here to say, however, that whenever pain enters our lives, God is faithful and true. He knows how to make a road in the wilderness when we don't see one. He can bring fountains of life out of the dry, dusty, barren deserts that seek to destroy us. He is able to resurrect life's song when the music has died. More than anything, He wants to redeem the painful circumstances and turn them around to actually work for our benefit. He doesn't always miraculously deliver us out of the situation, but He will give us the strength, mercy, and grace to go "through the valley of the shadow." His promise is: "When you pass through the waters, I will be with you; and through the rivers, they will not over flow you... For I am the LORD your God (Isaiah 43:2a, 3a, NASB). Tell me, which is the greater miracle? To be instantly delivered and rescued (like I wanted Him to do for me), or to be given the strength to go through the trial and endure?

I don't know about you, but this single mom and two fatherless girls have decided to keep walking, keep obeying, and keep trusting that "the judge of all the earth will do right" (Genesis 18:25). We're singing a new song, as we commit the keeping of our souls to our Faithful Creator to do what is right (I Peter 4:19). We invite you to join in on the chorus. It's a song that everyone can sing if they're willing. God never forces anyone to sing against their will. He leaves that decision to us. It's a choice we each can make. There are measures in the song that are difficult, and some of the rhythms and intervals are quite complex. But once you've learned it, you'll be convinced as we are that this is by far a better song than the little jingles we sang before!

So come on and sing along! The Master Musician is waiting for you, desiring to help you learn the melody and words! Everything you need to master the music has been provided. The decision is now yours to make. Will you come? It's a choice you'll never regret! You will find—perhaps to your own amazement— that you can be freed from staring at the grave of the tunes you formerly sang, to rise and *sing a new song!*

"I waited patiently for the Lord; And He inclined to me and heard my cry. He brought me up out of the pit of destruction, out of the miry clay; and set my feet upon a rock, making my footsteps firm. And He put a new song in my mouth, a song of praise to our God. Many will see it and fear and will trust in the Lord" (Psalm 40:1-3, NASB).

Appendix A

Your church can schedule Renee for a concert

Renee Coates Scheidt exudes a warmth and vibrance that can only come from knowing the love of Jesus. She sings and speaks of God's faithfulness to His children. Since beginning Renee Music Ministries, Inc. in 1990, Renee has performed in churches throughout the country. Her ministry includes a unique blend of songs and testimony as she offers "A Song of Hope for the Heart." Renee's versatility as a singer and communicator speaks powerfully to both young and old as she shares her message of faith and courage. Her life-changing message of grace flows from the depths of her experience. It is genuine. It is sincere.

Your church can schedule Renee for a worship service, conference, banquet, or seminar. Her ministry will have a lasting spiritual impact on those who hear her.

For more information about scheduling Renee, you can contact her by writing or calling:

Renee Music Ministries, Inc.
509 Versaille Drive
Pearl River, LA 70452
(504) 863-7024

What Pastors and Church Leaders Are Saying About Renee. . .

"It is a great pleasure for me to recommend Renee. She has proven to be faithful as she has walked through the fire. She has come through with a message of hope and comfort. A life-changing message of grace flows through her beautiful talent. Receive her and her ministry. You will be blessed and the kingdom will be enhanced."

Dudley Hall, President
Successful Christian Living Ministries
Euless, Texas

"Renee has bared her soul in a way that we are able to feel every emotion she experiences as we travel through this personal tragedy with her. She not only shares her pain, but also her difficult road to recovery as God walked with her and gave her His faithfulness and strength."

Jerry Evans, President
J & J Music
Chickasaw, Alabama

"Many artists are seemingly afraid to be vulnerable. . . . Renee is not. Many artists seem to shy away from people who are hurting. . . . Renee does not. Many artists appear to have lost their heart for the church. . . . Renee has not. As exceptional a talent as Renee is, her strong music background and versatility as a singer are sometimes overshadowed by her moving testimony and ability to communicate the gospel. And I can think of no better addition than these qualities to a Christian music industry where slickness and commercialism often blur the clear and simple message of God's love. Renee is a breath of fresh air! So, for a very enjoyable and life-changing worship experience, let me recommend Renee Coates Scheidt. . . in concert!"

Gary Driskell, Songwriter/Producer
Word Publishing Co.
Nashville, Tennessee

"As her pastor, it gives me great joy to commend to you the ministry of Renee. Her ministry is much more than just music. Renee presents a Life Message of faith, hope, and victory which is lived out in her own experience. She has journeyed through some of the most difficult adversities of life and experienced the victorious grace of God. She loves the Lord, and it's obvious when you've been around her for a brief time. I'm confident God will bless your life in a very special way through her dynamic ministry."

Dr. Bob Heustess, Pastor
Grace Memorial Baptist Church
Slidell, Louisiana

"Renee has a powerful testimony shared in a gracious, Christ-honoring manner through word and song. The reality of her love for the Savior and trust in His providential care is a direct result of her personal experience of being carried through turbulent, dark waters by His love. Renee has shared her rich voice of praise to God in music and testimony with our church. Her ministry has blessed us. Her joy has encouraged us, and her knowledge of His word has provided us an example to follow."

Robert J. Vetter, Pastor of Outreach and Missions
Providence Bible Church
Raleigh, North Carolina

Appendix B

About Rapha

Many people have asked me, "Where can I turn for competent, Christ-centered counseling?" In the past few years, I have been impressed with the quality of care people receive from Rapha Treatment Centers.

Millions of people in our country experience the pain of depression, divorce, drugs, alcohol, abuse, eating disorders, and anxiety. And each of these people affect many more. For example:

- 20% of adults experience major depression at some point in their lives.
- 12% of school children need psychological intervention at some time.
- Each year, 12% of Americans experience severe anxiety disorders.
- Approximately 30 to 40 million Americans abuse drugs or alcohol.
- Sexual abuse and addictions to gambling, sex, work, and many other behaviors destroy millions of families.
- Every addict adversely and directly affects about 4 other people.

If you or someone you know needs help, I encourage you to call the caring professionals at Rapha Treatment Centers.

The Rapha Perspective

The heart of Rapha is a combination of the finest medical care and Christ-centered therapy. Rapha's multidisciplinary approach addresses not only a person's mental and physical needs, but the spiritual needs as well. Those who come to Rapha learn a whole new way of dealing with painful emotions, strained relationships, and unhealthy patterns of behavior.

Rapha is a nationally recognized Christian health-care organization which provides intensive in-hospital treatment for psychiatric and substance abuse programs. Rapha has drawn enthusiastic endorsements from major denominational leaders.

For more information about Rapha's counseling resources for you or someone you love, call: 1 (800) 383-HOPE.

Endnotes

Chapter 3

[1]"My Tribute," Words and Music by Andrae Crouch, 1971, Lexicon Music.

Chapter 6

[1]Margaret Clarkson, *Grace Grows Best in Winter*, (Grand Rapids: Erdmans Publishing Company, 1990), p. 21.

[2]Robert Wise, *When There is No Miracle*, (Glendale, California: Regal Books, 1977), p. 44.

[3]R. C. Sproul, *Surprised by Suffering*, (New York: Walker & Co., 1988), p. 46.

Chapter 8

[1]*How Do You Keep the Music Playing?*, Words by Alan & Marilyn Bergman, c 1982, WB Music Corp.

[2]Ron Dunn, *When Heaven is Silent*, (Nashville: Thomas Nelson, 1994), p. 41.

Chapter 9

[1]James Martin, *Suffering Man, Loving God*, (San Francisco, California: Harper & Row, 1990), p. 33.

[2]Ibid., p. 65.

[3]Philip Yancy, *Disappointment With God*, (Grand Rapids: Zondervan Publishing House, 1988), p. 183.

[4]Ibid., p. 201.

[5]Ron Dunn, *Faith That Will Not Fail*, (Great Britain: Marshall Pickering, 1984), p. 25.

Chapter 10

[1]Doug Manning, *Don't Take Away My Grief*, (New York: Harper Collins, 1984), p. 60.

Chapter 11

[1]Robert Williams, *Journey Through Grief*, (Nashville: Thomas Nelson, 1991), pp. 93-94.

[2]Clarkson, op. cit., p. 21.

[3]Williams, op. cit., p. 74.

[4]Clarkson, op. cit., p. 20.

[5]Henry Cloud, *Changes That Heal*, (Grand Rapids: Zondervan

Publishing House, 1990), p. 49.

[6]Ibid., p. 49.

[7]Ibid., p. 32.

[8]Norman Cousins, *Anatomy of an Illness*, (New York: W. W. Norton & Company, Inc., 1979), pp. 39-40, 86.

[9]Jerry Dahmen, *I Love Life in Spite of It All*, (Nashville, Tennessee: Broadman Press, 1988), p. 185.

[10]Hal Lindsey, *The Terminal Generation*, (Old Tappan, New Jersey: Fleming H. Revell Co., 1976), p. 10.

Chapter 12

[1]*Hard Times*, Words and music by Gary Driskell, Word Music/ ASCAP, 1993.

[2]Jerry Bridges, *Trusting God Even When Life Hurts*, (Colorado Springs, Colorado: NavPress, 1988), pp. 180-181.

[3]Martin, op. cit., p. 32.

[4]John Claypool, *Tracks of a Fellow Struggler*, (Dallas, Texas: Word, Inc., 1974), p. 57.

[5]Bridges, op. cit., p. 32.

[6]Ibid., p. 177.

[7]Wise, op. cit., p. 52-53.

[8]Dunn, op. cit., pp. 146-147.

[9]Wise, op. cit., pp. 35-36.

[10]Cited In *Disappointment with God*, by Philip Yancey.

[11]Wise, op. cit., p. 48.

Chapter 13

[1]"Father to the Fatherless," by Renee Scheidt and Gary Driskell, Ariose/ASCAP, 1989.

Chapter 14

[1]Ron Dunn, *When Heaven is Silent*, p. 35.